THE NEGRO FAMILY IN BRITISH GUIANA

INTERNATIONAL LIBRARY OF SOCIOLOGY
AND SOCIAL RECONSTRUCTION

Founded by Karl Mannheim

Editor: W. J. H. Sprott

A catalogue of the books available in the INTERNATIONAL LIBRARY OF SOCIOLOGY AND SOCIAL RECONSTRUCTION, and new books in preparation for the Library, will be found at the end of this volume.

The Negro Family in British Guiana

FAMILY STRUCTURE AND SOCIAL STATUS IN THE VILLAGES

BY

RAYMOND T. SMITH

WITH A FOREWORD BY

MEYER FORTES

London, Routledge & Kegan Paul Limited
New York, Humanties Press
in association with
Institute of Social & Economic Research
University College of the West Indies
Jamaica

First published in 1956
by Routledge *&* Kegan Paul Limited
Broadway House, 68-74 *Carter Lane,*
London, EC4V 5EL
Reprinted 1965
Reprinted 1971
Printed in Great Britain by
Lowe & Brydone (Printers) Ltd.,
London, N.W.10

ISBN 0 7100 3355 9

CONTENTS

TABLES

ILLUSTRATIONS

FIGURES

MAPS

FOREWORD

By

MEYER FORTES

William Wyse Professor of Social Anthropology in the University of Cambridge

It has been my privilege to watch the growth of Dr. Smith's book from the time when it was only an aspiration for a field study to its final fledging. It has been an exciting experience. Following modern anthropological tradition, Dr. Smith has welded field observation and theory into a unitary argument. He has done it with the skill and economy of an old hand; so much so that his scrupulous checking of each step in the theoretical analysis against the detail of field observation may easily escape the reader. I stress this because Dr. Smith's manner is so self-effacing, his exposition so close-knit, and his main hypothesis so obviously right once it has been stated, that the quality of the field work behind the book may simply be taken for granted. But it is the quality of the field work that, in the end, distinguishes the best from the merely good monograph in social anthropology; and this best calls for special acumen and insight, and for the ability to share the feelings and ideas of one's hosts without sacrificing discipline and detachment.

These capabilities can only be encouraged, never taught, in the classroom. They come out in the telling detail, reported almost by the way rather than in the set piece on a conventional topic. Dr. Smith makes shrewd use of such telling detail. An instance is the description of the ambiguous attitudes of a child brought up by its grandmother when its own mother is also a dependant of the grandmother. It makes us see in a flash why Dr. Smith's analysis of the 'matrifocal' household from the angle of its child-rearing and economic functions, and not from the more usual side of the legal and moral notions of family and marriage, is so illuminating.

Even more effective is Dr. Smith's use of numerical data. His central theme is the Guianese Negro family. As is well known, there is no topic in the whole range of the social sciences that has been so much written about as the family systems of mankind. But a large part, if not most, of this voluminous literature is useless for scholarly purposes. Some of the best work on family systems is due to anthropologists; but, alas, it is too often marred by lack of rigour in investigation and by the fatal facility of generalization that goes with the narrative form of presentation. And strangely enough the deficiencies are most glaring with regard to an aspect of family structure that would seem, to common sense, to be particularly important. I mean the fact that every family in every society, no matter what its specific institutional form may be, has a life-cycle. For us this life-cycle of the family begins with the marriage of the founding parents, goes on through the different stages of child rearing and the dispersion of the children as they go out into the world and marry, and ends with the death of the parents. To ignore this process of development in family structure is surely to misunderstand its essential character.

This is Dr. Smith's starting-point and it is in elucidating its implications that he makes brilliant use of his numerical data. To be sure, this method is unorthodox in social anthropology. It is time consuming and tedious and it gives small scope for the purple passage. But it pays handsomely, at any rate in Dr. Smith's hands. It enables him to show that where others have seen only a confusing medley of family 'types' there is in reality a definite developmental sequence related to a few clear principles of conjugal and parental relationship.

These principles have been the subject of much discussion among social anthropologists. They have been shown to account for common features of family and kinship institutions in a wide range of societies. But there are still many unsolved problems connected with their nature and their modes of operation. One of these, and a fundamental one for the theory of family structure, is the question of what the French anthropologist Claude Lévi-Strauss calls 'elementary structure'. The question might be put in the form: Is there a minimal unit of social organization capable of fulfilling the functions of ensuring physical and social reproduction in a society? Or, to put it in other words, is there a limiting point of family organization beyond which social reproduction in man is indistinguishable from species reproduction in animals? The chimerical stage of 'primitive promiscuity' assumed by nineteenth-century anthropologists and still believed in by scholars who get their anthropology from 'The Golden Bough' or Engels, would have been such a limit. It has never been found in any known human society and it is futile to search for it. By contrast, we can ask relevantly whether or not there is in all human societies something like an elementary 'cell' of family organization susceptible of empirical identification and irreducibly necessary for the process of social reproduction.

FOREWORD

It so happens that the West Indies offer the social scientist a unique historical situation for studying the fundamental problems of the comparative sociology of the family, and students of West Indian family organization have been aware of this, as Dr. Smith shows in his survey of their work. But Dr. Smith's book puts the study of the West Indian family system on quite a new basis. The result is both a deeper understanding of the West Indian facts and a major contribution to the theory of 'elementary' family structure.

Dr. Smith achieves this by asking questions and following procedures that only a social anthropologist—and perhaps only one trained in the contemporary so-called British School of social anthropology—would think of. He shows that the question whether marital unions are proper or improper, legal or casual, and its legalistic corollary as to whether the children are legitimate or illegitimate, is a secondary one. The primary issue is the social relationship of filiation in which parents fulfil the tasks of upbringing and of endowing offspring with their place in society and their claims upon society. This relationship is basic to the Guianese Negro family as to every other type of family; and its 'elementary structure' is the unit of mother and child. But this unit, Dr. Smith demonstrates, has a developmental cycle through time in relation first to its domestic context and the local community, and secondly to the total social system of the country. And this is where the husband-father fits. He is the licit procreator (for *pace* the moralists who are so ready to see promiscuity in West Indian conjugal customs, a strict incest taboo is observed) and also the 'provi̍der' who links the domestic group with the economy of the total society. The 'matrifocal' unit is stable; instability in the conjugal relationship is a result of the male's productive and social roles in the total society. In the undifferentiated economy of the Guianese Negro village, the male earner is forced to go out to work for wages and this contributes to the instability of the marital bond.

I have given this very bare outline of Dr. Smith's main theme so as to indicate how he approaches his task. There is a naïve belief in some quarters that the distinguishing mark of social anthropology, as opposed to other social sciences, is that it deals with small 'face-to-face' communities. Dr. Smith shows the fallacy of this. He makes it clear that what distinguishes his approach as a social anthropologist is the method of considering every institution in the setting of the total social system. So he drives home the fact that a Guianese village is not a closed and isolated community. Its relationship to the total society affects the most intimate area of social life, the domestic group. But there is a limiting point to this influence. The nuclear unit of mother and child holds out against all external forces until the cycle of child rearing is finished. Dr. Smith thus confirms recent anthropological studies which bring out the central place of the mother-child unit in all family systems. But his observations have wider implications. In the past few years there has been a concentration of interest from many angles on the relationship of mother and child. The World Health Organization has held conferences on this subject and has published a book (Dr. J. Bowlby, *Maternal Care and Mental Health*, 1951) which has stimulated wide appreciation of the critical importance of the mother-child relationship for mental health. Dr. Smith's data will, I believe, throw valuable light on this problem as it emerges in the West Indies.

Dr. Smith's inquiry brings in many other aspects of the social and economic structure of British Guiana, but I should be trespassing too far on the reader's patience if I commented on them too. I must content myself with noting how the social differences between the three villages he studied and between different classes and races are most skilfully elucidated so as to throw his main argument into relief and to provide cumulative checks on his hypotheses.

I have said that I regard Dr. Smith's book as a major contribution to social science. I want to say this again. It was in order to have a privileged opening for putting this on record that I gladly agreed to write this Foreword. Dr. Smith's book is also a notable addition to the regional sociology of the West Indies, and I am sure its many practical applications will be quickly seen by public and private agencies concerned with family welfare in the West Indies.

Dr. Smith's book is, I believe, the first major publication of the Institute of Social and Economic Research of the University College of the West Indies. It is a beginning full of promise. It shows how fruitful it is to turn a young scholar on to a difficult topical issue of modern social life and give him the freedom to tackle it as a task of fundamental research and to write about it in a dispassionate, scientific spirit.

ACKNOWLEDGMENTS

The production of a book such as this necessarily involves the co-operation of a great number of persons and agencies, and it would be impossible to name them all here. I am particularly indebted to the Colonial Social Science Research Council for the generous grant which made possible the field work and the writing of the first draft of the book. Also to Trinity College, Cambridge, for the honour of electing me to the William Wyse Studentship in Social Anthropology. The University College of the West Indies extended the most cordial hospitality when I was in the West Indies, and the final draft of the book was written whilst I was a member of the staff of the Institute of Social and Economic Research there.

As one of Professor Meyer Fortes's first post-graduate students at Cambridge I learned from him the discipline of research, and his influence and teaching are apparent throughout this work. I am also grateful to Professor Talcott Parsons for his sympathetic interest whilst he was teaching at Cambridge in 1953–4, and for reading the manuscript and making many useful suggestions. With Dr. J. R. Goody I discussed most of the work whilst we were contemporaries at Cambridge. Professor David Schneider of Harvard University very generously read the initial draft of the book and gave me the benefit of his most constructive criticism.

When I first arrived in the West Indies I was fortunate enough to receive a stimulating and authoritative introduction to their problems and peculiarities from many persons at the University College in Jamaica, and to Mr. Lloyd Braithwaite and Dr. Elsa Goveia in particular I should like to offer my sincere appreciation of their friendship and guidance, then and subsequently. Also to Dr. Huggins for so generously placing the facilities of the Institute of Social and Economic Research at my disposal, long before I became a member of its staff.

In British Guiana I was given willing help and invaluable co-operation by hundreds of persons both in government service and outside. The Commissioner of Local Government, the Social

Welfare Officer, and their staffs, were always ready to go out of their way to facilitate my work. To the Department of Lands and Mines, I am particularly grateful for their help with maps and information on the villages, and to the Economics Division of the Department of Agriculture for their co-operation and advice.

In the rural areas I did not meet more than two or three people who were not always ready to offer me their hospitality, their assistance and the benefit of their knowledge. I cannot name all the school-teachers, civil servants, businessmen, doctors, policemen, lawyers, farmers and so on who were my friends and who helped the study in one way or another, but I should particularly like to thank my friend Dr. Frank Williams and his wife for the many pleasant hours I spent in their home in Berbice.

To the people of the three villages described in this book my debt is greatest of all, for they not only welcomed me into their homes and allowed me to pry into the most intimate details of their personal and community life, but they really allowed me to feel that I 'belonged' in their midst and was not merely an intruder. Whatever merits this book may have is a testament to their friendship and trust. In order to avoid them any embarrassment I have invented fictitious names and made individual identification impossible.

To my wife, who not only helped me in the field, but also typed the first draft of the manuscript and pointed out many of my errors, I would like to offer my deepest gratitude.

Any deficiencies this book may have are entirely my own responsibility, and the views or conclusions stated herein are not to be attributed to any of the persons or agencies mentioned above.

Mona, Jamaica.
20th December 1955.

RAYMOND T. SMITH

SECTION I

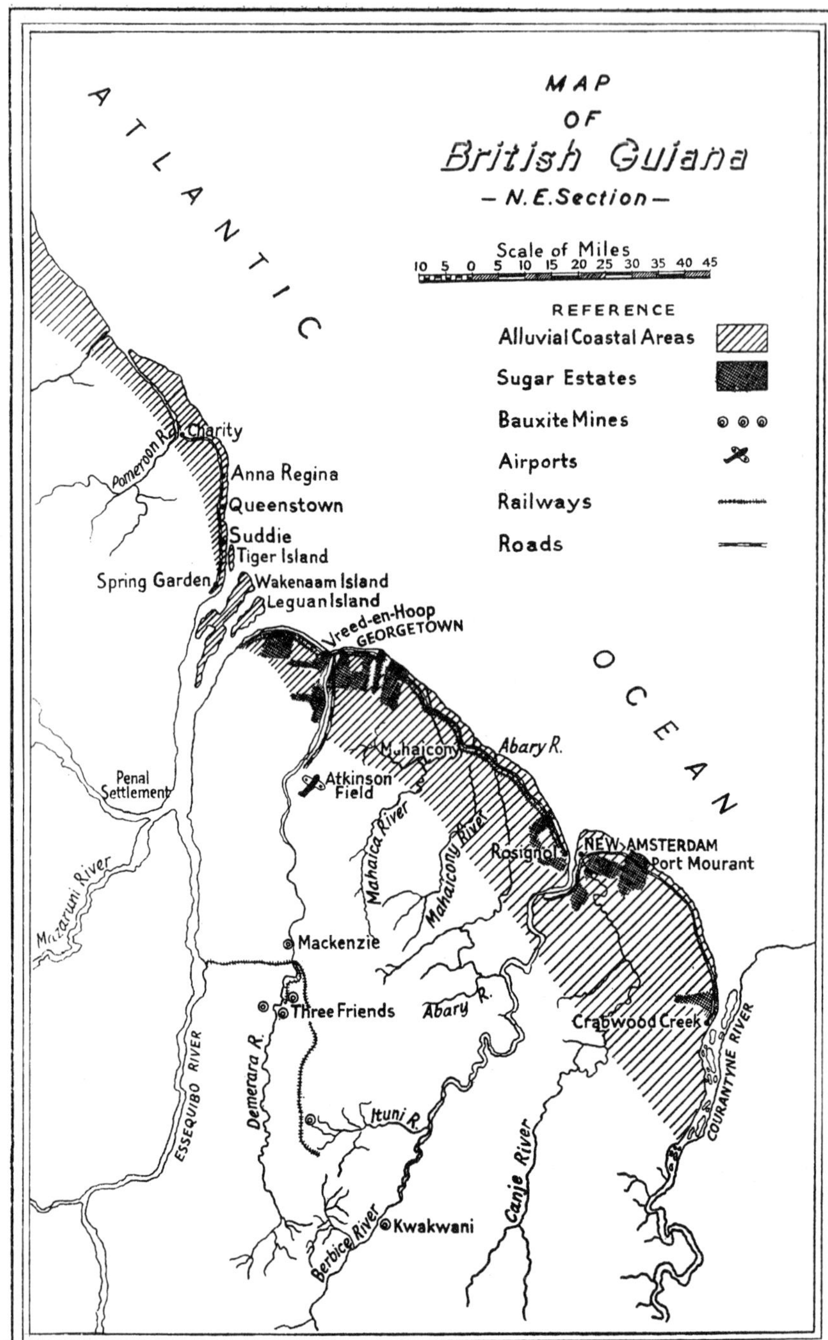
MAP
OF
British Guiana
— N. E. Section —
Scale of Miles
10 5 0 5 10 15 20 25 30 35 40 45
REFERENCE
Alluvial Coastal Areas
Sugar Estates
Bauxite Mines
Airports
Railways
Roads
ATLANTIC
OCEAN
Pomeroon R.
Charity
Anna Regina
Queenstown
Suddie
Tiger Island
Spring Garden
Wakenaam Island
Leguan Island
Vreed-en-Hoop
GEORGETOWN
Mahaicony
Abary R.
Atkinson Field
Penal Settlement
Mahaica River
Mahaicony River
Rosignol
NEW AMSTERDAM
Port Mourant
Mazaruni River
Mackenzie
Three Friends
Abary R.
Crabwood Creek
ESSEQUIBO RIVER
Demerara R.
Ituni R.
COURANTYNE RIVER
Canje River
Kwakwani
Berbice River

MAP I

CHAPTER I

INTRODUCTION

British Guiana lies on the north-eastern shoulder of South America, but its lines of communication run north and east, over the sea to the West Indian islands, to Britain and to the United States of America. Approximately 94 per cent of its ethnically diverse population lives on a narrow coastal strip separated from its continental neighbours by tracts of tropical forest and wide rivers. Whatever new links may be forged with Brazil, Venezuela, Dutch and French Guiana now that air transport is rapidly becoming a practical proposition, it is certain that at the present time British Guiana's main interests are bound up with those of the British West Indian islands, with which it shares a common language and culture. Despite its vast hinterland, and the possibility of the discovery of valuable mineral deposits and so on, it is at present 'under-developed' and the majority of its 436,431 inhabitants share the low standards of living and poverty which are so characteristic of the circum-Caribbean territories. But these factors are complicated by the existence of an intricate system of social distinctions based upon race and status. The process of welding six 'nations', East Indian, Negro, Portuguese, Amerindian, Chinese and European, into a unit where ethnic identity is not the basis of distribution of social rewards is not an easy one, and although British Guiana has gone a long way towards developing a sense of common purpose in its diverse population, it would be both unrealistic and inaccurate to ignore the marked cleavages which exist at the present time; cleavages which are based both upon ethnic and cultural foundations, and are inherent in the present structure and functioning of Guianese society.

The West Indian area has been relatively neglected by social anthropologists but it is becoming increasingly clear that it constitutes an extremely fertile field for the investigation of problems of social organization which lie close to some of the most crucial issues of the subject. This is nowhere more true than in the case of the study of the family, and whereas the West Indian lower-class family system has often been regarded as a pathological phenomenon resulting from the relative disorganization of West Indian society, it is our contention that this family system provides us with a special and extremely illuminating case of the operation of certain principles which have a general significance for social theory.

This book deals primarily with certain aspects of the social structure of three village communities in the coastal area of British Guiana, but in attempting to arrive at an adequate understanding of these relatively small sections of the population we are obliged to consider features of the total society of British Guiana, so interdependent and functionally related are the local communities and the total society of which they are a part. This is a fact which is often overlooked by social anthropologists when they turn their attention from small-scale, pre-literate, and relatively homogeneous societies to those more nearly resembling our own, or when they begin to carry out studies in Europe or North America using the techniques of anthropological field-study. Malinowski's insistence upon regarding every element of culture as relevant to the anthropologist's view of society, coupled with Radcliffe-Brown's postulate that a society must be regarded as an integrated whole, the function of each part being to contribute to the integration of the whole, have often been interpreted to mean that the field-worker must be able to encompass every aspect of a whole society by means of first-hand observation. So long as anthropologists confined their attention to small-scale homogeneous societies where the variations in the pattern of social life were small over the whole population, this was more or less feasible, though one often wonders just how much selectivity and generalization covering a range of social variation is made in even the best documented study. In larger and more extensively structured societies it is clearly impossible to cover every aspect of social life in the total society, and an almost natural tendency is to try to isolate a sub-unit, usually a geographical unit, of a large society, and attempt to study it *as though it were itself a total social system*. A convincing case can be made out for the selection of such a sub-unit in terms of working convenience when one is doing an intimate first-hand study of a people's way of life, but when it comes to the analysis stage of the work it may be quite unjustifiable to treat such a sub-unit as if it constituted a total system in itself. Some writers have even spoken of a local community, or geographically defined sub-unit, as being the microcosm representing the macroscopic whole of which it is a part (1). This position has been rightly criticized by Braithwaite (2), and our own experience has been that it is more realistic to forego the attempt to find a consistency between all the social institutions within the village as though it were itself a closed system with a well-defined boundary. We are now convinced that certain features of the social structure are only explicable if seen as part of a wider social system which cannot be regarded as being merely 'external' to the village. Consequently we shall have to deal with features of Guianese society in its widest sense, and particularly with the system of social stratification in the colony as a whole. Much social action at the local community level contributes to the integration of structures which cross-cut that community, and the boundaries of which are not coincident with it.

The question then arises as to what we shall consider to be the boundaries of our 'wider' or 'total' system, and for the purpose of the problems we shall explore in this book we shall refer to the 'total Guianese society'. That is, we shall treat the society of the colony of British Guiana as if it were a total social system for the purposes of our analysis, though it is clear that if one were investigating certain other problems, particularly of an economic or political nature, then British Guiana would have to be treated as a sub-system of a wider system, or systems, such as the British Commonwealth or the West Indies. Social systems are of such a nature that they are rarely completely self-contained, but whereas we may be justified in treating the whole of British Guiana as an autonomous unit for the purpose of the present analysis, we are not justified in treating the village in a similar fashion because there are direct interdependencies between those features of social structure within the village which form the subject of our inquiry, and certain social structures within the unit we call 'Guianese society'.

All writers dealing with the Negro family in the New World have remarked upon the important place held by women in the family system, and have been impressed by the apparent weakness of the conjugal tie on the one hand, and the strength of kinship ties and particularly the mother-child bond on the other. Such observations apply particularly to the lower-class Negro family, and whilst it is clear that many variations have been relatively neglected there is ample evidence to show that these generalizations are broadly true. When it comes to the question of why this should be so there is disagreement between scholars. Our task is a two-fold one. First to report accurately upon the situation as it exists in the population we have chosen to study and towards this end it is felt that the distribution figures which we present are an indispensable part of the report, and secondly to interpret the facts of field observation in the light of general sociological theory.

For the sake of brevity the title of this book has had to forego strict accuracy. To be able to generalize to the whole of the rural Negro group we should either have to study every Negro family in the rural areas, or take an adequate random sample of them. Neither procedure is practicable for a single field-worker. In fact field-work was carried out in three villages which have been given the fictitious (but typically Guianese) names of August Town, Perseverance and Better Hope. Field-tours were for the following periods of time.

August Town—West Coast Berbice—July 1951 to June 1952.

Perseverance—Essequibo—October 1952 to December 1952 inclusive.

Better Hope—West Coast Demerara—January 1953 to April 1953 inclusive.

The three villages were chosen on the basis of their general suitability as field-centres; the fact that their racial composition was predominantly Negro; that their populations were of such a size as to permit a thorough study of family structure in terms of field-work methods and resources; that they appeared to have different degrees of economic prosperity; and that they are varying distances from the urban centre of Georgetown. They were not chosen according to any rigorous sampling technique and therefore, strictly speaking, the conclusions drawn from the study cannot be generalized to other villages, though on the other hand, there is nothing to suggest that these three villages differ significantly from other Negro villages in the coastal area.

August Town, Perseverance, and Better Hope lie in the three counties of Berbice, Essequibo and Demerara respectively, and they are situated on the densely populated coastal strip which carries some 94 per cent of the total population of the country. The villages and plantations lie along the main, and almost the only, road in the colony like beads on a string and the cultivated area stretches inland for distances varying from about two to fifteen miles. The following summary gives a brief indication of the general characteristics of our three villages, the information being based on material collected in the field. Reference to the maps on page 24 and page 27 will give an idea of their general layout.

VILLAGE	POPULATION *Male*	*Female*	APPROX. AREA IN ACRES *Farm-land*	*Resi-dential*	APPROX. DISTANCE FROM GEORGETOWN IN MILES
August Town	797	930	520	250	56
Perseverance	324	361	572	130	34 road miles and two ferry trips lasting approx. 7 hours in all
Better Hope	422	541	688	200	7 road miles, and one short ferry trip lasting approx. 10 minutes

The field-work techniques adopted by social anthropologists are sufficiently well established to make a lengthy discourse on this topic unnecessary and the adequacy or otherwise of the data collected may be judged from the evidence presented in the chapters that follow (3). After a six-weeks period of familiarization with the rural areas of the coastlands, August Town was chosen as the first field-centre; a house, of the same type as the majority of houses in the village, was rented, and the field-work commenced. A certain amount of suspicion was encountered during the first few weeks, since no Englishman had ever lived in the village before, but this was easily overcome and good relations were quickly established. Participation in the life of the community was possible to a far greater extent than it would be in a more 'primitive' community, and since the local dialect is basically and recognizably English, there was no language difficulty. Surveys of various kinds were carried out, and a good deal of quantitative data were obtained without any difficulties arising in the way of refusals to co-operate in interviews and so on.

Field-tours in the other two villages were much shorter, but were carried out under exactly the same conditions. During the last field-tour in Better Hope, some time was spent in collecting information on other villages in the area, and on studying factors of significance in a wider context than that of the village.

INTRODUCTION

HISTORY OF THE THREE VILLAGES

As social anthropologists we are interested in the study of social structures as they exist over a limited time-span, usually broad enough to enable us to discern regularities in cyclical processes as well as to allow us to observe and record regular customary modes of social action (4). The three villages with which we are concerned came into being at a known point in time, and in a known manner, and we are able to give some idea of the relative stability in the form of local organization, economic activities, and so on, and this is of theoretical importance to our study as well as serving as a descriptive background to what has been recorded during the period of field-work.

Slavery and sugar cultivation made their appearance together in the British West Indies when, in 1616, the first plantation of sugar cane on British territory was made in Bermuda and in the same year one Negro and one Indian slave were landed from one of the Spanish islands (5). The history of colonization is the story of the demand for labour, and the building up of a diverse population through the importation of indentured Europeans, mostly criminals and deportees, but above all of Negro slaves from Africa.

British Guiana was originally discovered by Columbus on his third voyage, but attempts at colonization came much later. By 1580 a few Dutch settlers had landed on the Guiana coast, but Raleigh's expeditions of 1594 to 1597 were still mainly treasure-seeking enterprises and serious colonization was left to later Dutch traders and settlers who moved inland up the great rivers. Although the territories which comprise present-day British Guiana were under Dutch control for a great deal of the time between their discovery and their final acquisition bv Great Britain in 1815, this did not mean that British planters and traders were entirely absent from the colony. Apart from repeated forays against the Dutch by French and English expeditions in the latter half of the seventeenth century, English settlements were established on a permanent basis during the eighteenth century under Dutch rule. In 1796 a military detachment from Barbados under the command of General Whyte occupied the whole of Guiana, but by the Peace of Amiens the colonies of Demerara, Essequibo and Berbice were given back to the Dutch, only to be reoccupied in 1803 by an English fleet and officially ceded to Britain by the treaties of Paris and London in 1814.

Pinckard reports that at the end of the eighteenth century there was a large number of English traders in Georgetown as well as the English planters in other parts of the colony, but the towns of Georgetown and New Amsterdam were little more than administrative centres and the sites of the courts, for the real reason for the existence of the colony was the plantations and it was around them, and their production, that everything else revolved (6).

By the time that the abolition of slavery movement was under way the structure of West Indian society had emerged in a clearly recognizable form, and the broad outlines of that structure can still be discerned today. Plantation cultivation dominated by a white oligarchical plantocracy, and depending on the slave trade to furnish the necessary manual labour for production, resulted in the development of a rigid pyramidal structure with the lowest stratum in a clearly-defined legal position as slaves. Originally race and skin colour were relatively unimportant criteria of status, for all labourers regardless of whether they were African slaves or European indentured labourers occupied much the same position. The overriding consideration was to supply labour, and sentiments of racial superiority and inferiority seem to have increased in importance as race came to be a more crucial index of differentiation, with the rapid growth in the number of enslaved Negroes and the diminution in the number of white labourers. The formation of a mixed-blood middle-class, through the process of miscegenation, has been well documented (7). By the end of the eighteenth century, this group had assumed a position of great importance, and its existence gives the whole system its main distinguishing characteristics. The abolition of the slave trade and the eventual emancipation of the slaves established a more just relationship between the various strata without altering the fundamental structure of the hierarchical system in which they were arranged. Even in Haiti where a successful revolution resulted in the virtual expulsion of the French, the main outlines of the colour/class hierarchy eventually reasserted themselves and the light coloured Creoles replaced the French as the apex of the pyramid (8).

Of the social life of the slaves on the Guiana plantations we know very little. Certainly slaves were granted some privileges, and there was scope for them to develop a limited degree of internal organization and retain some of their own customs. An investigation carried out in Demerara in 1808 revealed that 'it had been customary for years for the negroes of every nation in a district to choose head-men or "Kings", under whom were several subaltern officers of the same nation. The duties of the "kings" were *to take care of the sick and purchase rice, sugar, etc., for them, to conduct the burials, and see that the corpse was properly enclosed in a cloth, and that the customary rites and dances were duly observed*' (9). It was also mentioned that the slaves contributed money for funeral expenses, and of course this is very similar to the prevailing West African pattern, both in the past and in the present. However, amongst the slaves an extended system of reciprocity such as this would be tied to the local community such as the estate, and further broken down on the basis of tribal affiliation, rather than on a strictly kinship basis. Even under the most adverse conditions, such an extended network of reciprocal relations would be necessary in order to carry out the minimum of rites in the event of death, and the present-day burial societies perform the same functions (10).

The ability to attend markets and to sell produce, as well as such articles as fish, crabs, pigs, poultry, fishing nets, baskets, pottery and prepared foods such as black pudding, souse (11), and cassava bread, must have been important in enabling some slaves to acquire enough money to purchase manumission, and this contributed to the growth of a free group of Negro and Coloured persons, who often owned slaves of their own.

Slave rebellions were as common in Guiana as elsewhere in the West Indies, and at various times groups of rebels and runaway slaves managed to establish settlements where they led an independent, if somewhat precarious existence. Pinckard reports that there were about eight runaway settlements in Demerara towards the end of the eighteenth century and they caused a good deal of trouble by their raids on the plantations. He describes the settlements as follows:

> Having fixed upon the spot most convenient for their purpose, a circular piece of ground was cleared of its wood, and, in the centre of this, they built huts, and formed the encampment, planting round about the buildings, oranges, bananas, plantains, yams, eddoes, and other kinds of provisions; thus, in addition to the trees of the forest, procuring themselves further concealment by the plantations which gave them food. The eddoes were found in great plenty, and had seemed to constitute their principal diet. Round the exterior of the circular spot was cut a deep and wide ditch, which, being filled with water, and stuck, at the sides and bottom, with sharp pointed stakes, served as a formidable barrier of defence. The path across this ditch was placed two or three feet below the surface, and wholly concealed from the eye by the water being always thick and muddy (12).

Shortly after Pinckard arrived in the colony all the bands except one were wiped out by a force of slaves and Amerindians, and by 1800 all the settlements had been destroyed. The members of the punitive expeditions got 300 guilders for every right hand they brought in, and from one foray they brought in seventy-six hands and a number of prisoners, all of whom were tortured and then killed. This put paid to the Bush Negro settlements, and no permanent groups survived as they did in Surinam (13) and Jamaica (14).

The estates at this time were concentrating on the production of cotton and coffee rather than sugar, and out of 116 estates along the coast from Georgetown to the Abary, only Plantation Kitty was growing sugar, all the rest being planted in cotton (15). Berbice produced coffee, and in August Town I was told by the older inhabitants that they had heard from their parents and grandparents that the estates on the West Coast did not grow sugar in 'slavery days' but cultivated cotton and coffee. However the plantation system was the same, and whether it was sugar, cotton or coffee that was grown at any particular time depended to a great extent upon the availability of markets, and price levels in Europe.

Between the beginning of the nineteenth century and the final emancipation of the slaves in 1838, there must have been a considerable influx of planters with their slaves from the over-crowded islands of the Caribbean, and Farley has referred to British Guiana at this time as an expanding economic frontier region (16). However, our main concern is with the establishment and development of the free Negro villages after 1838, and prior to that date there were only three tiny hamlets, probably inhabited by freed persons, in the whole colony, and the enormous development of the new village communities after 1838 was undertaken by ex-slaves who had all spent some time on the Guianese plantations. It is worth mentioning that even after emancipation the immigration of Africans continued, and between 1841 and 1865, 13,264 Africans entered British Guiana. No doubt many of them came from other West Indian islands, but some came from North America, and some came direct from Africa (17). In 1891 the number of African-born Negroes in the colony was 3,443 whilst by 1911 the number had fallen to 706.

The slaves had been participating in a money economy for a considerable time, particularly through their markets in the towns, and during their apprenticeship period from 1834 to 1838 they were able to devote a part of their time to working for wages, the planters being forced to pay them for any work they did in excess of a statutory seven and a half hours per day. After 1838 the now emancipated workers were free to choose their employers, and free to demand higher wages, and they thus began to accumulate a certain amount of capital. The planters were concerned lest the Negroes decided not to work at all, and it is reported that they even cut down many fruit trees to ensure that there was not a ready food supply to be had for the picking (18). For the same reason they were loath to lease lands on which the Negroes could build their own houses and plant gardens, and they attempted to keep them in the estate-owned quarters from which they could be evicted if they refused to work. Despite these attempts, the prevailing conditions resulted in many planters having to cease operations, and those who did not actually close down found it expedient to sell part of their surplus lands in order to offset their losses (19). The Negroes banded themselves together in groups and pooling their resources, purchased whole estates or sections of estates. The present-day villages of Victoria and Buxton on the East Coast of Demerara were the first two estates to be purchased, and by 1842 they were quite large villages (20). A Commission of Investigation appointed to determine the amount of land held by the freedmen, reported that out of a rural population of 79,000, some 15,906 were already settled in villages, and 3,322 wooden cottages had been erected. Cameron asserts that the farmlands of some of the new villages were worked communally with a paid manager and a clerk to keep accounts, and that in Buxton the impracticability of this system led to the villagers requesting government to partition their lands (21). The question of the 'communal' working of farmlands seems to be an open one, and though the main works of the village, including drainage and irrigation were certainly run in this manner, it is probable that each family planted its own gardens, and that the difficulties arose over the individual allotments of shares of land. Partitioning Ordinances were certainly passed in 1851 and 1852 which provided for the division of lands between shareholders in those villages requesting government assistance in this matter.

An interesting comment is made by Rodway on a subject that we shall find to be of great interest later on (22). A certain number of the freed Negroes had gone into the retail trades, for obviously there had to be agencies of distribution for essential commodities such as imported foodstuffs, cloth and hardware now that this function was no longer carried out by the management of the estates. Rodway suggests that the later ousting of the Negroes from this activity was due to the fact that the town merchants refused to sell to Negroes in an attempt to drive them back into the fields, but favoured the new Portuguese immigrants who had proved less satisfactory as field-hands. Even at a common-sense level this gives a new slant to the usually propounded theory that the Portuguese were just naturally better business men and so monopolized the retail trades.

The whole picture of the establishment of the free Negro villages is an exceedingly complex one and its detailed documentation in the wider context of the social, economic and political movements of the time remains as a task for the historian. It seems certain that the rapid development of freehold villages was partly due to the economic factors associated with the trade position of the West Indies which made land available, and which probably contributed in large measure to the growth of the emancipation movement itself (23). Another major factor was the ecological necessity for individuals to associate themselves into reasonably large units in order to cope with the problems of drainage and irrigation. With this brief background we are now in a position to examine more closely the development of the three villages with which we are primarily concerned.

August Town

In the pre-1838 era a planter named Mr. James Blair owned four cotton estates in the vicinity of what is now August Town. They were known as Nos. 16, 17, 18 and 19, and after emancipation, groups of slaves from No. 19 on the one hand and Nos. 17 and 18 on the other, bought two sections of August Town lands. This is a traditional account, and the same tradition also asserts that all of Mr. Blair's slaves were related even then, and this accounts for the close relationship between the people of August Town and certain other Negro villages further down the coast, for their ancestors came from Blair's estate too. The Congregational Church which stood at Rodborough, the present site of the Congregational Manse, was dismantled and the materials were divided into three sections which were used to build three new churches in three villages of which August Town was one. This helps to bolster the tradition of a common origin for the three villages and for the Negro communities of the lower part of the coast of Western Berbice. Whether the details of this story are historically accurate or not is of little concern to us, for its main purpose seems to be to validate the relationships which exist between the communities today. Certainly the main outlines seem likely to be correct for Pinckard mentions having visited Mr. Blair's estate at the end of the eighteenth century (24).

The main event in the historical tradition is the founding of the village itself shortly after emancipation. The first section of August Town known as St. Paul's section was purchased by a group of forty-nine persons. A copy of the Transport (conveyance) passed at that time shows that they were represented by one man who appeared before His Honour Samuel Firebrace, one of the Judges of the Supreme Court of Civil Justice of British Guiana, on the 12th day of October, 1840 (25). In 1841 a magistrate made a tour of the rural areas, and in his report to the Governor he remarked upon an estate called No. 21 (the numerical designation of St. Paul's section) and on the neat cottages built by the 'labourers'. He thought it seemed to be quite a village already.

> The cultivation of provisions is being commenced at the back of the estate. This property is owned by forty-nine people and cost 2,000 dollars. The majority of these people I was informed by one of their body, Jacob Wilson, work upon a sugar estate called number 17, and come home only at night. (26).

The second section of the village to be purchased was named Troy, and this was bought in 1841 by a group of ex-slaves from Nos. 17 and 18 sections of Blair's estate. Although these two units, Troy and St. Paul's were, and are, contiguous, they formed two separate units for many years. A bitter feud is supposed to have developed between the two sections over the disputed position of the boundary lines between them at the very back of the cultivation area. The drainage trenches separating the two sections take a sharp turn into St. Paul's land at one point, before turning back into the previous direction of division, and if they are still taken as the dividing line beyond this point it means that St. Paul's loses a small area of land. The St. Paul's people contended that the boundary should be a continuation of the straight compass line, and they reputedly took the matter to court and got a decision in their favour. However, this resulted in a prolonged series of fights, reciprocal burning of crops, impounding of animals, and working of destructive magic. Most important of all, a ban on intermarriage between the two sections was maintained until somewhere around the 1870's when the marriage of a Troy woman to a St. Paul's man marked the beginning of frequent intermarriage. It is interesting that this traditional account places the first intermarriage at a point corresponding to the farthest extension of known kinship reckoning, and this division of the village into two sections with a tradition of mutual hostility is particularly interesting since something of the kind is found in most Negro villages throughout the country (27).

When the two sections were purchased and settled each had its own internal organization and its own elected headmen. The fact that most of British Guiana's coastlands lie below the level of the sea at high tide means that an elaborate system of drainage and irrigation works has to be maintained if the land is not to be perpetually under water, and if farming is to be at all possible (28). This means that the system of social organization has to be of such a nature that the tasks involved can be properly executed. It was not, and is not, possible for each proprietor to drain his or her own pieces of land individually, and the history of village political organization is dominated by the recurrent theme of problems of drainage and irrigation. We do not know a great deal about the very early working of the system in August Town, except that the headmen were elected to supervise the proper execution of the necessary works. Some villages seem to have run into difficulties quite early, for one of the demands of the central government was that every village and estate should be responsible for that section of the public road running through it, and as early as 1845 we find Queen's Town, Essequibo, petitioning government to enact an ordinance making it compulsory for every villager to contribute to the upkeep of the road and its bridges. Plaisance, Demerara followed in 1849, and monetary contributions in lieu of labour contributions were introduced. The central government gradually came to exercise a greater degree of supervision over the internal organization of the villages, and the history of the various ordinances affecting the villages has been well documented by Cameron (29), and in less detail by Hinden (30). It appears that there was always a certain amount of difficulty involved in enforcing the obligations of villagers to contribute to the maintenance of the village works and the early appeals to government were primarily for a system of effective legal sanctions to bolster the authority of the village headmen or overseers. Most of the early legislation was concerned with providing these sanctions, but one also hears stories today of the way in which villages sometimes worked out their own control system. Thus in August Town it is said that anyone defaulting on their obligations to work was arraigned before a 'court' of the whole body of the proprietors, and if the negligence of the offender was established then he could be beaten by the headmen. For August Town we are fortunate enough to possess a copy of an agreement which was signed by all the shareholders as early as 1865. This document is in the possession of one of the villagers, and although it was originally dated 1865, it was recopied at later dates in exactly the same form, and it is quite possible that this particular document is a copy of an even earlier one. Judging by the style and punctuation it appears to have been drawn up by the villagers themselves, perhaps with the help of a minister or local official, and it sets out very clearly the rights, and obligations of every shareholder. Due recognition is given to the values prohibiting 'African' dancing and Obeah, and these must have been fairly common at the time to merit mention in a document such as this (31). It is abundantly clear that a democratic form of local self-government had been established as a natural response to the situation confronting the settlement. That this form of local control eventually became less efficient was not due to the natural inabilities or political ineptness of the villagers, but rather to the change in the pattern of activities of the shareholders, and the same factors are responsible for the 'inefficient' running of the village today under a local government system with a large measure of outside control. The following is an exact copy of the document, apart from the fact that the place-names have been changed. Where a cross appears in the middle of the signature, this indicates that the person was completely illiterate.

Rules for the administration of St. Paul section,

August Town

Be it known to all whom these presents shall come we the undersigned proprietors of plantation No. 21 called Saint Pauls on this tenth day of July 1865 hereby enter into mutual agreement in the presence of the undersigned witnesses.

1st. We do hereby agree that whenever there is Estate work required to be done each and every shareholder shall at once turn out and do it, or send a fit and proper person to do the same or failing to do he or she shall pay a fine of 32 cents per day which shall be recoverable by a Magistrate. All the public outlet and dams to be refit in good order and attended to, the Estate to well drained and put in good condition.

3rd. A Committee to be chosen yearly from the majority of shareholders who shall vote for the election of such committee which shall consist of five men who shall advise the Headmen as to what is necessary to be done for the good of the Estate for the year ending 31st July 1866 if their successors inherited shall neglect their duty a fine of sixty four cents shall be imposed, each and every shareholder shall with his family have equal rights to and from the waterside a back along the public roads or dams. Any other person or persons trespassing shall be dealt with according to law.

4th. Any person keeping a shop not interested in the village to pay a fine or sum of one dollar per month for the transporting of his or her goods through the coker trench. Firewood to be bought from the shareholders.

5th. Should any person not interested in the village graze Horses Asses pay a sum of three Dollars per Annum for each and every head.

6th. We do hereby agree to have a burial ground or else the dead to be carried to a church or chapel such Burial ground to be well drained and kept in good condition No provision to be planted on the aforesaid ground.

7th. We also agree that there shall be from the surveyors pall a ten feet trench to prevent all stock from grazing aback.

8th. No strange person shall be allowed to cut cordwood unless being provided with a Licence from the committee.

9th. And be it known to all shareholders that no ungodly dance shall be held in the village Mingy Mamma Mingy drumming, persons found in such act to be carried before Magistrate of the district.

10th. Should any person be found practising Obeah or receiving money under false pretence to be dealt with according to law.

11th. There must be a meeting held quarterly for the benefit of the public work of the Estate Roads Bridge Coker etc. Carpenters to be elected by the Members of the Committee and exempted from diging trenches etc. there must be fourteen days notice given to every shareholder.

12th. We Nominate and appoint Jacob Rowley and Sancho Cameron to be our Headmen in the purpose of superintending the general business of the Estate and in case of failure or neglect in the said business a fine to be imposed of sixty four cents.

This done signed by the shareholders in the presence of the sub scribed witnesses.

Witnesses
Robert Bowling
George Houston

I hereby agree to the terms of this agreement
[Names of the proprietors of the village]

Jacob Rowley
Sancho Cameron X
Watson X Joseph
Stewart Thompson
Bass X Schrewder
Collingford X Sam
Hector X Wilson
Corydon X James
Brian X McFarley
Job X Stupid
King Gillis
James Watts
William Liverpool
Pith X Dover
Frank X Nicolson
Phebe X Archibald
Penny X Romeo
[Indistinct] Alexander Cain
[Indistinct] Bowling
Pompey Joseph
Felix X Wilson
Dianah X McDonald
Quamey X Johnson

William Author
John Whinfield
Harry Benjamin
Lucy X Acman
Rory X Maria
Samuel X McFarley
Eve X Rigby
Sandy Moria
Frances X House
Sabina Young
Amba X Blair
King X Thompson
Pondorah X Acman
Frank X Joseph Rigby
Sarah X Edwards
Hero X McDonald
Joan X McFarley
Phillis X Acman
Edward Gillis
Matair X [Indistinct]
[*Unreadable*]
Blenhem X [Indistinct]
George Cook
Febuary Watts

After emancipation the new villagers needed to earn money with which to provide themselves with at least those essentials which had been provided for them by their masters when they were slaves. Clothing, cooking utensils, and certain items of food such as salt-fish, salt-beef, and pickled meat, now had to be bought for cash and since there was a limited market for farm produce grown on small holdings cash had to be obtained by selling one's labour to the planters. The security of having one's own house, and at least the produce of one's own garden, gave the ex-slaves a favourable position from which to bargain with the planters, and the strikes of 1842 show that there was a lively appreciation of the new situation. This was short-lived and when the planters prevailed upon the home government to allow the wholesale importation of indentured labourers, first from Maderia and China, and then more significantly from India, the Negro was effectively robbed of his hitherto disconcerting bargaining power (32). He continued to work on the estates for part of the time, particularly during the cane-cutting seasons when a reasonable amount of money could be earned in a relatively short time by the concentration of considerable physical effort. Attempts to grow cash crops such as cotton, coffee and arrowroot met with little success in the villages, and farming activities came to be little more than glorified kitchen gardening for home consumption.

In 1863 the Eastern half of Plantation Belle Vue or Lot No. 22, was surveyed and partitioned into forty-four shares. The present-day oral tradition is that the proprietors of St. Paul's section bought this land, comprising some 250 acres, in order to bring the size of their holdings into line with that of Troy section, and it is true that the surnames of the majority of the original proprietors of Belle Vue correspond with those of the original proprietors of St. Paul's section (33). However a number of new surnames appear on the Belle Vue list and there is no means of telling who these people were or where they came from. They may have been the children of St. Paul's women by men from other parts of the country, or they may have been new settlers. Today Belle Vue has its own village council but it holds joint meetings with August Town and the same individual is chairman of both councils. It is very much a part of the social unit of August Town and should be really considered as a sub-unit of the same order as Troy and St. Paul's being closer to St. Paul's and in some respects an extension of it. It is separated from St. Paul's section by a narrow private estate owned by an East Indian family, and on the other side of Belle Vue there are two private estates separating it from an East Indian village. It is on this Belle Vue boundary of the village that there has been a slight inter-mixture of the Negro and East Indian groups. A few Indian families actually live on Belle Vue land, and the adjoining estate is owned by an East Indian family which has kinship ties with many August Town Negro families through the intermarriage of a male member of the family with a woman from August Town. Thus the physical boundary of the two villages August Town and the East Indian village is a stretch of private land owned by families with kinship ties in both villages.

The opening up of the gold and diamond mining enterprises in the interior of the colony from around 1880 onwards, resulted in village men going off on extended trips as a regular feature, and the tapping of balata from the wild forest trees also became a well established male occupation requiring lengthy absences from the village (34). Today the older men in any village love to tell stories of their days in the interior, of the rivers and forests and mountains, of their feats and their exploits, and of the 'buck Indians'. This is their world of fantasy and the women roundly mock them and call them liars behind their backs. More recently, work in the Bauxite mining towns of Kwakwani and McKenzie has provided an avenue of employment for August Town men and resulted in their spending long periods of time away from home.

Perseverance

Perseverance was settled as a village rather later than August Town. According to local informants the land belonged to a Dutchman named Brummell prior to 1838, and it was later owned by the well-known Hogg family of England, and also by a private corporation. It was certainly an abandoned estate when it was taken over by the ancestors of the present inhabitants, and there may have been squatters living there prior to its legal acquisition which is placed around 1882. Various accounts of the origin of the settlers are given, and one informant claims that 'you had people from Africa and from Dutch Guiana. All them African people them die out'. Other informants claim that some of the people came from the nearby estates of Devonshire Castle and Better Success. Kirke, writing in 1898, says:—

> Better Success was an old, abandoned estate, where lived a number of Africans in a state of primitive barbarism. The front dams of the estate had been broken down by the sea, and the tide swept in and out, under and around the houses of the inhabitants, which were built on greenheart piles; the road was washed away, and the only means of approach was in bateaux. I once went to this place to open an inquest over a man, who was supposed to have been murdered. I was astonished to see such numbers of fine stalwart people. Their food was principally fish and rice; the former caught in great numbers out of the sea, the latter grown by coolies on a neighbouring settlement.
>
> As the tide was up, the people were wading through the water in all directions, most of them without clothes; only the older women seemed to think it was necessary to cover their nakedness in any way, although a few of the men sported a ragged pair of trousers or an old shirt. There are several settlements of these Africans in various parts of the colony. They are a fine, hardy race, hard working and prosperous, very different from the ordinary Creole black man. They are the descendants of thirteen thousand Congoes, Mandingoes and other tribes, who were taken out of captured slavers and landed in the

> country, where they readily found employment. The language these people talk is very peculiar, and perfectly unintelligible to a stranger. (35).

This account of Better Success (which is now a privately owned estate), corresponds very closely to the kind of picture outsiders have of Perseverance, although there is no tradition of Perseverance villagers being descended from Africans brought in after emancipation. Prior to 1950 Perseverance had practically no effective drainage or sea defence and the villagers were renowned for their semi-aquatic life, their supposed health and vigour, and for their independence. There appears to have been a minimum of effective organization for maintaining the village works, but there was certainly some organization, and the pattern of land holding, etc., was substantially the same as that in August Town. Perseverance villagers worked on the sugar estates, and when the last estate on the Essequibo Coast closed down in 1925 this was regarded as something in the nature of a major catastrophe. Men now had to go further afield to find work as they do at the present time.

Better Hope

Like August Town, what we have called Better Hope is really composed of two separate settlements, and also like August Town they were purchased soon after emancipation by groups of ex-slaves. There is still a traditional distinction made between Better Hope proper and the contiguous section known as Eldorado, and the official title of the village as a whole is Better Hope and Eldorado. The history of this village does not differ materially from that of August Town and we shall not dwell upon it at length. The main difference is that being close to Georgetown it has been much more affected by urban influences, and it came into the centralized local government system much earlier than did August Town.

This historical sketch has been kept as brief as possible. The intention has been to give a clear background to the present-day village structure and to highlight those antecedent developments which seemed most relevant. The resultant impression is of groups of people forcibly transported to the estates of British Guiana from Africa and various other colonies of the New World, where they were fitted into a complex social system, occupying a given place within the total structure. They developed enough cohesion in their sub-group to be able to establish village communities of their own after emancipation, and these were characterized by their ethnic identity, their peculiar culture or customs, their peculiar dialect and by their special place in the social system of the colony as a whole. The further introduction of new ethnic groups in the nineteenth century modified the position of the Negro groups still further, but by the tail-end of the century the structural situation was essentially the same as it is today. We have no reason to believe that the 'culture' of the Negro villages has changed substantially over the last hundred years or so despite the continued 'culture contact' situation, and it will be part of our thesis that the peculiar 'culture' of the Negro villages is correlated with their structural position in the Guianese social system.

ECOLOGY AND ECONOMY

It is crucial to make clear the fact that the village is not a bounded economic unit, except in so far as we decide to treat it as one for the purposes of description. Farming activities and animal husbandry are balanced against participation in the labour market of the colony as a whole, for villagers sell their labour for wages outside the village as well as cultivating the soil within it. This has important consequences for apart from the fact that it results in men spending considerable periods of time away from their families, it also ties in with the fact that the purchasing power of money is a more important asset than are non-consumable items of property such as land, which might in other circumstances form the basic means of production for household groups.

Although British Guiana has an estimated area of 83,000 square miles, approximately 94 per cent of its population of 436,431 live on 3,000 square miles of coastland. Approximately 85 per cent of the total area of the colony is forest land and 10.5 per cent is open savannah sparsely populated by Amerindians and a few cattle ranchers, gold miners, etc. The relative inaccessibility of the interior lands and the great fertility of the coastal ribbon have been factors of some importance in the trend of development of the colony, but such ecological factors merely coincided with the primary interest in plantation cultivation in the most intensive period of settlement to produce the characteristic pattern of population distribution that we find today. There has been no expanding frontier development despite the often expressed desire to open up the interior of the country.

Water control is necessarily the major ecological problem of a country whose population is concentrated on a narrow coastal belt lying for the most part below the level of the high tides, and experiencing very heavy rainfall.

The general principles upon which the drainage and irrigation system of a village is built are fairly simple. A wall is thrown up along the seashore and another wall is built at the back of the estate to keep out accumulated rain-water which would otherwise drain through to the sea. This water can be conserved for irrigation purposes. In an area where there is a sufficient degree of organization, these two walls, the sea-wall and the back-dam, will be extended either way to link up with those of adjoining estates. Down each side of the estate, side-line dams and trenches are built, the trenches being skilfully graded so that the accumulated water can be drained down through a sluice gate to the sea, this gate being closed against the sea at high tide (see Plate VIb). Fig. 1 presents a schematic diagram showing the general layout of any typical coastal estate (villages are of course estates, and this diagram refers to village estates), and shows the main essentials of a drainage system. This basic layout is capable of a great many modifications of course, and some of the sugar plantations are much more complicated pieces of engineering. However in the three villages with which we are dealing the system is fundamentally the same as shown in the diagram.

The proper maintenance of such a system requires a great deal of effort and an overall plan of administration. Someone has to be employed to open the sluice gates and to close them again at the appropriate times; the trenches must be kept clear of silt and weeds; and the dams must be rebuilt as they begin to wear as the result of heavy rainfall or the constant passage of animals, carts, etc. Since there is no stone easily available, village dams are usually built up from packed mud which wears very quickly, especially since the tops of the dams serve as roads and pathways. A few villages metal the top surface of their dams with brick (burnt earth) but even this does not prolong the life of the dam very much.

It would be difficult to over-emphasize the importance of the peculiar nature of the country and its effect of imposing a pattern of corporate group life almost as a condition of existence, but on the other hand it must be remembered that there was never any iron necessity for this. Some villages in British Guiana have let their drainage and irrigation works deteriorate to a point where they live a semi-aquatic existence and just don't bother about the repeated flooding of their lands. For many years the inhabitants of Perseverance did practically no farming on their village lands, and the fact

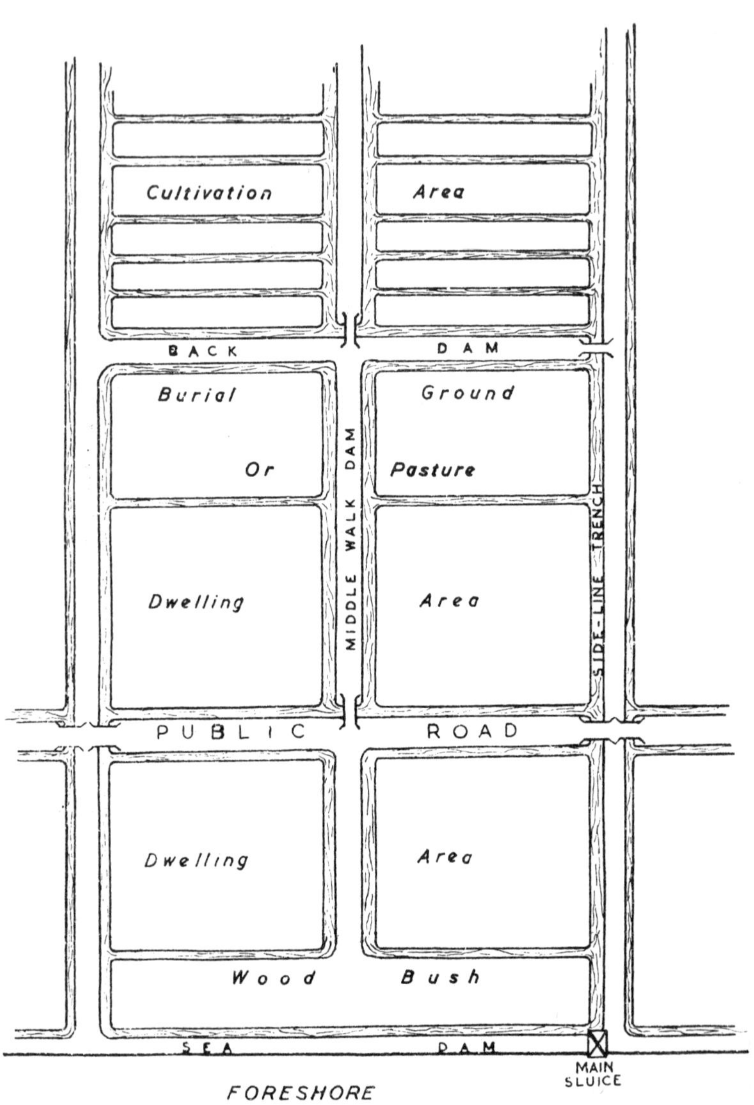

FIG. I.—SIMPLIFIED DIAGRAM OF A VILLAGE DRAINAGE SYSTEM

that they had to wade waist deep in water to get to the public road was of little consequence to them. Such villages often specialized in fishing, particularly for shrimps, and the possibility of finding employment on the sugar estates has always meant that the Negro villager is not wholly dependent on farming as a means of livelihood. Of course only a limited number of villages at any one time could be completely unproductive or the production of food crops would fall below a necessary minimum, but farming has been, and is, very much a secondary occupation to the Negro. On the slave plantations small plots of land were given to the slaves for the purpose of growing food and the fact that slaves often sold their surplus produce in the markets did not make them farmers. After emancipation the new villages were established and operated by a remarkable feat of co-operation, but this co-operation has always been difficult to maintain, not least of all because men have found it difficult to meet the demands it made upon their labour when they wished to sell that labour for wages outside the village. By the time a village has come under the aegis of the local government system, real co-operation has been replaced by a system of cash payments which are obligatory under the law of the colony as a whole. Ever since the villages were first established the tendency has been in this direction, and the initial feats of co-operative endeavour never crystallized into a strong continuing system. The present-day local government system has been described by Simey (36), Hinden (37) and Laing (38), but these writers tend to ignore the fact that in practice the villages are heavily dependent on agencies of the central government both for supervision and administrative assistance and often for financial aid (39).

If we try to look at the economic system of the village as a whole we find that there is really no sense in which the village functions as a sub-system of the total economy of the colony. There is instead a series of lines where the economy of the whole society cuts across the village as a unit. For example, villagers participate in the economic life of the sugar estates, but these estates are external organizations so far as the village is concerned. Similarly farmers produce rice which is sold to external agencies, and they may even engage tractors to do part of the cultivation, but the tractors are also external to the village. Whilst we must bear in mind this intrusion of external economic factors, for the purpose of simple analysis such as we require at the moment we may look at the village as though it were a distinct unit and try to see how the economy fits on to its political, territorial and social organization.

Farming

Farming is the first sector of the economy with which we shall deal, and there is a fairly close degree of correspondence between the organization of agricultural activities and village structure. Successful farming depends upon adequate drainage and irrigation and this is most directly organized at a village level, even though a large measure of administrative control rests with officials of the central government. It is not organized by individual farmers or by households. In all three villages the farm lands are divided into large blocks on which different kinds of crops are grown. Thus we speak of the 'provision area', the 'rice lands' and the 'cattle-grazing area' (see Map 2). Each village is made up of lands which are the freehold property of the villagers, but in the case of August Town there are certain lands used for rice cultivation and for cattle grazing which are leased from the Crown on a long lease at very low rental. They do not all come under the direct control of the village council although they are really an extension of the village lands, but there is a basic similarity in their mode of control. In the first place these lands must be drained through the village drainage system and the local authority takes full responsibility for this. Secondly, the lands are leased from government in exactly the same way that the village lands were purchased after emancipation. That is, two men take out a lease on behalf of a number of villagers and then the land is allocated in strips between the participating shareholders who all contribute towards the rental, the cost of building low dams or 'empoldering', and the cost of buying any wire fencing that may be necessary. One block of Crown land is actually leased by the council and allotted to farmers in this way. Rice is always cultivated in large blocks divided into individual holdings, and is kept distinct from the 'provision' area, which is similarly divided into strips. The reasons for this are obvious, since rice fields require to be flooded at certain stages of the plant's growth.

In the provision area, which is freehold land in all three villages, the land is divided into individual strips known as 'beds' (see Map 2) and they run laterally across the village from the side-line trenches to the middle drainage trenches. Originally each bed was an individual holding but through sub-division a single bed may be divided into as many as four separately owned sections. In August Town the majority of beds are about 800 × 30 feet in Troy section, and 450 × 57 feet in St. Paul's section, averaging a little over half an

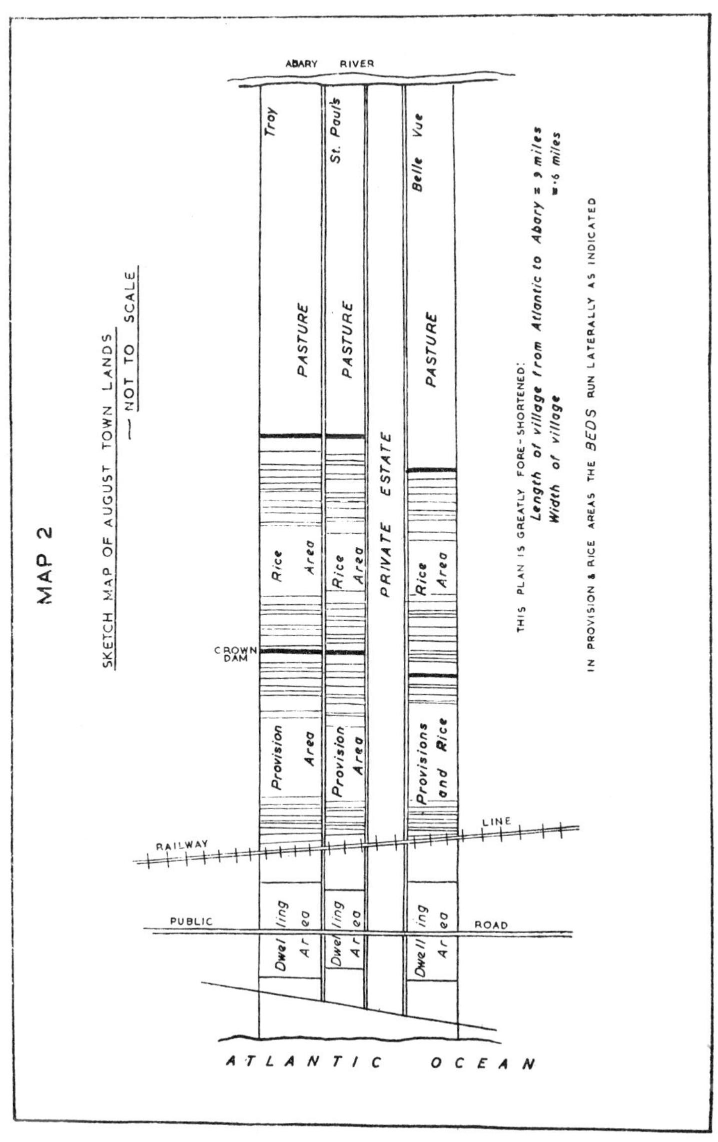
MAP 2
SKETCH MAP OF AUGUST TOWN LANDS
— NOT TO SCALE
ABARY RIVER
Troy
St. Paul's
Belle Vue
PASTURE
PASTURE
PASTURE
PRIVATE ESTATE
Rice Area
Rice Area
Rice Area
CROWN DAM
Provision Area
Provision Area
Provisions and Rice
RAILWAY
LINE
PUBLIC
ROAD
Dwelling Area
Dwelling Area
Dwelling Area
ATLANTIC OCEAN
THIS PLAN IS GREATLY FORE-SHORTENED:
Length of village from Atlantic to Abary = 9 miles
Width of village = ·6 miles
IN PROVISION & RICE AREAS THE BEDS RUN LATERALLY AS INDICATED

MAP 2

acre per bed in both sections. The greater part of Belle Vue section is now used for rice cultivation and when it was repartitioned in 1952, it was divided into varying sized lots, but very few were over one acre, and the majority were less. Perseverance was also repartitioned in 1951, and individuals who had consolidated a few holdings may have beds of three or more acres, but again the majority of beds are in the region of one acre, and even where there are large beds, it is most likely that they are being cultivated by several different persons (40).

On these small plots of land a variety of crops is grown, the majority being for home consumption or for sale within the village. Cassava, yams, sweet potato, plantains, eddoes, tannia, squash, pumpkin, corn, ockro, boulangers, peas, beans, calalloo (spinach), and fruits and nuts are often grown mixed up together, without any attempt to separate the various plants. This is not always the case and there may be definite grouping of the plants, but the term 'mixed provisions' is commonly used to designate the crop growing on a particular bed, and it is to be taken as a literal description. Before a provision bed can be planted it has to be cleared of bush and this is done by the 'slash and burn' method. The undergrowth is hacked down by cutlass and burnt before the bed is forked over ready for planting. After the initial clearing of a bed it is worked for about five to seven years before being allowed to return to bush for fallowing for upwards of five years. During the period when the bed is being worked, crops are planted almost continuously, and reaped as they ripen or as they are required. Cassava in particular can be planted at any time of the year, and it can be left in the ground without deteriorating until it is required. There is therefore no well demarcated cycle of planting and harvesting seasons so far as ground provisions are concerned, and the harvest festivals celebrated in the churches are based upon the English church calendar, being delayed just a little to coincide with the rice harvest in late September or October.

The bulk of the produce of provision farms is consumed by the producer or sold within the village, but some is bought by itinerant dealers who are mostly Negro women from other villages, or East Indians. The quantities sold are usually quite small and the transactions will rarely exceed a few dollars at the most (41). Selling within the village is done by women or children who go around from house to house, or by women at the one market of the week held in August Town. From Perseverance a few farmers take provisions to markets at Charity or Anna Regina (each 7 miles away), and there is also a government depot at Charity which buys produce for transport to Georgetown by schooner. The farmers in Better Hope sell their produce either to middlemen ('hucksters') who transport it to Georgetown and the sugar estates, or they sell it themselves in the local markets. The general rule amongst rural Negro cultivators is that you sell wherever you can, whenever you need money sufficiently badly to take the trouble to seek a market. This is not true for all farmers, and in Perseverance and Better Hope the proximity of markets with a constant demand leads some farmers to produce regularly for it.

Apart from provision farms there is a certain amount of produce grown in kitchen gardens on the house lots, particularly in Better Hope where animals are more satisfactorily controlled and less constant attention to fences is required. Again the bulk of kitchen garden produce is used for domestic consumption, and the methods of cultivation are exactly the same as in the case of provision farms except that manure from the animal pens may be used. Very few villagers grow provisions on land outside the village as there is no shortage of this type of land within the village boundaries. In fact it is much more likely that a few beds of provision land will be rented to outsiders, including East Indians from neighbouring settlements.

In the early days of village settlement some attempt seems to have been made to grow cash crops such as cotton and coffee, but these attempts were never very successful. Markets were not particularly good, and the village cultivator could not hope to compete with the plantations. Sugar has never been widely grown as a peasant crop in British Guiana and the few cane farmers there are in the colony are all concentrated on the East Coast of Demerara near to a few large plantations which buy their crop. Out of a total colony sugar production of 217,306 tons in 1951, only 1,070 tons were produced from canes supplied by small farms (42). It is rice which has developed as the basic cash crop for the small farmer, but in the Negro villages the cultivation of rice is still very much a supplementary activity for the great majority of farmers, yielding only part of their total cash requirements. East Indian and Chinese immigrants established rice cultivation on a commercial basis and the Negro villages seem to have taken it up when the milling and marketing facilities had been developed to a point which made it worth their while. Originally they grew only a small amount for subsistence purposes and only began to sell surpluses as the demand increased. At the time of the study there were some 540 acres of Crown lands under rice in August Town, and in addition to this, rice was grown on about 120 acres of freehold land in Belle Vue section. Some August Town farmers were also planting rice on rented lands lying outside the village boundaries. Perseverance had 213 acres of village land under rice in 1952, and Perseverance farmers were cultivating some 140 acres of rice on various rented and leased lands outside the village. Exact acreages were not collected for Better Hope but it was clear that far fewer villagers planted rice than in the other two villages, and much more of the village land was rented out to non-villagers, and particularly to East Indians.

The methods of cultivation employed by the Negro farmer tend to be extremely rudimentary and the real progress in establishing a flourishing rice industry based on a high degree of mechanization is being made by the East Indians rather than the Negroes. The only mechanical farm equipment owned and operated by any member of the three Negro communities studied was that owned by a Coloured (mixed Negro and European) man in August Town, and where mechanical equipment was used at all on Negro farms it was hired from outside the village.

Despite the possibility of planting and reaping two crops every year owing to the double wet and dry seasons, very few Negro farmers take the trouble to try for a double crop. The ploughing of the rice fields begins as soon as the weather is dry enough after Christmas, and some August Town farmers began to plough before the end of January in 1952. February and March are the main ploughing months, and unless tractor-driven ploughs are hired the work is done by light ox-drawn ploughs of a very simple design, the plough share being bought in one of the Georgetown hardware stores.

Towards the end of March, as the rainy season approaches, the padi is sown by 'shieing' or hand broadcasting. August Town farmers scatter about seventy pounds of seed to the acre, which is twenty pounds more than is strictly necessary, but since they generally use seed kept from the previous crop rather than high grade selected seed-padi the excess probably compensates for a low germination rate. Once the seed has been scattered, it is left to germinate when the rains come and no further attention is paid to it until harvest time (43). Of course water control is very important during the period when the rice is growing, but this is a matter for the sluice-watchman to decide in collaboration with the village overseer. By building temporary dams, or 'stop-offs', it is possible to keep the rice fields flooded whilst ensuring adequate drainage for the other farm areas and the dwelling area, but of course it is impossible to regulate the amount of rainfall, and a lack of rain at the crucial period of growth can be disastrous. The more laborious method of transplanting prepared seedlings is not very popular amongst Negro cultivators though it is more common in Perseverance than in the other two villages.

As the padi begins to ripen around the beginning of September the main job of harvesting gradually gets under way, and this is the one activity in the village which mobilizes the labour of men, women, and, to a limited extent, children, all at one time. However, there is practically no co-operative activity involved. Each farmer is concerned with his own crop, but the available resources of labour and equipment manage to get distributed in such a way that every one is able to harvest his or her crop. There is very little development of a system of reciprocal kinship obligations, and although ties of kinship or friendship may be invoked as the basis for reciprocal help, the main mechanism operates through the medium of monetary exchange. Reaping requires the greatest number of hands, and the bulk of this work is carried out by women who are paid according to the area they cut. We shall have more to say about this in the next chapter. In Perseverance this system of monetary payment is not quite so highly developed, but a farmer who has planted more rice than can be reaped by the members of his own household group will certainly have to pay for labour, either in cash or by returning an equal amount of labour under what is known as the 'day for day' system. In August Town, cash payment for rice cutting is the rule even between members of the same household group.

Mechanical reaping is very little practised in either village and even in areas where mechanical equipment is available, it is not always possible to use it owing to the fact that the heavy-grained stalks tend to fall down flat in front of the mechanical cutters. Threshing is either carried out by bulls which tread the grain from the straw, or in the case of Perseverance, by beating the heads of the sheaves on a table with a slotted top, the grain falling on to sheets spread beneath (see Plate IVb). The threshed padi is packed in 140 lb. bags which are transported by donkey or bullock carts to the dwelling area or to the railway line to await shipment to the mills. A part of the crop will probably be retained for domestic consumption and for seed for the following year, though some farmers lodge the padi they require for domestic consumption with a miller, and during the course of the year they can withdraw it in the form of milled rice on payment of a milling fee. This amounts to about $2.00 per bag of padi, which yields about half a bag of clean rice. In Perseverance there is one small mill catering for domestic needs and padi can be milled there by the bucketful as it is required. Alternatively women may pound the padi in a mortar and winnow it on a special winnowing tray, but this method is rarely used today in any of the villages.

Padi which is surplus to domestic requirements is sold either to one of the government rice mills, or to a private miller through a village agent. In either case the net return per bag of padi was approximately $4.75 in August Town in 1951, and a normal yield for an August Town farmer would be about fifteen bags of padi to the acre. The cost of cultivating one acre would be in the region of $50.00 so that the farmer would make a profit of about $21.25 on each acre if he paid for the land to be ploughed and the crop to be reaped. This figure takes no account of rent, rates, or depreciation on capital equipment such as carts, sickles and so on. Whilst the profit is fairly high if looked at from the point of view of return on capital invested, the income derived from this source is certainly not high when it is remarked that one of the biggest August Town rice farmers planted only twenty-two acres of rice in 1952. Not all the padi reaped is sold of course, for a certain amount is retained for home consumption, and this cuts down cash income considerably where the acreage planted is small. One general consideration to be borne in mind is the risk of failure in planting rice at all, for unfavourable weather conditions, or faulty drainage and irrigation, can quite easily render the crop a total loss.

Animal Husbandry

In any coastal village in British Guiana livestock is very much in evidence, and cattle, sheep, goats, pigs, donkeys, fowls, turkeys, ducks, cats and dogs wander about the village under varying degrees of control. In many of the Negro villages there is a perpetual battle raging over the allegations of damage to crops by uncontrolled animals, and actions for damage are frequently heard in the courts. This is not merely the result of bad management, but is also tied in with the fact that there is very little systematic feeding of livestock, and pasturage is generally inadequate.

There is no systematic breeding of cattle for particular purposes,

a. House yards. Slight flooding after a shower of rain

b. East Indian vendors at the village market

Plate I

a. House building. Stage I

b. House building. Stage II

This photograph was taken several months after the one above

PLATE II

but the agricultural department has made some attempt to raise the standard of the stock by introducing Zebu and Holstein bulls which are made available to the villager for crossing with his creole cattle. The creole cattle are generally small, the bulls weighing about 800 pounds and the cows about 500 pounds when fully grown, and they quite definitely give the appearance of being under-fed. No attempt is made to develop dairy cattle as opposed to beef cattle, and all cows are milked, and all eventually killed for beef. In August Town there is a large expanse of grazing land beyond the rice area which is leased from government and used as a communal pasture by those cattle owners participating in the joint lease. The pasture is some four to five miles from the dwelling area and it generally falls to young boys to drive the cattle to and from the pasture when it is necessary. After the rice harvest the cattle are put to graze in the rice fields which means that there is a certain amount of natural manuring. Perseverance has no satisfactory grazing area at all that it can call its own, but there is a neighbouring estate owned by an East Indian where cattle can be grazed upon payment of an agistment fee of 60c per head per month. A few farmers lease Crown lands for grazing but this pasture is about five miles from the village. Fewer villagers keep cattle in Better Hope and they use the village foreshore or a small grazing area between the dwelling and cultivation areas.

Milk yields are low and the general procedure is to milk the cows after they have been corralled away from the calves overnight. The calf is allowed to feed for a few moments until the milk is flowing, and then the cow is milked before being turned out with the calves for the rest of the day. Eight pints of milk per day is considered to be a fairly high yield and many cattle owners milk out considerably less, so that there is no real attempt at specialized milk production. Most bulls are castrated during the animal's first year and are then used for draught purposes. The number of cattle kept by farmers is generally small and in Perseverance no villager had more than six animals, with the exception of one East Indian store-keeper who had about thirty-five head, and one Negro carpenter who kept about forty head on leased lands outside the village. In August Town the figures would be very little different, except that there would be a greater number of persons owning about ten animals, as there are more adequate grazing facilities. There is one butcher in August Town who slaughters one animal per week, and this is not always obtained from a village cattle-owner. The meat is sold in the village, but the choicest cuts go to the Government Compound at Fort

Nelson, and the rest is distributed amongst those of the 1,700 villagers who can afford to buy it. Perseverance has no butcher and any fresh meat that is bought comes from a village seven miles away, but fresh meat is not a regular part of the diet of the majority of Perseverance villagers. In Better Hope there is a fairly large abattoir and the number of animals slaughtered per week varies. However meat is distributed more uniformly through the population than in the other two villages owing to the greater quantities available and to the higher purchasing power of the majority of families, as well as being sold on other parts of the coast.

Cattle, or indeed livestock of any kind, are not counted as a symbol of wealth or status, but in the system of internal differentiation in the village there is a tendency for the wealthier persons, who are generally non-Negroes, to own the largest number of animals, but this is a result of their pattern of economic activities rather than a sign of their superior status.

Pig rearing is more highly developed in Better Hope than in the other two villages, and pigs are usually kept in pens in the vicinity of the house and fed with prepared pig feed. Wherever the making of coconut oil has become established as a small scale industry, pig rearing on a slightly larger scale becomes feasible since the pigs can be fed on the by-products of the oil extraction process. At the time of the study there were very few oil manufacturers, who could maintain their production because of the government plan to increase the production of copra by offering the growers high prices and imposing limits on the sale of locally made crude oil. Consequently many manufacturers who had been rearing pigs as a side-line were forced to slaughter their pigs when they could no longer compete with the government in purchasing copra. The price of prepared pig feed is generally too high for August Town or Perseverance farmers and the number of pigs they keep is usually determined by the degree to which they are able to allow their pigs to 'graze' or scavenge about the village. Even when this is done the animals' diet must be supplemented by home-made mash composed of boiled wild grasses and household surpluses, such as there are. Most pigs are hybrid, being 'creole' stock crossed with Berkshire or Tamworth breeds. They are generally killed for home consumption on special occasions such as at Christmas time, but in August Town and Perseverance one or two are killed for sale from time to time. Better Hope rearers can always find a market for pigs in the town and some are slaughtered for local consumption.

Sheep and goats are kept almost exclusively for sale outside the village, and particularly to buyers from the East Indian communities. Goats are not milked. There are quite considerable numbers of goats and sheep in both August Town and Perseverance, and they tend to be kept in reasonably large numbers by a few persons rather than each household having one or two. They are put out to graze on a small pasture or in the 'wood bush' near to the village, and it is not at all unusual to see sheep spending a considerable amount of time in swampy ground with water up to their bellies. It is usually the older men, who are less spatially mobile, who keep sheep and goats, whilst pigs are frequently reared by women. Both sheep and goats cause a considerable amount of damage to growing crops, particularly to kitchen gardens in the dwelling areas where they wander freely in most villages.

As a result of continuous hybridization, a 'creole' variety of poultry has been developed which is hardy and fairly small, but strains of such varieties as Rhode Island Reds, Plymouth Rock and Leghorn can be distinguished. Almost every household keeps a few fowls which scratch around the yard and are fed a little padi when there is enough to spare. There is generally a brisk trade in eggs, and some women go around buying from different households to meet orders from outside the village. The consumption of eggs within the domestic group is almost solely confined to ceremonial occasions when cakes are made. The fowls themselves are consumed on similar occasions and the rest are sold to buyers from outside the village. Again a pattern of trade with East Indians has grown up in August Town, and regular visits are paid to the village by Indian buyers.

A few donkeys are kept as draught animals, and there are one or two horses in August Town and Better Hope which are used either for riding long distances to the backlands or for racing at holiday seasons.

Methods of earning cash wages

Apart from the money accruing from the sale of padi, earned wages account for the bulk of the cash intake of the village. These wages come from a variety of sources, but work on the sugar estates is one source common to all three villages, and it has always been the typical kind of employment open to residents of the rural areas. Such work is largely seasonal, and is generally paid on a task basis, which means that there is a minimum of 'time-keeping' or regular working hours. It is during the cane-cutting seasons that the Negro labour force is recruited most fully, when extra hands are needed to supplement the main supply of resident East Indian labour. On many estates, special ranges of bachelor quarters are provided to accommodate seasonal labourers. From August Town a number of men travel across the Berbice river to an estate near Canje Creek where they stay during the cutting season, occasionally travelling back to the village whenever they feel like it. The fact that they go to work on an estate so far away when there is a cutting estate within daily walking distance of the village is extremely interesting. The reason given for the preference for the more distant estate is that they like the manager there, but this seems to be a rationalization of a more fundamental predisposition to spatial mobility on the part of men. Not all August Town cane-cutters go to this estate but certainly a majority do.

In Perseverance the situation is rather different for there have been no sugar estates on the Essequibo Coast since 1925 and therefore men have to travel to Demerara to find work. The whole of the Essequibo Coast is regarded as a depressed area, and there is certainly very little scope for finding employment there, with the result that there is both a marked seasonal migration and a certain amount of permanent migration to other parts of the colony, and particularly to Georgetown. Out of a total adult male population (over 18 years) of approximately 151 in Perseverance, it is estimated that about ninety to one hundred men regularly spend the cane-cutting season working on estates in Demerara. There is the same tendency for all the men to go to one estate that is found in August Town, and in the case of Perseverance the main group goes to Plantation Diamond on the east bank of the Demerara River. The rest go either to Plantation Uitvlugt or Plantation Leonora, two neighbouring estates on the west coast of Demerara. In Perseverance, the pattern of regular seasonal migration is firmly fixed, and for the majority of Perseverance men this tends to be the only type of labour which takes them away from home. By and large, the regularity of the migrations tends to give a certain stability to the economic activities of the men which is not found to the same extent in August Town.

The wages paid to sugar workers are not high as the averages for the whole industry show. In 1951 the average weekly earnings of adult male, non-resident piece workers was \$9.72 (£2 0s. 6d.). Since the majority of men from Perseverance and August Town who engage in this type of employment are temporarily living away from home it means that they have to meet their own expenses for food and washing, at least, before they can calculate how much they will send home to their families. Many cane-cutters make much more money than the average wages might indicate, for the Negro prides himself on being a strong and able worker, and when he does turn out to work on the estates he usually does a good job. Despite this fact it is abundantly clear that the wages earned by a good worker during the two cutting seasons would be quite inadequate to keep himself and his family for the whole year. There is practically no attempt to spread the earnings over a long period of time, and the money is usually spent as fast as it is earned, and in some cases even before it is earned. After the rice harvest is in, one actually hears men saying that they are going off to the sugar estates to earn their 'Christmas money'. This means that they are going to accumulate enough ready cash to celebrate the Christmas holiday in an appropriately festive manner.

In addition to this seasonal work cutting the sugar cane, there are opportunities for other types of work on the estates. A few August Town men work as labourers on the maintenance of the sugar estates' drainage and irrigation works, and for this type of job a system of indirect employment is generally used. One man acts as a contractor to the estate manager, and he employs a group of men to work for him, usually paying them on a piece-rate basis. Most of the work involves digging ditches and making up dams and is paid by the rod. (One rod = 12 ft 4 in.) Women are also employed on some of the lighter tasks such as weeding, and this affords an opportunity for young women to earn money in their own right. Perseverance men usually leave the estates when the cane-cutting season is over, for it is hardly worth their while to stay on waiting for a few days' piecework now and again. Better Hope supplies a certain number of factory workers to the adjoining estates and some villagers are highly skilled technicians. Sugar boilers are amongst the *élite* of the sugar industry and their skill commands high wages both in British Guiana and in the other West Indian islands, where they often go to work for six months or so at a time. These technicians enjoy prestige within the village community, often ranking almost as high as the school-teachers. Neither Perseverance nor August Town has a comparable degree of differentiation of this kind, and Better Hope is the only one of the three villages to have a sizeable group of regularly employed skilled artisans.

For generations men from the coastal Negro communities have supplied the bulk of the labour for the mining industry, and this is still an important source of employment for many village men. From about 1890 onwards, men from all three villages took part in the rapid opening up of the gold and diamond fields, but today there are relatively few men engaged on work in these smaller mining enterprises (44). The growth of the bauxite industry after the first World War, and its rapid expansion during the second, provided a new outlet for the migrant Negro worker. For some reason August Town men went to the bauxite workings in large numbers, and in keeping with the tendency for the men from one village to keep together during their migrations to the sugar estates, August Town became almost 'specialized' in bauxite (45). Almost 200 men and youths from August Town are employed at either Kwakwani or McKenzie City at any one time (there were 338 adult males in August Town at the time of the study, and though many of these migrate periodically to the sugar estates etc., the men at McKenzie and Kwakwani are not included in this number), and the migrations to these two mining towns appear to be taking on an aspect of greater permanence than formerly. This is very difficult to estimate, but it does appear that more young men are taking their wives and children with them than was the case in the past. The bauxite industry is highly mechanized and the resulting differentiation of occupations into skilled and semi-skilled jobs means that a young man has the opportunity of some sort of progressive advancement, and the old uniformity of the 'labourer' category is broken up to some extent. There is a positive inducement for some of the men to stay on as regular employees rather than regarding the work as just another labouring job to be held for a short time before seeking a change. No studies were carried out at either of the bauxite towns but it would be interesting to discover how much internal social differentiation has developed within the Negro groups there. In the case of August Town then, employment at the bauxite mines forms a very special part of the village economy, and it has gradually tended to become distinct from all the other forms of employment in the mining industries of the interior. It forms a special part of the village economy because workers send a considerable part of their total earnings back to relatives in the village, and particularly to their mothers and to the mothers of their children (46). Other occupations in the interior lands are definitely regarded as temporary jobs, and they include gold and diamond mining, balata bleeding, employment with companies extracting other minerals such as manganese, and an occasional job in connexion with the driving of cattle down from the savannahs to the coast. Neither Perseverance nor Better Hope have a comparable number of men working in the bauxite industry, but a few men from both villages engage in the other activities at any one time, and probably most of the older men have worked in the interior of the colony at some time or other.

Economic specialization within the village.

Although we have stressed the lack of occupational specialization our description would be both incomplete and misleading unless we briefly outlined the actual differentiations which do occur. It is part of our thesis that the Negro group in British Guiana constitutes a functionally differentiated sub-group of the total social system of the colony, and this differentiation runs through the economic system. Whilst this is a primary consideration to be borne in mind in any discussion of the village as a unit we are now concerned with the actual range of specialized occupations which occur within the actual territorial unit. The village is not solely composed of Negroes, and the presence of Chinese, Portuguese, East Indian and Coloured persons gives us a link with the total social system which serves to emphasize the fact that even the village as a unit is not coincident with the boundaries of the Negro sub-group. There are villages in British Guiana which have almost equal proportions of Negroes and East Indians, but of course this does not destroy ethnic distinctions.

Shops and the retailing of imported or non-village products are mainly in the hands of non-Negroes, and we shall delay their consideration until a later chapter when we are concerned with an examination of other than purely economic factors (47). We may just note here that the shops form an integral part of the village economy for they are the main channels through which money flows out of the village. It enters in the form of earnings from the sugar estates, bauxite mines, government work etc., and from receipts for farm produce sold outside the village. In the case of Better Hope the system is not so closed, for money is often both earned and spent outside the village by its resident members. However, shops in all three villages do supply a range of essential commodities, and there is a definite tendency to buy locally rather than going farther afield. The principal items stocked by the village shops and stores are as follows:—

GROCERY SHOPS

Rice	Marsala and coriander seeds	Onions
Salt-fish	Cooking oil	Flour
Salt-beef	Lard	Yeast
Salt-pork (pig-tails)	Margarine ('salt butter')	Sugar
Smoked herring	'Irish' potatoes	Matches
Salt	Garlic	Kerosene
Pepper		Patent medicines
Curry powder		Cigarettes

Various canned goods, coffee, tea, etc., which are only rarely purchased by the average village household.

STORES

Cloth	Shirts	Cooking utensils
Thread	Cutlasses	Plates and other domestic ware
Needles	Sickles ('grass knives')	Glasses
Shoes	School books, pens, etc.	
Hats		

Various small items of hardware such as spoons, penknives, cheap children's toys, etc.

CAKE SHOPS

Cakes, bread, sweets, aerated drinks, cigarettes.

RUM SHOPS

Rum, beer, wine.

Whisky and brandy are usually stocked but have very little sale except in case of sickness.

It is clear that the rural shops do not present a wide range of consumer goods, and most of the higher status persons in the village make a point of buying household furnishings and luxury items from the towns. In some villages persons such as school-teachers form co-operative purchasing groups and buy their foodstuffs monthly from a Georgetown firm. The city and town stores are quite definitely organized to cater to customers on a class basis and the average villager would feel rather uncomfortable in one of the more expensive stores. In fact it is only a very small minority of persons who would consider buying in town at all, except in the case of Better Hope, and even then they would tend to buy in the lower-class stores staffed by Chinese or East Indians rather than in those staffed by light coloured girls. Cumper mentions the limitations on spending opportunities for lower-class workers in Jamaica and argues that this is one factor affecting the worker's response to wage incentive schemes (48). Despite the limited range of commodities available in rural Guiana shops one does encounter seemingly anomolous situations. For example, persons with a low standard of living will buy relatively expensive commodities such as 'Ovaltine' in a very small shop in Perseverance. This seems to be symptomatic of the lack of concern with 'economizing' or showing planned selectivity in purchasing which is very similar to the situation obtaining in the lower status groups in a Scottish mining community reported on by C. S. Wilson (49).

We have already discussed the major productive activities of village inhabitants and indicated that they tend to be followed by everyone to some extent. Rice growing, provision farming, stock rearing, and estate work are not specialized occupations, but are components in a general pattern of employment followed by most male villagers, particularly in Perseverance and August Town. Work in the bauxite mines and various occupations in the interior of the colony have also tended to be supplementary rather than exclusive pursuits, the difference being that they take up a longer period of time. Perseverance most nearly approaches the pattern of mixed activities with the bulk of the male population going off to the sugar estates in the cutting season and returning to their farms for the rest of the time. But there is yet another range of occupations which we can most easily call 'trades' which enter the picture.

In any Guianese Negro village, one can always find a relatively large number of men who call themselves carpenters. A few will spend the major part of their time actually working at this trade, but the majority only get a job now and again. Even those who spend most time working at the trade will also probably grow rice, plant provisions and keep stock, and this applies to all the trades we shall mention. Only in Better Hope is the division of labour carried to the point where we find men who work full-time as carpenters, masons, painters, sugar-boilers, shoe-makers, etc. Whilst it is true that there is a high demand for carpenters in a country where houses are constructed almost entirely from wood, this does not explain why there should be a surfeit of men who are able to turn their hand to this trade as a means of earning money. It is likely that there is an element of prestige involved here which fits in with the over-all value system of the society, and on the other hand there is a block to the development of a high degree of specialization which is the result of the solidarity and lack of internal differentiation of the ascriptively based lower-class Negro groupings (50).

In August Town there were two tailors, one a Negro and one a mixed Negro-Portuguese, and at the time of the study there was a blacksmith-wheelwright who was a 'stranger' from New Amsterdam. The shoemaker was a village-born Negro who also planted rice and provisions, and all the village council employees—overseer, sluice watchman, and two rangers—were local Negro part-time farmers. One off-shore fisherman worked a boat with his brother, but whenever the nets got damaged by sharks he would go and work on the sugar estates in order to accumulate enough capital to repair them. Two or three men were barbers, but hair-cutting is very much a spare time occupation and no specialized ritual or ceremonial features adhere to it. One Coloured man kept a hire-car, but his main occupation was as a truck driver and mechanic for the Public Works Department. One bicycle-repair shop was run by a mixed Negro-Portuguese, but he also cultivated a large provision garden, in which he planted special crops such as tomatoes. When the Public Works Department requires brick for resurfacing the road the district foreman usually orders it from a contractor who 'burns a heap' of earth. One man in August Town was an active contractor for this kind of job and he employed villagers to work with him, including women who carry the earth in baskets on their heads.

Women's primary function is as mothers and housewives but they engage in a whole range of money-making activities as well as running farms and keeping livestock. We have already dealt with some of the jobs which women take, such as estate work and helping with the burning of the earth to make brick for the road. The breaking of this brick prior to laying it is also a woman's job, and women sit in the sun by the side of the road breaking the large rough lumps of red brick with a small hammer. They are paid on a task basis and may make up to about $1.00 per day if they work continuously during the daylight hours. The rate of payment is $2.50 for breaking up one truck load. This is just one of the many 'rough' jobs that women may do but they are all casual occupations and are the least desirable of all women's jobs. Dressmaking is a much more highly-rated feminine occupation, and even married women may work at home as dressmakers without their husbands feeling ashamed. The mere possession of a sewing machine usually indicates that the household is better off and may even symbolize respectability to some extent. A certain number of women find jobs as domestic servants with higher status families such as the head-teachers, government officials, or on the sugar estates, and some women work as washers for wealthier families or for single men.

There is some danger of over-simplifying the occupational pattern in trying to present it concisely, and it must be borne in mind that the following list is merely an enumeration of the major economic activities which are open to men and women. Any particular individual may engage in several occupations in as short a time as one week or even one day, so that this is not a list of specializations. It must also be noted that the list covers all three villages and all occupations do not occur in all three. For example Perseverance has no blacksmith, no butcher, no tinsmith, and no crude oil manufacturers, nor are there any government servants such as sanitary inspectors or midwives resident in the village.

TABLE I

LIST OF PRINCIPAL OCCUPATIONS

OCCUPATION		*Participated in by men*	*Participated in by women*
1. *Within the Village*			
(*a*) *Farming*			
Provision farming	clearing bush ..	X	Very rarely
	Planting ..	X	X
	Weeding ..	X	X
	Reaping ..	X	X
Rice farming	Ploughing ..	X	—
	Broadcast planting	X	Rarely
	Hand transplanting	X	X
	Reaping ..	X	X
	Threshing ..	X	—
Animal husbandry	Cattle keeping ..	X	Occasionally
	Goats and sheep	X	Occasionally
	Pigs	X	X
	Poultry	X	X

OCCUPATION	*Participated in by men*	*Participated in by women*
(*b*) *Local authority work*		
Maintenance of drainage and irrigation system	X	—
Administration (Overseer, rangers, sluice watchmen)	X	—
(*c*) *Trades*		
Carpenter	X	—
Tailor	X	—
Painter	X	—
Mechanic (including bicycle repairs) ..	X	—
Blacksmith/Wheelwright	X	—
Shoemaker	X	—
Mason	X	—
Butcher	X	—
Off-shore fisherman	X	—
Dressmaker	—	X
Tinsmith and Guttersmith	X	—
(*d*) *High status jobs*		
School-teacher	X	X
Midwife	—	X
Health visitor	—	X
Sanitary inspector	X	—
Public works overseer	X	—
Agricultural instructor	X	—
(All serve a larger area than one village)		
(*e*) *Other*		
Small scale trading of farm produce ..	Rarely	X
Selling prepared foods	—	X
Shopkeeper (i) Cake-shops	X	X
(ii) Larger shops ..	X	—
Cook	—	X
Domestic servant	—	X
Washer	—	X
"Huckster" (buying and selling farm produce, poultry, eggs, etc.) ..	—	X
Copra and crude oil manufacturer ..	X	Rarely
Baker, cakemaker	X	X

OCCUPATION	*Participated in by men*	*Participated in by women*
2. *Outside the Village*		
(*a*) *Sugar estates*		
Cane-cutter	X	Sometimes assist men
'Driver' or foreman	X	—
Shovelman	X	—
General labour such as weeding, etc.	X	X
Trades such as carpenter, cooper, etc.	X	—
Sugar boiler	X	—
Punt operator	X	—
(*b*) *Bauxite mines*		
Principally men who go to bauxite mines and engage in a series of occupations from unskilled labourer to storeman, barman, mechanical shovel operator, etc., but a few women go to the bauxite towns to find work, mainly as cooks, washers, etc.		
(*c*) *General*		
Gold and diamond mining	X	—
Labourers for Public Works Dept. (includes burning brick, breaking brick, etc.)	X	X
Domestic servant	—	X
Tradesmen (e.g., carpenter)	X	—
Work as agricultural labour for large farmers, government rice plantations, etc.	X	X
Police	X	—
Post Office workers	X	—

Conclusion

The relative non-differentiation of the village population is a crucial fact, and it is only in Better Hope that real specialization becomes important though even there it is only slightly developed. This has important implications for our central problem of family structure, for it means that economic and occupational factors do not operate as variables in correlation with varying types of family structure **within the groups we are studying.** Economic and occupational differences are of vital importance when we come to discuss the village populations in relation to the total society, and at this level they are certainly correlated in some way with variation in family structure, though it is not necessarily a primary correlation. Within the villages, the important fact is that to a very large extent any individual could replace any other individual in the occupational system without too much difficulty, though we would except the schoolteacher and government servant group from this generalization and one has to realize that it is only an approximate generalization. Age and sex factors have to be taken into consideration, as well as the few specializations we have mentioned. The generalization would apply most nearly to Perseverance and would be only very approximate in the case of Better Hope, which is another way of saying that Perseverance is the most homogeneous of the three villages in this respect.

Another important point we have made is that men spend a considerable part of their time away from the village working for cash wages. This is reflected in the following table which shows the sex ratios of the adult populations of the villages at various ages. Men who are away on extended working trips are not included, although those who go away on short seasonal migrations of only a few months are shown.

TABLE II

AGE AND SEX OF ADULT POPULATION

AGE GROUP (YEARS)	AUGUST TOWN		PERSEVERANCE		BETTER HOPE	
	Male	*Female*	*Male*	*Female*	*Male*	*Female*
21–30	62	124	40	50	24	27
31–40	68	93	39	42	12	25
41–50	79	72	30	18	18	17
51–60	53	60	18	13	13	15
61–70	38	48	11	15	8	9
71–80	12	29	5	7	6	5
81–90	2	12	1	0	0	5

N.B.—These figures are based on 100 per cent censuses in the case of August Town and Perseverance and a sample of eighty-four households in the case of Better Hope. The discrepancy between the figures in this table and those in Table V is due to the fact that certain cases of households whose inhabitants were either non-Negro or marginal to the village community have been excluded from Table V.

It is clear that the preponderance of females over males in the lower age groups is highly significant, and August Town with so many young men at the Bauxite mines shows the greatest disparity.

a. A village wedding

b. Pounding padi for domestic consumption. Note the mud-thatch house in the background

PLATE III

a. A rice plough, see page 30

b. Threshing padi, see page 31

Plate IV

SECTION II

CHAPTER II

THE HOUSEHOLD

THE household, consisting of a house and the group of people who live in it, is one of the most important functional units of the social system, and the locus of practically all the joint action of members of the domestic group. It is within the framework of some household group that each individual finds food and shelter, and the household group is a child-rearing unit. In a small building some twelve feet by twenty feet, one often finds upwards of ten people, and of that number the majority are invariably children. Households come into being through the association of men and women in some kind of conjugal relationship, though there are certain exceptions to this when a woman establishes a household without the co-operation of a male partner. Each household group normally 'cooks one pot' and all members are fed from it, none of the food being allocated to anyone who does not live in the house. There are exceptions to this rule, but they are not of frequent occurrence. To grow up in a particular household gives an individual certain customary rights, duties and obligations, which are often quite irrespective of exact 'blood' relationship, and this helps to emphasize the importance of 'growing' with someone, no matter what the legal considerations involved may be. The complete absence of corporate kin groups or even of hereditary offices or social positions, results in a lack of continuity between the household as a kin group and other social groupings. However, kinship does create ties and affective bonds between the members of different households, and the fact that in August Town particularly, the whole village is sometimes referred to as 'all one family' illustrates the importance of the generalized extension of the sentiments of solidarity which arise within the household group, and which find expression in a local setting.

The term often employed to describe the members of a household group, especially in August Town, is 'house people' and this designation is extended to include the spirits of the dead, as well as particularly intimate friends who can visit the house freely and make themselves at home in it. When a new bottle of rum is opened, a little is always thrown out on to the floor of the house or on to the ground in the yard if the drinking is taking place outside. It is characteristic of the system that these libations are for the dead 'house people', but at the same time the spirits of the dead are not personalized, and the same offering would be made in a new house in which no one had ever died as in an old house that had been the scene of many deaths. A non-member of the household wili throw the rum as readily as a member.

In this chapter we shall describe the material aspects of the household before going on to a consideration of the composition of the household group and the internal relations of its members.

Houses

The design of houses is fairly uniform throughout the villages studied, but there are variations in size and construction which it is important to note, for there is some correlation with other factors. For example, it is usually the smaller houses that contain the largest number of persons.

The cheapest type of house to build is what is known locally as a 'mud-trash' house, and this is built almost entirely from locally procured materials. (See Plate IIIb.) Raised on low wooden blocks, about two to three feet from the ground, its framework is built from roughly trimmed poles cut from trees, or from the *courida* bush (1). The walls are wattled and filled in with mud, perhaps mixed with cow-dung to bind it, and then smoothed over with liquid mud both inside and outside. Roofing material varies according to locality, and whilst villagers in August Town use bundles of long grass, in Perseverance it is usual to use the leaves of the Troolie palm which grows in abundance in the river areas of the Essequibo Coast, and which are actually sold in the markets by persons who collect them in the more inaccessible reaches of the rivers. Mud-trash houses rarely exceed about twenty by ten feet in ground dimensions, and the most expensive item in the whole building will be the floorboards which are purchased from a saw-mill, or from a dealer in town. An internal partition divides the house into two rooms. Doors and shutters are made from wood and are usually put together by a carpenter, unless old ones can be procured ready made. Cooking may be done inside the house on a coal-pot which burns charcoal, but usually a kitchen is either built as a separate shelter outside, or as a lean-to attachment to the main building. A house such as the one described would be worth anything from fifteen to forty dollars in August Town, its value consisting mainly in the materials used and not in the house itself, for few people would trouble to buy a mud-trash house, except for the boards it contained. Unless regular repairs and maintenance are carried out deterioration is fairly rapid. A well kept mud-house is not unpleasant to live in, the thatch affording considerable protection from the sun and absorbing much less heat than corrugated iron. The mud will have to be replaced at least every year and as the frame becomes rotten sections will be replaced. A good thatch will last anything from five to seven years.

Average number of persons per mud-thatch house

August Town 5.57; Perseverance 6.00; Better Hope 0.

Proportion of mud-thatch to total number of houses

August Town 22.1 per cent; Perseverance 9.25 per cent; Better Hope 0

The standard house in the rural areas of British Guiana is a wooden building, raised anything from three to eight feet on wooden piles set on concrete or wooden blocks. (See Plate Ia.) Constructed from local woods prepared in saw mills and sold by the foot as dressed boards, or from softer imported woods, it is usually about twenty feet by fourteen feet in ground plan and is roofed with corrugated iron sheets or shingles made from local wood. Divided internally into two rooms it may have a kitchen built on as an attachment, or cooking may be done in a separate small kitchen on the ground outside. Access to the house is by permanent wooden steps. The quality of this kind of house can vary considerably, not only according to the state of repair, but according to the general finish and whether glass windows or shutters are used. In August Town the value of such a house could vary between 100 and 1,000 dollars depending on the state of repair etc., but the cost of building a simple two-roomed house, with an attached kitchen was in the region of 750 to 800 dollars at the time of the study, and costs were rising daily. Owing to the difficulty of finding enough capital to pay the total sum involved in building a house all at once, most houses are built in stages, often covering a period of years. Materials are first purchased as money is available, and then a start will be made on the actual building. As soon as cash runs out, work stops and the frame of the house may be left for months before any further work can be done. (See Plate II.)

Once the main body of the house is complete it is habitable, but an ambitious owner can easily extend the size of the house by adding a front and a back gallery as he is financially able. A house with both these additions will have two or three bedrooms, a dining recess, and a front lounge as well as the main living-room. This represents the ultimate development in size of the normal rural house, but there are one or two larger houses to be found in most villages, usually incorporating a shop of some kind. Various modifications such as building a lower room or a kitchen underneath the house are possible, and this is sometimes done when the danger of flooding is not too great. In Better Hope one finds a number of tenements, which are long buildings, divided into not more than three separate dwellings, inhabited by three separate domestic groups, with at least two of them paying rent. This type of dwelling is very common in Georgetown of course, but is not found in either Perseverance or August Town. In August Town there are a couple of cases of persons renting a section of a house (a lower flat in both cases), but this is hardly a permanent arrangement.

Average number of persons per two-roomed board house
August Town 5.13; Perseverance 6.33; Better Hope 3.63.

Proportion of two-roomed board houses to total number of houses
August Town 52.7 per cent; Perseverance 61.1 per cent; Better Hope 49.4 per cent.

Average number of persons per house with more than two rooms
August Town 4.28; Perseverance 6.66; Better Hope 4.71.

Proportion of houses with more than two rooms to total number of houses
August Town 25.2 per cent; Perseverance 21.3 per cent; Better Hope 40.0 per cent.

In Perseverance a considerable number of wooden houses are roofed with Troolie Palm and although these have been included with the other two-roomed board houses it should be noted that they are less valuable. Also in Perseverance one finds a few houses with split manicole (2) wooden walls rather than wattle and mud, but they are of the same general pattern as the mud-walled houses and certainly no more valuable. Both Perseverance and Better Hope have a number of one-roomed dwellings, and we have already referred to the tenements in Better Hope which usually consist of one room only. In Perseverance 8.35 per cent of the total number of houses are very poor one-roomed dwellings containing as many as nine individuals in one case, and 38 per cent of all houses in Perseverance are thatched with Troolie Palm rather than having the more valuable corrugated-iron roof.

Each house stands on a precisely defined lot, or piece of ground, and the owner of the house is usually also the owner of the lot on which it stands, though this is not always the case as we shall see presently. Houses can be, and often are, moved from one lot to another without dismantling them, and such a move is quite a communal affair, usually being carried out on a moonlit night with the co-operation of a large number of men who slide the house on skids from one spot to another. The whole proceeding is supervised by a carpenter who 'ties' the house by nailing strengthening supports inside it. Traditional house-moving songs and 'boasts' are sung during the actual pulling of the house. At least this is the case in August Town, though a house-moving was never observed in the other villages. One house-moving witnessed in August Town was carried out because the owner's daughter was being troubled by a spirit, and he had been advised by an Obeah-man to move the house to another spot. Reluctant at first, he was finally persuaded by friends, and the house was moved about 250 yards to the opposite side of the public road.

The law stipulates that each house must have a pit-latrine, and in fact most houses do have one on the same lot, though some households share a latrine, or use the bush on the outskirts of the village. It is not considered improper to micturate anywhere outside the house, provided one is not seen, and few people would trouble to go to a latrine for this purpose after dark. Once the house has been closed up for the night (and it really is closed up with all the windows shut tight), it is unusual for anyone to go outside, and practically every house has a chamber pot. One informant said that this is the first thing a woman will acquire when she sets up house, and she will always make sure that it is kept scrupulously clean: cleaner in fact than her cooking pots.

Most villagers take great care over personal cleanliness, and it is usual for everyone to bathe at least once every day. Some house-lots carry a small shelter which is used as a bathroom, where one bathes from a bucket using a calabash to pour the water. Alternatively persons will bathe when it is dark, early in the morning or late at night, whenever they can find sufficient privacy. Children bathe openly in the yard, or in one of the drainage trenches.

Small kitchen gardens, animal and fowl pens are also found on many house lots, though the presence of pigs, goats and sheep wandering uncontrolled in the dwelling area makes it difficult to maintain a kitchen garden unless constant attention is paid to the fencing. A fence is erected around the whole lot if the owner can afford it, but the majority of lots remain unfenced. In Better Hope the movements of animals in the dwelling area are much more effectively controlled, more lots are fenced, and the cultivation of kitchen gardens is more feasible. Some households have a rice store-room built on the lot, and here padi for household consumption will be stored. Such rooms are kept locked and are guarded at night by the dogs which are to be found in every village. Even the poorest household will keep a dog, which is usually terribly emaciated, since dogs are fed very little and there is practically nothing for them to prey upon.

Furnishings inside the house vary from practically nothing, except a few empty rice bags to sleep upon, to quite a considerable number of chairs, tables, cabinets, beds, wardrobes, etc., and the houses of many of the school-teachers and village upper-class group are quite expensively furnished. The majority of houses will have at least one bed, even if it has a board bottom and a home-made mattress filled with grass or leaves. Apart from this the bedroom is usually bare, except for a chest or box in which clothes can be stored, and occasionally one finds a wash-stand with a basin and water jug. This latter is very rare in Perseverance and August Town except in the homes of the more wealthy villagers. In the living-room it is very common to find an old settee or settle, with or without upholstery, which can be used as a bed at night. Most houses have at least one table, a number of chairs, and a few boxes which can be used as seats. The centre piece of all except the very poorest homes is a cabinet on top of which glasses and dishes are displayed. It would seem that these are quite definitely for display, and a good housewife will keep them clean and shining. In one house with six inhabitants the total furnishings and household effects were as follows:—

1 table	2 flat irons	3 knives
2 chairs	3 iron cooking pots	5 enamel cups
1 couch	1 frying pan	8 enamel plates
2 beds	1 cutlass	1 stew pot
1 small water tub	4 spoons	3½ *dozen glasses*

The total value of the whole lot was estimated by the wife of the head of the household at $45.00. In this particular case there was no cabinet in the house, but the glasses were stacked on a shelf in the living-room.

It was noticeable that in Perseverance much less care was taken over the cleanliness of houses than in either of the other two villages. Whereas in August Town and Better Hope it is customary to scrub out the house at least once every week, in Perseverance it was clear that many houses had not been scrubbed for much longer than this. The majority of houses in all three villages remain unpainted, and quite often the inside walls are papered with old newspapers and magazines which help to keep out draughts and cover up cracks as well as being decorative.

Wood collected from the bush is the normal fuel for cooking and it is burned on an open hearth set on a shelf at convenient working height in the kitchen. This shelf is in a little recess, the hearth is surrounded by bricks covered with mud and cow-dung, and the pots are supported on iron bars. (See Plate Va.) Occasionally a more elaborate stove is built with an enclosed fire space and a series of holes in the top over which the pots are placed. One rarely finds cupboards in the kitchen though some houses will be equipped with a mesh-covered meat safe. Generally there is little cause for storing food since it is consumed soon after it is obtained. A bunch of plantains may be hung from the roof, or a supply of cassava may be stored in one corner, but it will not be kept very long. The only food which is stored in any quantity is rice, and the few households that keep a store of rice have a special room under, or outside, the house in which the unmilled padi is kept.

The kitchen is the province of the women, and the head female of the house usually owns all its contents and has complete jurisdiction over its running and management. It is here that the main work of the household takes place, and it is here that women sit to talk when they visit each other during the day-time. Small children crawl over the floor whilst their mother or grandmother is busy preparing food or cooking it. Apart from cooking, one of the other main duties of the woman is washing clothes, and this is usually done in a tub in the yard using rain water, though in Perseverance most women wash clothes in the drainage trenches, beating them with wooden beaters to get out the dirt.

The living-room is the place where the household group congregates in the evening to sit and talk over the day's happenings, or listen to 'old-time story', or 'Nancy stories' from one of the older members (3). When the male head of the household comes in the children are expected to be quiet and well behaved, and if by any chance he is entertaining his friends, the children will be pushed off into the kitchen or the bedroom. This is also the place where the food is served to the male head of the house, for whilst the other members of the household will eat anywhere around the kitchen or on the steps outside, he is served alone at the table. An interesting modification occurs when the head of the household is an old man, for then he is much more likely to eat in the company of one of his young grandsons if there are any living with him. Whenever friends are entertained with any kind of formality it is the living-room which is the centre of activity, but at any formal gathering in a house one always finds a definite tendency for all the women guests to gravitate towards the kitchen, leaving the men to their conversation and their rum.

Sleeping arrangements vary a great deal, but it can be assumed that the male head of the household always sleeps on the bed, and whether the wife regularly shares his bed or not depends on how they are getting along together. In the majority of cases she does, and all except the younger children sleep on rice bags and old clothes, called 'beddings', which are spread on the floor of the living-room. The children dispose themselves in small clusters depending on their age and sex. Sleeping arrangements vary according to the age of the head and his wife or common-law wife, and according to the composition of the household group. It is usual for everyone to change their clothes when they go to sleep and even very poor people possess night-dresses and pyjamas. Sometimes of course, an old shirt or dress has to suffice. Every attempt is made to preserve complete privacy for sexual intercourse but as can be imagined this is somewhat difficult under such crowded circumstances, and it is not unusual for couples to make the most of opportunities which arise during the daytime when the younger people are out of the house.

OWNERSHIP OF HOUSES AND HOUSE LOTS

Before considering this question it is as well to note that within the household group each individual can own things in his own right, and each individual with the exception of young adolescents also has a definite right to dispose of his income as he wishes. The fact that each individual is expected to contribute to household expenses and the cost of food, giving the contributions to the mother, or to the woman in charge of the household affairs, does not vitiate this right. Even small children are given a fowl or a goat, which they consider to be their very own, though of course they cannot dispose of it as they wish. Children are also given money to put in the church savings group or in the Post Savings Bank, and when this money is withdrawn it will normally be used to buy clothes for that particular child. Under these circumstances it can be seen that a woman can hold quite a considerable amount of property in her own right, including land and houses. There is also a very definite feeling that a married woman has a right to half of all her husband's property, though it is not common for this claim to be made explicit. A married man who owns the house he lives in has a positive obligation towards his wife, and cannot easily put her out of the house. Even though he has to be consulted on all matters concerning the household, his spouse has the major voice in its actual running, and more often than not her husband will merely endorse her decisions. In the case of a couple living in a common-law union the situation is not so very different, especially when the union has been established for some time and there are several children. However, a woman in this position is conscious of the fact that she has no legal claim on her mate, but the existence of a number of children does modify her position even in regard to the law, for if her common-law husband does put her out, she can take him to court and he will be forced to maintain the children. The fact that this situation rarely arises is a good indication of the strength of the woman's position in this type of union.

In a sample embracing all but a few households in the Troy and St. Paul's sections of August Town, it is found that of 154 households with a male head, the household head owns the house in 82 per cent of cases, whilst out of ninety-seven households with a female head the household head owns the house in 65 per cent of cases. These percentages would be much higher if we were to exclude rented houses which account for 10.4 per cent of male-head households, and 11.4 per cent of female-head households. So far as the households with a male head are concerned, ownership of the remaining 7.6 per cent is by the head's wife, his brothers or sisters, and in one case jointly by the man's wife and her siblings. It is clear that in the great majority of cases a man who is head of a household owns the house in which he lives. This is equally true for households with a female head, for if we exclude the rented houses and also

10.3 per cent of houses which are owned by men working away from the village and temporarily headed by their wives, then we find that only 4.1 per cent of houses are owned by the head's sons, sisters, or jointly by the head's siblings because they have been inherited as 'children's property', and therefore other persons retain a nominal claim. No house in the sample is owned by the brother of the female head. It is clear then that headship of the household is closely correlated with ownership of the house, though it must not be thought that this is an explicitly stated criterion of headship, and few people in August Town would put headship in terms of house ownership.

When we come to examine the ownership of title to the land on which the house stands, the picture is much more complicated owing to the fact that land is much more frequently inherited jointly than are houses, and consequently many people may retain a claim to a share in a house lot, even though it is clear that the owner of the house is really the *de facto* owner of rights to the land, and he or she will probably be paying the rates on it. In any case a majority of both male and female house owners also hold title for the land on which the house stands, and the complications of the claims of kin have been considered elsewhere (4). Suffice it to say here that only one case has been noted in this sample, of a house owner paying rent for the land on which the house is built, and even where the land is not held by the owner of the house, it is occupied by consent of the title holder or holders, who are almost invariably kin of some kind who would not expect rent. It is sufficient that the occupier pays the rates on the land. Few house lots are valued at more than $75.00 so that even with a rate of 10 per cent, the total amount to be paid in any one year only amounts to $7.50 for the larger house lots.

HEADSHIP OF THE HOUSEHOLD

Heads of households have no precisely defined functions nor is there any very clear social concept of household headship. The household as such has practically no corporate functions such as working land in common or owning things as a group. The rôle of household head is much less important than the person's rôle as husband, father, mother or grandmother. Nevertheless, every household does have one person whom we can define as the head and this device gives us a starting point for analysis. The limitations of the definition will become clear as we proceed.

Male heads

By far the greater number of male household heads are married with their wives living with them, or in common-law relationships with women which involve co-residence. A man in this position is clearly recognized to be the head of the household and he is expected to keep the house building in order and to provide food and clothing for his partner and her children. It is his duty to maintain his property and to pay the rates on the land even if it belongs to his wife. In many cases where a wife holds legal title to the land on which her husband's house stands, it is only because the land has been put in her name so that it cannot be seized if her husband defaults on the payment of a debt. It is the male head's right to be consulted on all matters concerning the household and he has the right to expect the deference and respect of the other members of the household. The fact that he may get this only in a very modified form is another matter. In point of fact, it is usually his spouse who is the most knowledgeable person in family affairs, and who makes the majority of decisions affecting the whole household. The male head of the household does not lead the whole group in any co-operative activities though he may recruit the help of his sons at rice planting or harvest time, and his small sons will have duties such as driving his animals to the pasture. This is not a very well developed pattern though, and as soon as the sons are old enough to work on their own account they will no longer help their father in his farming. Sometimes at harvest time his wife or daughters may help with the rice cutting but they will expect payment with which to buy new clothes, unless it is a very poor family and all the rice is retained for domestic consumption. On social occasions outside the home the head does not appear in company with other members of his family. This is true for all three of the villages.

The age at which men attain headship of a household group is important and it can be seen from the following tables that in all three villages the average age of male household heads is well up in the 40–50 year age group, and there are relatively few young men who are established in this position. Perseverance has more young men in the position of household head than the other two villages, and since it is in some ways the poorest of the three villages the point is of some interest. It is correlated with the fact that in Perseverance young people get married or set up a common-law relationship at a much earlier age than in the other two villages, and this will be considered in more detail when we deal with marriage and mating. It is also connected with the fact that there are an almost equal numbers of males and females in the age-groups from which household heads are drawn, and this contrasts quite sharply with the other two villages where females outnumber males in practically every age group. This is clearly shown by reference to Tables III and V. The discrepancies between the number of males and females

TABLE III

AGE DISTRIBUTION OF MALE HOUSEHOLD HEADS

AGE GROUP	AUGUST TOWN		PERSEVERANCE		BETTER HOPE	
	No.	%	*No.*	%	*No.*	%
21–25	2	1.0	0	0	1	1.7
26–30	7	3.5	12	13.8	4	7.0
31–35	15	7.6	8	9.2	5	8.8
36–40	26	13.2	16	18.4	5	8.8
41–45	38	19.3	12	13.8	13	22.9
46–50	20	10.2	12	13.8	4	7.0
51–55	21	10.6	8	9.2	7	12.3
56–60	20	10.2	6	6.9	6	10.5
61–65	15	7.6	5	5.7	6	10.5
66–70	19	9.6	3	3.5	1	1.7
71–75	5	2.5	1	1.1	2	3.5
76–80	7	3.5	3	3.5	3	5.3
81–85	1	0.5	1	1.1	0	0.0
86–90	1	0.5	0	0.0	0	0.0
91–95	0	0.0	0	0.0	0	0.0
TOTALS	197	100.0	87	100.0	57	100.0

N.B.—For August Town, thirteen household heads who are living outside the village have been included for the purposes of this table. Most of them are living at McKenzie or Kwakwani and sending money home regularly to their families. They would not normally be included in the permanent village population for the purposes of enumerating, but it was necessary to include them in this table since they are the effective heads of their households despite their absence at the time of the study. They are also included in Table V.

TABLE IV

AGE DISTRIBUTION OF FEMALE HOUSEHOLD HEADS

AGE GROUP	AUGUST TOWN		PERSEVERANCE		BETTER HOPE	
	No.	%	*No.*	%	*No.*	%
20–25	1	0.9	1	5.6	1	3.3
26–30	2	1.9	1	5.6	1	3.3
31–35	2	1.9	0	0.0	1	3.3
36–40	5	4.6	1	5.6	1	3.3
41–45	14	13.0	0	0.0	0	0.0
46–50	10	9.2	2	11.2	3	10.0
51–55	13	12.0	3	16.5	4	13.3
56–60	11	10.2	1	5.6	3	10.0
61–65	13	12.0	1	5.6	4	13.3
66–70	13	12.0	3	16.5	4	13.3
71–75	6	5.6	4	22.2	1	3.3
76–80	8	7.4	1	5.6	2	6.7
81–85	7	6.5	0	0.0	5	16.7
86–90	2	1.9	0	0.0	0	0.0
91–95	1	0.9	0	0.0	0	0.0
TOTALS	108	100.0	18	100.0	30	100.0

in August Town and Better Hope is particularly striking in the lower age groups and this is a reflection of the fact that so many young men leave the village in search of work. In Perseverance they tend to leave only for short periods of time, to work on the sugar estates and therefore they have been included in the enumerations. In the middle age range in August Town and Better Hope the proportions more nearly approach equality, and then females tend to predominate in the later age groups.

A comparison of Tables III and V shows that once men pass the age of 40 years they have usually become household heads, only a few being left as subsidiary members of their parents' or siblings' households. It must be noted that there are twenty-five men and six women in August Town; one man and one woman in Perseverance and six men and ten women in Better Hope who live absolutely alone, and they have been listed as household heads.

TABLE V

AGE AND SEX OF ADULT POPULATION

Age Group	August Town		Perseverance		Better Hope	
	Male	*Female*	*Male*	*Female*	*Male*	*Female*
21–25	28	59	22	33	7	20
26–30	27	54	18	17	17	7
31–35	31	44	19	22	5	14
36–40	36	44	20	20	7	11
41–45	42	37	15	8	14	8
46–50	32	31	15	10	4	9
51–55	29	40	9	9	7	7
56–60	22	19	9	4	6	8
61–65	16	25	6	8	7	5
66–70	20	20	5	7	1	4
71–75	5	19	1	5	2	2
76–80	7	10	4	2	4	3
81–85	1	8	1	0	0	5
86–90	1	2	0	0	0	0
91–95	0	1	0	0	0	0
Totals	297	413	144	145	81	103

N.B.—Percentages have not been given in this table since the comparison of the relative numbers of males and females in each age category is more important than comparisons between villages.

TABLE VI

SEX RATIOS OF HOUSEHOLD HEADS

Village	Male		Female	
	No.	%	*No.*	%
August Town	197	64.5	108	35.5
Perseverance	87	83.0	18	17.0
Better Hope	57	65.5	30	34.5

TABLE VII

SEX RATIOS OF ADULT POPULATION

	MALE		FEMALE	
Village	*No.*	%	*No.*	%
August Town	297	42.0	413	58.0
Perseverance	144	49.7	145	50.3
Better Hope	81	44.0	103	56.0

The higher proportion of male heads in Perseverance is correlated with the fact that the whole age structure is pitched lower than in the other two villages and there is not the same preponderance of females in the higher age-groups. There are also fewer opportunities for women to find work in that area, so that their dependence on the earning power of men is greater.

Female heads

Female heads of households are nearly all women who have passed the menopause, and consequently finished their period of child-bearing. This is shown in Table IV. Whilst most of them are widows, common-law widows, or separated, a few have passed straight from being daughters to being mothers and household heads without ever having lived in any kind of marital or quasi-marital union with a man. The position of female heads is largely defined by the fact that they are mothers and grandmothers, and the household with a female head grows naturally out of the other type of household group. The bond between mother and child is the strongest in the whole matrix of social relationships, and it endures through time as a strongly reciprocal relationship. A woman with children will always find ways to provide for them even if this involves handing them over to another person, and it does frequently happen that a child is reared by a person other than its biological mother. Most frequently this person is the child's maternal grandmother and we shall examine this type of situation later (5). When a woman's children grow up she can always depend on them for help, in the form of money or presents of food, and they will make sure that she has a roof over her head as long as she lives. Women own land and work farms, as well as working on the sugar estates for cash wages and they also have a range of peculiarly feminine occupations open to them. Breaking brick for the Public Works Department to lay on the public road is a feminine occupation, as are dressmaking, washing, and petty trade (6). There are openings too in domestic service, and the teaching profession absorbs a few women. In addition a young woman who is not living with a man will have need of sexual satisfaction and she will form friendships with men who will give her presents, and if a child is born the father will have to contribute to its support, even if the woman has to take him to court for it. A woman who has reached the stage of being a household head will almost certainly have grown-up children who will be contributing to household expenses. One of her sons may pay the rates on the land which she owns, other sons will send her money. Grown daughters who are living at home will be able to work occasionally, and they may be getting money from the fathers of their children. A woman in her late forties or fifties is usually quite secure whether she is titular head of her own household or not. She has her home (either her own or her husband's house) and she has her children to look to for loyalty and support. She commands respect because she is a mother; she is the most knowledgeable person where family affairs are concerned and she has learnt a good deal of self-reliance in the running of a home. As one married woman said, 'You can't trust men to do anything for you really, so if you want a new fence for your garden, or a new oven built, it's best you make up your mind to do it yourself.'

Headship of the household is then largely a matter of one's position as a father or mother, and to some extent of the ownership of the house and perhaps the land on which it stands as well. A man of about twenty-four years of age who was living in a common-law union with a girl of the same age in a small house standing on the same lot as her mother's house, showed no sign of being anything but a subordinate member of the household. In several cases in August Town one finds an elderly woman with a family of her own taking in a common-law husband or even marrying a man who comes to live in her house. In such cases there is no doubt that the woman is recognized to be the dominant person in the household and the man is in a very precarious position and liable to be expelled from the house on the slightest provocation.

HEADSHIP OF THE HOUSEHOLD AS A JURAL CONCEPT

Immediately we begin to consider the headship of the household from a legal point of view in terms of the collection of rights, duties and obligations attached to this position we run into difficulties which are inherent in the very definition of what constitutes 'law' in this particular sub-system of Guianese society. The law of British Guiana is based mainly on English common-law, and it can be invoked by any member of the community through the magistrates' courts. However, customary usage in these villages differs quite considerably from the legal code, and the courts only recognize such customary practice in a very limited way. Custom itself is extremely flexible and deviance from the norms of social behaviour is frequent, whilst conformity is not severely enforced by clear-cut sanctions. In discussing family matters with informants one of the most frequent answers to questions is, 'it all depends on the individuals involved'—implying that the particular relationship developed between people will be a very important determinant of their response to any given situation, within the range of alternatives permitted by the social structure.

The male head of a household group is quite definitely considered to be responsible for his spouse and his children and this fact is emphasized by women, who, being without a husband or common-law husband, often speak of having no one to take care of them. Young women often speak of marriage as having someone to be 'responsible' for you, and responsibility in this context refers to the provision of food and clothing, shelter, and money for incidental expenses. It also refers to protection; protection from physical harm and from the possibility of malicious slander and gossip. A man with any pride cannot see his wife and children inadequately housed or fed, nor can he allow others to 'take advantage' of them without taking the offender to court. Theoretically a woman can sue her husband for support if he deserts her, but in fact few cases of this kind occur. Once a husband and wife have parted she will normally only expect him to support the children.

A man is legally responsible for his wife's debts, and occasionally one does find a man whose wife has left him placing a notice in the papers saying that he will no longer be responsible for his wife's debts, but this is probably as much a gesture of knowing what is the 'town' method of doing things as due to any fear that she will in fact run up debts in his name. Very few women would incur a debt without their husband's knowledge if they knew that they would be unable to repay it themselves, and unless a woman was threatened with court action it is doubtful whether her husband would interfere, particularly if the debt was for other than household expenses.

Debts incurred by villagers are never very large and they are not allowed to continue over long periods of time. Custom dictates that each individual is responsible for his or her own debts, and they are normally contracted in the individual's own name.

The majority of households have what is known as a 'canister' in which money is kept to be used in time of emergency or on special occasions. This 'canister' is theoretically controlled by the head of the household, particularly since he is the one who will normally contribute the greater part of the contents, and money from it may be used for paying for farm labour, buying clothes for the children, paying fines, paying doctors' bills, buying materials for building, paying for labour, or a host of other items. It is evident that the accumulation of such savings is never very great, and it would be difficult to characterize this as an important household institution as we shall see later when we come to examine domestic economy in more detail.

The right of a man to exercise authority over the members of his household by beating them is tacitly recognized, but a man who habitually beats his wife will not keep her for long, and women do not hesitate to go to the police if their husbands ill-treat them. Punishment of the children is most often carried out by the mother, though they are often told that their father will beat them if they misbehave. (If the father is living in the same house with them.)

Behind the apparent dominance of the male household head, one almost always finds a woman who acts as the focus of domestic relations, caring for the children and organizing the everyday life of the group. This is probably true in most societies, but the important thing about the case we are now studying is that the woman may be almost completely independent of her spouse at certain stages of development of the household group, and this is a point we shall take up in Chapter V. If the man deserts her, she automatically assumes full responsibility for the continuance of the household. Although a man is always supposed to provide for his spouse and her children without her having to work for money, many women do in fact trade or sell things which they have made at home or produced in their own gardens. At rice harvest time they work as reapers and the money they earn is normally their own to use as they wish.

Despite the pronounced independence of women in this position, and the large measure of control over household affairs which they enjoy, they are never completely dominant so long as their husbands or common-law husbands are present, for it is socially prescribed that he should be the authoritarian figure in the household. It is when he dies, or leaves the household, that the woman assumes complete control and she finds no difficulty in doing this, particularly if her own children are grown up. One of her adult sons probably takes responsibility for the payment of rates on her land, and for financial claims made upon the household but he does this as a duty towards his mother, and not because he has assumed control of the household group.

In this chapter we have considered the physical aspects of household layout and construction, size of household groups and the ownership of houses and house lots. We have also discussed the question of headship of the household group and tried to see what this means in terms of the age at which persons become household heads, and the legal and customary definition of what headship implies. It is clear that headship is not a rigidly defined concept, and the reasons for this will become clearer as we examine the kind of activities in which the household group engages.

CHAPTER III

ECONOMIC FEATURES OF THE HOUSEHOLD GROUP

IN considering headship of the household we have been led into an examination of the organizational features of the household group as a functioning system, and one of the primary fields in which this organization comes to life is in the handling of everyday economic problems. It is also in this field that many of the interrelations of the household to the wider social system are most clearly seen, and to some extent we shall try to keep these two aspects separate for the purpose of analysis.

Since it is common practice in British Guiana to refer to a 'Negro peasantry' and make the assumption that villages are peasant communities, composed of small farmers and their families struggling to make a living from the soil, it is necessary to stress time and again the fact that the household in a rural Negro village community is not by any means the kind of corporate productive unit encountered in the general run of peasant societies. It is not tied to a farm which is the basis of its existence, and the productive activities of its members do not fall into place as parts of a total pattern of exploitation of a *natural* environment. For any particular household the overriding consideration is the acquisition of cash income, and cash is in turn the means of acquiring necessary goods and services. Subsistence crops and the unsold portion of products accruing from agricultural activity generally, are regarded as supplementary to the money income of the group, in the same way that kitchen garden produce is regarded in this country. A striking example of the truth of this statement is to be seen in the fact that all magical practices concerned with acquiring wealth are directed towards getting money, or 'gold', and not towards ensuring the productivity of farms or the increase of animal stock (1). No instance of anyone employing any kind of supernatural aids to farming was encountered during the course of field-work. On the other hand, rational techniques for improving the yields of farms and the quality of produce are extremely difficult to introduce into the Negro communities, and the methods of agricultural production are just about as rudimentary as they could be. This is a generalization of course, and the few exceptions to the rule do not invalidate it. Where better methods are employed one's immediate reaction is to find out if the operator is a non-Negro, and in the majority of cases this is so.

Men are expected to earn money. Within the context of the household this is easily their most important function in the economic field, and to this end they spend considerable periods of time away from the house, and in most cases, away from the village. The occupations which they pursue are such as to preclude their working in family units with a degree of authoritarian control over a team of sons. Furthermore the avenues of employment which are open are mainly for unskilled labour where there is very little differentiation in rates of pay as between one man and another, irrespective of age.

After leaving school at the age of 14 or 15 years a youth continues to do odd jobs on the farm lands and around the house, as well as taking care of stock. These are all jobs he has been introduced to since his boyhood, and which he is able to do with a minimum of direction from his father. He may begin to work at a trade as apprentice to a carpenter, tailor, blacksmith or shoe-maker, and if he does, it is most unlikely that the man he will work with will be his father. He gets no pay apart from an occasional 'pocket-piece' from his master, and it is more than likely that he will only be one of a number of 'apprentices'. In any case it is only in a minority of cases that he will persevere and become a full-time tradesman himself. There is no rigid apprenticeship system which requires a tradesman to serve his time before becoming a recognized craftsman, just as there is no overall standard of skill in the various trades. A youth is much more likely to flit from job to job in the village and spend only a small part of his time working with his master. The village tailor in August Town had various boys 'apprenticed' to him, but one did not often find them in the shop, and it is significant that the tailor had plans for his sons to take up quite different occupations.

By the time a young man reaches the age of 18 to 20 years, he is ready to begin earning money in the same way as the adult males. He goes to work on the sugar estates, or moves to the bauxite mines in search of a job. The money he earns does not come under the control of the male head of the household to which he belongs, and any money he contributes to household expenses is given to his mother, presuming of course that she is alive, as in a typical household.

A man sets up his own household when he is able to assume responsibility for a spouse and children, and assuming responsibility means providing a house, food and clothing. That he delays this move for a considerable period of time is clear from the last chapter (2), and the fact that Perseverance men establish separate households at an earlier age than in the other two villages demonstrates that the difficulty involved in a man's accumulating enough money to provide a house is not the only operative factor. It is certainly one factor to be considered and is often enough advanced as a reason for delaying the establishment of a separate household.

The observed fact remains that the majority of young men remain nominal members of their parents' households during the whole of their twenties. This does not mean that they are living at home during this period though, and in the case of August Town, one of the most noticeable facts about the village is the almost complete absence of young men, the majority of them being at the bauxite mines. There they can earn relatively high wages, but more important still, they are responsible for themselves. They no longer depend on their fathers to provide for them, and they can actually contribute to their mother's support. If the mother is sole head of the household then the son will feel a definite pride in being a major contributor to the running of the household, and he will in all likelihood assume responsibility for the payment of the rates on the land and in many ways take the place of the male head of the group. Such a state of affairs will often lead to his postponing the setting up of his own household, based on a conjugal tie, until his mother dies. There are a large number of female household heads who depend mainly on their sons for support in this way and the sons may have a number of children of their own with a woman, or women, with whom they have never lived.

Once a man does marry or set up a common law union he tacitly accepts a responsibility, and this is stressed much more than his acquisition of rights over the woman's services. In courtship young men boast to their girl friends of their ability to take care of them and provide them with all kinds of luxuries, and engagement is marked by the presentation of gold jewellery to the girl.

The requirements of a small sized family in the way of cash are considerable, relative to the normal sources of income. It is estimated that a household group consisting of two adults and three children needs approximately $8.00 per week (at the time of the study) in order to maintain even a low standard diet. The following day's menu for a group consisting of two adults and three children gives some idea of the amount of money required for a fairly typical day's food consumption for the average village family (3).

Menu—19th November 1952

Tea—7 to 7.30 a.m.
Bread and margarine (cheap local salted margarine).
Bush tea.

Breakfast—11.30 a.m.
Rice.
Potatoes.
Fish.

Supper—5.30 to 6 p.m.
Coconut rice.
Pigtail.

Item	*Amounts and cost in B.W.I. Dollars*
3 pts. rice	.27
1 coconut	.03
Skinfish (approx. 6 ozs.)	.06
1 onion	.01
$\frac{1}{8}$ pt. fryol	.04
5 bread rolls	.10
$\frac{1}{2}$ lb. potatoes	.06
1 oz. margarine	.07
$\frac{1}{2}$ pt. milk	.04
$\frac{1}{4}$ lb. sugar	.02
$\frac{1}{4}$ lb. pigtail	.14
7 ockroes	from garden
Soursop leaves for tea	picked locally
Total	.84

This menu takes no account of such essential items of domestic requirements as matches, salt, pepper, kerosene oil, soap, starch, coals for ironing, and so on, and even when these have been added we have only covered a sector of the total budget for the group. Of course many families are unable to spend so much every day, even when all the mechanisms of credit and petty trading are in operation, and they have to forgo the evening meal, making do with a hot, sweet, drink only. Other families are able to afford more, and such items as eggs, cheese and fresh meat appear in their daily diet now and again.

The mistress of the house receives money and garden produce from her spouse, and she is solely responsible for its management once it has been handed over to her. Because men's incomes tend to be irregular, women's expenditure is equally unplanned, and unplannable. In Perseverance there is more regularity in this respect since men will send money home regularly during the cane cutting season, but even here amounts vary according to the availability of work. In August Town men often divide their time between estate work and their farms, and although the time spent on the farm will ultimately bring some return it does not come in fixed amounts. Consequently women have to resort to various expedients to stretch their purchasing power over time. Obtaining credit at the shops is one obvious method, and this is an extremely common practice. However, the debts never assume an unmanageable size, and they are usually fairly short term. Indebtedness to shopkeepers rarely comes up as a problem in any of the villages studied and this is in quite sharp contrast to the situation in many of the East Indian communities. Another method of spreading purchasing power over time as well as through the community is the great volume of internal petty trade. The buying and selling of farm vegetables in small quantities serves this purpose admirably, for a villager will readily buy a few plantains, or a coconut, or a few greens from another, even though she has some on her own or her husband's farm. She does this to 'help out' her neighbour, knowing that she will be able to sell something herself when the need for a little ready cash arises. This is quite a different process to the marketing of surplus produce, and the often quoted remark that West Indians seem to live by taking in each other's washing is not so far from the truth in so far as it refers to these mechanisms of distribution of resources.

This small scale buying and selling within the village gradually shades off into slightly more specialized women's trading. The making of cassava bread is one of the more common activities and a woman will gradually become known as a regular maker of these flat dry cakes, made from grated cassava baked on a kind of griddle. Another woman may become known as a cake-maker, and her services may be in demand for weddings and parties as well as for her regular baking for Saturday sale. One woman in August Town used to make ice-cream regularly each Saturday evening and others manufacture black-pudding and 'souse' (pig's trotters, pig's head or cow's cheek, pickled).

When a woman first sets up house with a man it is extremely unlikely that she will participate in any of these money making activities. The accent is upon the ideal pattern of the man being wholly responsible for her maintenance, and in any case it is most likely that any trading she did previously was under her mother's guidance and control. She may have worked for cash on the sugar estates, in domestic service or in some other occupation particularly if she had children, but this ceases, ideally, when she enters a conjugal relationship. For one thing it is an adverse reflection on the man's ability to maintain his spouse if she goes out to work, and in one case a man who had been living with a woman for many years beat her when he discovered that she had been out collecting crabs with the idea of selling them. Not only did he beat her but he released the crabs, and this was so intolerable to the woman that she left him to go to her natal village until he went and begged her to return.

The fact that there are children to be cared for is an important consideration, and once a woman is mistress in her own house she pretty soon has her hands full. The following is a broad outline of the normal daily routine for a woman running her own household.

Daily routine—Females

5.30 to 6 a.m.

This is the normal time of rising though some women may rise earlier, particularly if they have to cook food for their spouses to take with them to work. On rising women usually bring a bucket of water and bathe, or they go and bathe in the trench before it is fully light. As soon as it gets light at around 6.30 a.m. they start the fire (or 'catch fire') to make 'tea'. This usually consists of a drink made from 'weed' (wild plants), or cocoa, or drinking chocolate made locally and sold in the shops at 2c per stick, or most common of all, what is known as 'milk tea'. This is merely hot water with a little milk and sugar and spice added. All hot drinks are referred to as 'tea' and tea itself is known as 'green tea'. Very few villagers drink coffee or 'green tea' unless they belong to the better-off group such as teachers. Rice porridge, boiled cassava or plantain, cassava bread, shop bread or 'bakes' (which are simply cakes of flour fried in oil), may be eaten with the tea.

Whilst the tea is being made all except small pre-school age children are made to get up, and they carry out various odd jobs such as feeding fowls and bringing in goats and pigs or going to the shop to make odd purchases. Cows are usually milked by men or older boys.

Before eating, the children are sent to bathe in the trench, or from a bucket in the yard, and the smaller ones are bathed and dressed by the woman.

7.30 to 8.30 a.m.

Food is shared out to the children by the woman who cooked it, and they are sent off to school. The very small children are then bathed, dressed and fed before the woman eats her own food and washes the dishes. At least once every week and usually twice, clothes have to be washed, and the clothes are starched, and then ironed, on the two succeeding days. The house itself is scrubbed once every week, and sometimes twice, except in Perseverance as we have mentioned already (4).

10 a.m.

Around this time the fire is lit to cook 'breakfast' which is the main meal of the day. The few women who have to go out and work for wages during the day will cook early in the morning and leave the food for the children to share themselves when they come home from school. Whilst the breakfast is cooking, the woman will find some odd job to do, and breakfast is served when the children come from school at 11.30 a.m.

11.30 a.m.

Breakfast. The children are almost invariably fed first, and they will eat quite separately from the adults, spreading themselves around in groups based on age and sex. They frequently quarrel about who has most and may try to steal each other's food. If the male head of the household is in for breakfast he eats separately. Men and women never eat together. The exceptions to this rule are so few that they are insignificant. The natural consequence of the fact that everyone eats separately is that food is not always eaten hot. Quite often a little food is left in the pot for later and this is referred to as 'bambye' which is probably a corruption of 'bye and bye'. After breakfast the washing up is done by the older girls, and the children go back to school at 1 p.m.

The afternoon is the time for a little leisure and for visiting friends or relatives. Daughters visit their mothers, and, as everywhere, women gossip and discuss their neighbours' shortcomings. This is not the sole afternoon occupation though, for there is ironing and mending to do, cassava bread to be baked, and most important of all firewood to be collected. This is collected in the bush on the fringe of the village, or from wild trees in the cultivation area, and although boys often go to collect firewood, it is primarily a woman's job.

3 p.m.

The children come home from school and change into old clothes before being set to do odd jobs such as bringing water, going to the shop, sweeping the yard and so on, after which they are free to play. A light lunch may be eaten at 3 p.m. consisting of 'bambye' or cake bought from a cake shop. Preparation for cooking the evening meal begins around 4.30 p.m., though on many days nothing is prepared save another 'tea'.

After the evening meal is over and the dishes are washed the whole household may congregate and talk over the day's happenings, or tell 'Nancy' stories, but more often than not the adult males will go out to meet their friends on the public road or in the cakeshop, where men play dominoes or cards. At around 8 p.m. the 'beddings' are spread for the children who gradually go off to sleep, and everyone is in bed by 9 or 10 p.m., unless there is some special event such as a dance, political meeting, wake, wedding, or other public function.

This is merely a bare outline of the more important tasks women have to perform as housewives, and it pre-supposes that there is a husband or common-law husband earning enough money to keep the group going. Complications arise when the man is unable to earn enough to carry out his obligations, and when this happens the man often just disappears, or at least goes off to some other area in search of work, leaving the woman to manage as best she can. For a man to feel that he is quite unable to support his spouse and children is intolerable, for this is his main distinguishing feature as a husband and father, and the males' constantly expressed fear of women as robbers can be seen as a sort of defence mechanism against this ever present possibility of failure on their part to provide for their families.

In households where there is no man present as male head several situations may exist. A female household head who is a widow or common-law widow probably receives cash from her adult children. In addition she may have daughters and their children living with her in which case there is probably some cash income from the fathers of the children, no matter how sporadic it may be. This money is paid to the mother of the child, who gives the mistress of the house either a part of the money, or buys food herself to hand over for the common pot. If the father of the child contributes no money, then it is not unusual for the maternal grandmother to assume full responsibility for the care of the child, including buying its clothes (5). This is all the more likely if the child's mother has left the village or has left a child behind when she goes off to set up house with a man. However, the child's mother will generally attempt to raise enough money to contribute a fair share of the cost of keeping it, and more particularly will she endeavour to buy the child's clothes. In order to do this she may go out to work, either on the sugar estates or in domestic service, or she may take odd jobs carrying earth for the contractors who burn heaps to make brick for the road. In such a situation there is always a delicate balance between the amount of money the young woman can earn or acquire to contribute to the support of her child, and the degree of authority she exercises over it, or the amount of 'motherhood' she can claim in relation to it.

A woman who is left alone with small children is in a much more difficult position for she has to raise cash as well as try to look after her children, and the likelihood is that she will not only work for pay, but she will also have a series of liaisons with men who give her presents in exchange for her sexual favours, if she is young enough. She may have men coming to live with her, but such unions are generally short-lived owing to the fact that the man never really becomes effective head of the household in a situation where the young woman already has a large measure of independence. Such women may depend on a brother for occasional help but there is never any suggestion that the woman is being kept by her brother.

It is clear that in any household group there is always one woman who is the manager of the internal economy of the group and this is a part of her general function as a leader in domestic activities. In Bales' terminology relating to small group interaction patterns (6), she would be primarily an 'expressive leader', but she is also an 'instrumental leader' in many important respects. Instrumental leadership may be divided amongst a number of individuals at certain stages of the development of the household group, but the rôle of husband-father as head of the household, responsible for the group and being the chief provider of cash and economic resources is well established in the system and those households which are headed by females are almost by definition without a male head. Thus women will often say that they are poor and have to work hard because they have no husband to take care of them. The absence of a male is thought of as a deficiency in this sense.

At this stage it will be useful in presenting a picture of the over-all configuration of the household economy to examine one or two particular cases selected on the basis of the type of household group involved and its stage of development.

Case No. 1

The first case is that of a household group consisting of a man aged 46 years, his wife aged 40 years and eight children ranging in age from 18 months to 13 years. They live in a three-roomed wooden house which has a corrugated iron roof and an attached kitchen, but the house is very sparsely furnished and the floor of the bedroom needs repair. It was built in 1936 and is now beginning to deteriorate. The head of the household owns the house and the lot on which it stands, and he also owns two other unoccupied house lots in the village, the three having a total area of .549 acres. He also owns two beds of land in the cultivation area. The first has an area of .992 acres and half of it is planted in corn, the other half being abandoned to bush. The second is .278 acres and is planted in mixed provisions for household use. In addition to this the head rents 1.5 acres of rice land on an adjoining estate, and this is all planted in rice. The rental for this land is $6.00 per acre per crop, and since only one crop per year is planted the rent paid is $9.00. Once the crop has been reaped the owner is free to rent it to someone else for the small crop, or to graze cattle on it, so that the tenant only has rights to the use of the land for that period during which his rice is actually growing on it. The wife of the household head has planting rights in a Perseverance cultivation lot which is registered in the name of her mother's sister's daughter. This woman (the title holder) does not live in the village and so the land is used by the head's wife and her brother. The total area of the lot is 1.462 acres and the head's wife has about one quarter of it planted in rice, the rest being planted by her brother.

The total amount of land operated by this household (actually planted) is then, approx. 2 acres of rice land, .278 acres of mixed provisions and .496 acres of corn. Scattered throughout the holdings mentioned (including house lots), are twenty coconut trees, two orange trees, ten banana trees, eight mango trees and two star-apple trees. The household group also possesses eight goats and twenty fowls of which ten are hens over 6 months of age. They possess no other livestock.

Just in front of the house is a small cake shop operated by the head, or his wife, in which they sell bottled drinks, cakes, bread, matches, cigarettes, sweets, and various home-made drinks such as ginger beer. This shop makes a maximum profit of $4.00 per week. The household head refers to himself as being a carpenter, but in fact he rarely works at his trade. He spends most of his working time on a fishing boat which operates from the village, fishing off-shore and selling the bulk of the catch in Georgetown. For this he gets a share of the cash made on the catch, and this may amount to as much as $15.00 to $20.00 in one week though the pay fluctuates considerably according to the catches and the market prices, and according to the amount of time which has to be spent on repairing nets. Since this man does not own the boat he need not always join the crew as there are other men who can take his place on some trips, and in any case he rarely spends more than three or four days per week on the boat. His wife does not normally work for money apart from keeping an eye on the cake shop, but during the rice harvest she works as a cutter, and during November 1952 she made $14.00 at this work.

The family has very few debts. The head owes $10.00 to the Co-operative Credit Bank which he borrowed to help to pay for planting his rice, and he will pay this back out of the proceeds from the sale of padi, plus an interest of 3½ per cent per annum. The wife has a small running debt with the grocery shop which she clears every week if possible, and this rarely exceeds $5.00. The head has $60.00 in the Post Office Savings Bank which is a reserve in case of sickness etc., and he also keeps a canister with money which is used for running expenses. Two of the children have sums in the School Savings Society of $1.68 and $1.00 respectively. The wife has no savings of her own, generally spending what money she gets almost as soon as she gets it. She estimates that she needs to spend $14.00 per week on food etc. for the whole family, over and above that which comes from the farm. From the 1951 rice crop they reaped sixteen bags of clean padi, of which ten bags were kept for domestic consumption and seed, but in 1952 they planted a little more, though the unfavourable weather conditions meant that the yield was approximately the same. During November 1952 the head's wife spent $17.48 on clothes for herself and the children, and the bulk of this was money she earned by cutting rice.

Other expenses for the whole household were such things as rates, which amounted to about $17.00, and the rent for the rice land which is another $9.00. During the 1952 rice harvest the head had to pay men to assist him with the beating of the padi as well as paying cutters, and his total expenditure on this was in the region of $50.00.

Small subsidiary sources of income are from selling farm produce such as coconuts, bananas, corn, and an occasional goat or fowl. Over a whole year it is doubtful whether the total income from these sources amounts to more than about $100.00 at the most. What is quite clear is that the household cannot function at its present level without the wages of the household head. If for some reason he loses his job on the fishing boat he will have to go and seek work on the estates or elsewhere. This man has worked on the estates and in the gold fields at one time or another, and he does not regard his job on the boat as his permanent job. It is just the thing that he is doing at the moment. In fact he considers himself to be a carpenter, and this is undoubtedly what he would put down on any census return as his 'occupation'. This is a family where the woman is still largely dependent on her husband's earnings, but even so she organizes the whole of the spending for the household in connexion with food, and her own, and the children's clothes. The head takes care of the farm and all expenditure connected with it, and he gives his wife money as he can afford it and as she needs it. She has very little scope for earning money herself, apart from during the rice harvest, and if she needs clothes or wishes to travel to see a relative or buy a present for someone, she either has to ask her husband for the money or take it out of the money she handles for the housekeeping. Eight children and two adults consume quite a large quantity of food and there is very little margin for extra expenditure. Her husband has one outside child towards whose support he contributed a little money until the child was 16 years old, and that was an extra drain on the income.

Case No. 2

The second case is a household with a female head who is 52 years of age. She is illiterate and was very uncertain about the dates of the birth of her children, and even her own age. However, she got her first child when she was very young, certainly before she was 18 years old, and when she became pregnant she went to live with the father of her child. They lived together for 22 years in a common-law union and during this time she had eleven children, of which four died, three of them in infancy. Her last pregnancy resulted in a miscarriage at 5 months. Shortly after this her common-law husband left her to go and live with another woman in the same village, and she says that he was beginning to be very troublesome and she got tired of the way in which he would be perpetually going about with other women. For the past twelve or thirteen years she has been running her household alone, and it now consists of herself, her two adult daughters who are 21 and 23 years of age, and four small children. Three of the children aged 8, 4 and 1 year are the children of the elder daughter, each one having a different father, and the other one aged 9 years is the child of the daughter aged 21 years. The head also has two sons aged 21 and 17 years, both of whom work away from the village, sending no money to their mother, but they come home occasionally and help her with the farm work, and they do give her presents now and again with which she buys clothes. Another daughter lives in a small house on the same lot with a common-law husband, but she cooks separately and runs a separate household.

The house is a two-roomed thatched cottage with a separate kitchen, all in a bad state of repair. There are no furnishings apart from a small wooden bench and an old wagonette which serves as a table. The lot on which the house stands belongs to the head, and this is the only house lot which she owns. Her own estimate of the value of the house is $20.00. She has recently bought .845 acres of land in the provision area, but has not yet obtained title to it. This is planted in mixed provisions and scattered over the lot are eight coconut trees, four mango trees, one star-apple tree, and there are forty banana trees planted. This woman also rents two acres of rice land on an estate which is three or four miles from the village, and she pays $8.00 per acre per crop for it. In all then, the household group cultivates .845 acres of mixed provisions and two acres of rice. The household head also owns one pig, one donkey, two hens and five dogs, and she possesses one hoe, one cutlass and an agricultural fork.

This household depends to a large extent on the produce of the farm for food, but even so it is estimated that they spend about

$4.00 every week on food from the shop. Some of this money comes in the form of intermittent payments for child maintenance from the fathers of the daughters' children, which theoretically totals $8.00 per week for the four children. However, these payments are not regular, and one of the fathers went to prison during the period of the study for failure to pay, being many months in arrears. Neither of the adult daughters has a regular job, but all three women work on the farm, and they will take odd jobs such as carrying wood or cutting rice whenever they can get them, which is not often. The bulk of the cash comes from the sale of provisions and bananas, which the household head takes seven miles to market on a donkey cart. During the crab season which lasts from mid-July to mid-September, the whole household group catches crabs on the village foreshore and the head carries them to market. Crabs bring a fairly high price, selling for as much as twenty cents for three or four crabs. The money obtained from the sale of produce and crabs is almost invariably spent as soon as it is obtained. The general practice is for women to crowd the stores on market day buying cloth and various items of clothing with the money they have made. Some food, such as fresh meat or fish, may be bought and a little money will be saved for the food requirements of the next few days, but certainly this woman spends most of her money as soon as she gets it, and she is fairly typical in this respect. No member of this household group has any savings.

The household head used to operate as a village midwife, but this source of income has stopped since a government midwife began to work in the district. Despite the poverty of the group, the head is renowned as a woman with taste for clothes and she somehow manages to buy these fairly regularly. She does not buy clothes for her daughters' four children, for each daughter gets whatever she can from men friends or the fathers of their children for this purpose. The head owes $65.00 to the Co-operative Credit Bank which is the outstanding balance of a loan contracted for the purpose of repairing the house, and for paying for the provision land which she finally bought. She has no debts at the shop, and always tries to pay as she goes. Her two daughters often do the cooking and they also buy food as it is required with any money they may have. She is generous to her daughters when she has money, and out of $70.00 she made from the sale of padi in 1952 she gave them $10.00 each to buy clothes. They, of course, contributed their labour freely during the cutting of the rice.

One cannot draw up a precise balance sheet for the income and expenditure of a group such as this, for existence is a continuing process and resources are balanced against expenditure in a complex and piece-meal way. This woman has managed, and manages, to keep a household together and she does it effectively despite the low standard of living which the group enjoys.

Case No. 3

The final case we shall quote is slightly more complex, and although the family still belongs to the village group, and the lower class, it is in the slightly 'better off' category now. The household group consists of a man aged 57 years, his wife aged 52 years, and eight children ranging in age from 28 years to 8 years. The group occupies two house buildings, but one is practically unfurnished and merely serves as a dormitory for the older sons, having only one room. The other building has two rooms and an attached kitchen, and is reasonably well furnished with a large double bed, washstand and trunks in the bedroom; table, four chairs, a small sideboard and a meat safe in the living room. Light is provided by a wick-burner oil lamp, and cooking is done on an open hearth in the kitchen. There is also a pit latrine, a bathroom, a rice room and a small animal pen on the lot. The head of the household is a 'driver', or contractor, on a sugar estate about ten miles from the village, and this is a fairly permanent job. Tasks such as trench cleaning or making up dams, cutting cane, etc., are given to this man by the European manager or overseers, and he in turn employs labourers to carry out the work. The estate authorities pay him for the job, and he pays the men according to the amount of work each one has done. Two sons who are members of the household group, aged 28 and 25 years respectively, work regularly for their father and he pays them in exactly the same way that he pays all the other men working under his command. One other son aged 17 years does not work on the estate as yet, but he has a part-time job delivering newspapers which brings him $3.00 per month. The head's wife sometimes does washing in order to earn a little money for her own personal use. Some friends of hers take in washing from the East Indians of a neighbouring village, and they will always give her a part of the total if she wants it, and she does her share in their yard, not at her own home.

It was impossible to ascertain how much money is earned each week by the head of the household, partly because the amount is irregular, and partly because he only spends a portion of his income on his family. At the time of the study there was a 21-years-old daughter (unmarried and childless) living at home, and she was doing most of the cooking and running the finances for the feeding of the group. Every week the head of the household would bring approximately $7.00 worth of food from a shop on the estate where he worked, and in addition he handed over about another $7.00 in cash to the daughter for the purpose of buying food. This was rarely handed over in one sum, but was given in smaller amounts spread over the week. The head also gives his wife $3.00 per week for her own personal use. There is a household canister which contains money which, theoretically is kept in case of sickness, but it acts as a central fund, and also serves in some sense as a symbol of the authority of the household head. The head himself puts varying amounts of money into this canister. Sometimes he will put as much as $10.00 per week, or he will put in a lump sum when he sells a pig. The two adult sons earn between $9.00 and $15.00 each week during the busiest seasons on the estate. The eldest son contributes absolutely nothing to household expenses, nor does he give any money to his mother. He often sleeps away from the house with friends and never seems to save anything at all. The other adult son pays nothing towards food, but he gives his mother $1.50 every week for her personal use, and he also puts between $3.00 and $5.00 per week in the canister when his wages are good. In addition to this he 'cares' one of his younger brothers aged 13 years, buying most of his clothes and school books and giving him small sums of money to spend on sweets, etc. He also has a bank account of his own and takes a great pride in saving. The 17-years-old son who delivers newspapers puts the bulk of his money in the canister.

This is a household group with a relatively high, and comparatively stable, income, but even so we can see that both income and expenditure is diffused according to the various statuses and relationships within the group. The head is personally responsible for paying the rates on all the land (three house lots and one provision bed), and the provision of food for the group is unequivocally his responsibility. The one provision bed is worked by the adult son who contributes to the group canister, and the produce is used by the group. This son also keeps fowls but those are his own private property and the money he obtains by selling them, and their eggs, is his alone. The canister in this household is a stable core of the whole economy in one sense, but the fact that the only person who is allowed to take money out of it is the head himself, emphasizes his authority. The daughter who was doing most of the housekeeping could 'get away' with removing small amounts from the canister for food, but this was only because she was a great favourite of the head, and she never abused the privilege by taking too much or too frequently. The head's wife always knew how much was in the canister, and when the head removed a large amount in order to pay for timber to build a new kitchen for one of his 'girl friends' in another village, his wife created a great fuss. She was particularly indignant because part of the money had been obtained from the sale of some pigs which she had originally bought with her own money. Because the head paid for the feed for these pigs he had claimed them as his own, but she did not consider that this gave him the right to spend the money from their sale on anything except the needs of his own household group. Money from the canister would be used for buying clothes for the children, except for the boy who was being kept by the adult son. The head's wife bought her own clothes and she also bought most of the clothes for her favourite daughter aged 10 years out of her own money.

The head always kept a great deal of his earnings for himself and he had quite a number of 'outside' children which he helped to support. At the time of the study he had a paramour with whom he would spend several nights per week, and his wife accepted the situation, though she never hesitated to complain about it in public. If he ever failed to give her the weekly allowance which she considered her due, then she would certainly create a great fuss and make life as unpleasant as possible for him, even to the extent of 'shaming' him by complaining to his European employers.

Although this woman handled practically none of the money used for the day-to-day running of the household, there was no doubt that she was the centre of the household group, and she was its main unifying force. Even her married daughters looked to her for guidance, and when they were hungry or short of money they would come to her for food or small gifts of cash. They would also ask their father for money, and he would occasionally give them a little.

This household is not a 'farming' family at all, and although the head keeps a few pigs and goats (there are seven goats which nominally belong to an eight-years-old son, but the head decides when they shall be sold and receives the money from the sale), and one son keeps fowls and works a small bed of provisions, the group would not be considered a 'farm family' even for the purposes of the agricultural census (7). The total income of all members of the group is higher than for most village families and yet this household is not differentiated in any way from the poorer families. Its members share the common village culture and participate in all normal village activities. It does not use its cash income to build up an accumulation of 'display' possessions such as furniture, a radio, etc., and the household dwelling is indistinguishable from any other of its type. Nor is the money used to purchase more land, and land has very little value as capital unless it is actually being worked; in this village at any rate.

These three cases have been cited in order to give a concrete demonstration of the way in which domestic economy is organized. The three households are not necessarily 'typical', but the manner in which they handle their finances and resources is comparable to that obtaining in the majority of lower-class rural Negro homes.

THE HOUSEHOLD AS A UNIT OF CONSUMPTION

The manner in which the household group organizes its expenditure and the tastes and consumption patterns of its members are of importance so far as the total economy of the colony is concerned. All we can do here is to indicate very briefly the main outlines of the patterns of consumption which seem to throw light on the value system of these groups.

Food must necessarily account for a large part of household expenditure, but there is a very marked tendency to maintain a fairly uniform diet, and whilst extra luxuries such as canned meat and cakes may be bought when money is more plentiful, the main items on which extra income is spent are clothes and rum. Saving for the sake of saving is not a characteristic of most villagers, and once a certain amount of money has been accumulated it is usually spent on something or other. The principal occasions on which food luxuries are bought are parties of various kinds, and the concept of the appropriate foods to be eaten on these occasions is fairly rigid. Chicken curry and *rôti* (8), chow mein made with chicken, cake and ice-cream together with ginger-beer, aerated drinks and rum are the standard party fare, and it is significant that these items do not come within the local conception of what constitutes 'food'. In August Town the term 'food' is reserved for staple items such as rice, and ground provisions, and it would include curry eaten with rice as well as other dishes served with rice and provisions. Even in households with a higher income level, including the schoolteachers', there will not be a marked difference in basic diet even though it may be better balanced and contain a higher proportion of meat, butter, eggs and milk. For any given household then, food consumption varies within fairly narrow limits both as regards variety and quantity, and this is borne out by the statements of the storekeepers as to the commodities which they can profitably stock. The occasional purchase of a luxury item such as Ovaltine or Marmite, does not invalidate this generalization, and odd expenditure on expensive items such as this is fairly rare.

The purchase of houses must be regarded as a special form of expenditure, incurred at infrequent intervals, and requiring a fairly sustained effort in accumulating the necessary capital. We have already pointed out that the building of a house is usually spread over a period of time, and the money is usually earned outside the village. Building probably occurs with greater rapidity at times of relative prosperity, and when wages were high during the war there was undoubtedly an increase in the number of new houses erected. Loans for this purpose are to be had from the co-operative credit banks, and probably a majority of the loans issued by these banks are used for building new houses or extending and repairing old ones.

The payment of rates on land, and houses (in the case of Better Hope), is a recurrent form of expenditure, on the whole paid unwillingly and on threat of the loss of lands or property. In August Town and Perseverance many men clear their debt to the local authority by working on the village projects instead of handing over cash. Provision is made for villagers to make periodic part payments, and whilst this is not an uncommon practice, probably the majority of land holders wait until 'crop time' when they can pay off outstanding debts to the local authority out of the receipts from the sale of padi. Payments of this nature, rates, purchase price for houses and land, expenditure on labour and materials for farming, are primarily the responsibility of men, either in their rôles as husband-fathers or as sons, but this is not to say that women do not sometimes undertake them all.

Expenditure on furnishings for the home varies considerably as between households and at various times of the year. In the houses of members of the higher status group such as schoolteachers one may expect to find considerable elaboration in the interior decoration of the home. Most of the pieces of furniture will be bought in

Georgetown or New Amsterdam, and the whole scheme of furnishing will be in accordance with urban middle-class standards. In the majority of village households the furnishings will be made in the village or by carpenters and cabinet-makers in neighbouring villages. A few pieces of furniture may be bought in town from one of the cheaper dealers. The uniformity in design of furniture throughout the whole of British Guiana is a fact worth noting. Locally made basket chairs are widely used by the lower-class and these tend to be almost standard design, the only difference being between four-legged and rocker chairs. Wooden chairs made from local woods usually have a woven seat and once again are made in exactly the same pattern by almost all cabinet makers, this time being made as rockers, armchairs or armless. These chairs are more frequently used by the higher status rural households or by the urban middle-class. In poorer homes the old-fashioned ottoman with a wooden unupholstered seat is commonly found, together with locally-made 'straight chairs', or boxes used as seats. Small sideboards or 'cabinets' are frequent items of furniture and the possession of drinking glasses glass dishes, etc., which are usually displayed on top of the cabinet is fairly general (9). The standardization of furnishings is of course paralleled by the standard design of houses (10), and it seems likely that uniformities of this nature go hand in hand with the lack of status differentiation and social mobility and are not merely a sign of lack of ability to execute new designs.

At holiday times, and particularly at Christmas, houses are thoroughly cleaned, furniture is varnished, and curtains are made for the windows. It is also at holiday seasons that new items of furniture are likely to be acquired, and knick-knacks to adorn the 'cabinet' may be purchased.

Cash which is surplus to immediate requirements for food, rates, and miscellaneous household expenses such as soap, kerosene, coals, starch, etc., is most frequently spent on rum by the men, and clothes by the women. Women budget for the children's school books, slates, etc., and make sure that they have shoes and decent clothes to go to school in. Money spent on court cases, doctors' fees, and on consulting obeah men is in the nature of emergency spending and may either be taken from the 'canister' or raised by borrowing, pawning gold jewellery, by withdrawing cash from a 'box' (11) or from the P.O. Savings Bank if an account is held. It may also be raised by selling livestock if the person possesses any.

There are not a great many alternative ways of spending money.

Diet, house furnishings, entertainments, church subscriptions, and running expenses for the farm are all more or less uniform, or at least very within relatively narrow limits throughout the main village group. Practically all money is spent within the village, or in the case of men, close to where they happen to be working. Expenditure tends to be immediate rather than planned over a period of time and this is consonant not only with the irregularity of income but with the system of values which lays stress not upon status differentiations and hierarchical mobility, but on immediate satisfactions and 'living well' with neighbours, friends and fellow villagers.

Conclusion

It would be desirable to conclude this chapter by presenting some kind of quantitative picture of household income and expenditure. However, the difficulties involved in collecting anything like an adequate sample of household budgets in this particular society, carefully recorded over a long period of time, were too great with the limited resources available. A series of budgets were collected in August Town but they have unfortunately been lost. The kind of study necessary in order to arrive at precise numerical formulations has been carried out by Mr. K. Straw in Barbados (12). All we intend to do here is to present a schematic outline of the principal sources of household income, and to list the principal categories of household expenditure. This is a very generalized list, and it applies particularly to the main Negro section of the village population unless otherwise indicated. We have already listed the principal occupations in Chapter I and so there is no need to recapitulate them here. (13)

A. PRINCIPAL SOURCES OF HOUSEHOLD INCOME

(*i*) *In cash*

Wages of men-folk
Wages of women-folk
Cash from sale of padi, farm produce, and livestock
Cash from sale of prepared foods etc., made by women
Profits from petty buying and selling

(*ii*) *In kind*

Farm produce
Locally caught fish, crabs, etc.
Locally reared livestock

B. HOUSEHOLD EXPENDITURE

(*i*) *Food—principal items*

Rice
Salt fish
Salt-meat (beef and pork)
Smoked herring
Cooking oil
Cooking butter (margarine)
Potatoes
Onions
Flour
Yeast
Sugar
Salt
Pepper
Curry powder
Garlic
Fresh meat (infrequently)
Milk
Vegetables from farm or kitchen garden
Fruits from farm
Coconuts
Bought vegetables
Bought prepared foods

(*ii*) *Rent and rates*

Even where persons are renting a house in the rural areas, the proportion of income spent on rent and rates is still fairly small. Even a moderately sized house of the type that might be rented by a head-teacher would only cost between ten and fifteen dollars per month, and a small two-roomed house would only cost about four or five dollars per month. Rents are somewhat higher in Better Hope than in the other two villages. Rent and rates on cultivated land represent part of the working costs and they are usually paid out of the income from the sale of produce. Where a household owns land which is not being cultivated then the rates on this land form a drain on the household income.

(*iii*) *Purchase of houses, furnishings, etc.*

This is not a recurrent form of expenditure, but small amounts will be spent on repairs and the purchase of cooking utensils etc., from time to time.

(*iv*) *Fuel and light*

Most villagers collect their own firewood, and light is normally provided by small kerosene lamps using perhaps two pints of oil per week, which costs about fifteen cents. Most houses keep a low light burning all night.

(*v*) *Clothing*

This is a major item of expenditure for all families and accounts for a considerable proportion of the total income being the next largest item of expenditure after food.

(*vi*) *Luxuries and entertainment*

The amount of money spent by men on rum is fairly high especially at holiday times. Tobacco does not constitute a major item and there are few heavy smokers in the villages. The shops often sell cigarettes in ones and twos rather than by the packet, even though they only cost about seventeen to twenty cents per packet of twelve cigarettes. Entertainments involving the spending of money are relatively few. Dances, concerts, and church fairs occur infrequently and only in Better Hope do persons go to the cinema. When a family can afford it, they will hold birthday parties which involve fairly heavy expenditure for it is obligatory to provide the guests with rum and luxury foods such as cake and ice-cream.

(*vii*) *Sickness, death, weddings, birth, obeah consultations, legal expenses*

Expenditure on all these items is really emergency spending, and if the household group does not have enough money saved up, or does not get enough from the burial society in the case of death, then the money may be borrowed or raised by selling stock, pawning jewellery, etc.

(*viii*) *Travelling*

Men spend quite a lot of money on travelling in search of work, and a certain amount of money is spent on travelling to visit relatives in other parts of the colony.

(*ix*) *Domestic help*

Only households in the higher status groups such as school teachers have domestic servants. The general rule is to employ one young woman who acts as cook and general servant. The servant is provided with food and paid a small wage, sometimes as low as four dollars per month.

(*x*) *Investment in capital equipment*

This is extremely low. Farmers possess the bare minimum of tools and there are no tractors or mechanical farm equipment owned by any Negro farmers in any of the three villages.

(*xi*) *Savings*

If savings are taken over a long-time span of say one or two years, they tend to be very low indeed. Short-term saving for a specified end is the rule and saving for the sheer sake of accumulating money, or for long-term goals, is rare.

This list covers most of the principal items of expenditure for the average village family and gives some idea of the fluidity of the economic situation, which makes it difficult to speak of 'weekly' income and expenditure. Both income and expenditure are balanced out over much longer and irregular periods of time.

CHAPTER IV

COMPOSITION OF THE HOUSEHOLD GROUP

In the literature on the West Indian family, writers have frequently mentioned the fact that the household is an important social unit and they have sometimes tried to indicate the nature of these units. Professor and Mrs. Herskovits writing of a village in Trinidad, state explicitly that:—

> 'The definition of the Toco family, in any functioning sense, must give a prominent place to the individual household' (1).

Having said this, they then proceed to base their discussion on the case of one family group only, though they do give some very rough figures on the approximate number of children per household in a sample of 106 households. The figures were compiled from the statements 'of third persons concerning their neighbours and friends' and consequently are not very reliable. The Herskovitses show considerable insight into the nature of the problem involved in studying the family system in this area, but their predominating interest in 'African survivals' soon leads them away from it, and the greater part of the chapter on 'The Functioning Family' is taken up with a description of the customs surrounding childbirth, child rearing and courtship. The preliminary insight into the basic importance of the household as a social unit is never developed, and the formulations concerning the nature of the household group are never given any precision.

Simey is similarly vague on this subject, though he is writing from a much more general point of view, and he does quote certain information collected by Mr. Lewis Davidson in Jamaica. He tells us that:—

> The family group is, indeed, one which is brought together in a very casual way, and this obtains for the Christian as well as the Disintegrate family. Mr. Davidson discovered the striking fact that amongst all the

> 270 families he studied in Jamaica, *not a single one* consisted only of parents and their children (2).

Since we do not know what Mr. Davidson's object was in studying these families nor the methods he used it is difficult to evaluate this piece of information, but it does seem that there is at least an implied comparison with what is conceived as the ideal type of European family group consisting of the nuclear family only.

Madeline Kerr, also writing of Jamaica, states that:—

> The members of a Jamaican household must not be identified with the family. Sometimes the household does consist of mother, father and own children only, but more often it contains a collection of people tied by kinship or sometimes only by proximity (3).

Again there is the implied comparison with the ideal European type 'family' and we are left with a very vague impression of what actually does constitute a household group in this society, and if there are variations we certainly don't know the frequency of their occurrence.

Henriques has a more detailed discussion of the domestic group and proposes a four-fold classification according to the type of conjugal union on which the domestic group is based, with one residual category to take care of those groups where there is no male head present (4). Simey has proposed a similar type of classification based on the work of Mr. Lewis Davidson (5). Henriques is well aware that his four types of domestic group do not constitute mutually exclusive categories, and he specifically states that:—

> 'This classification is not rigid as a domestic group can during its history experience several or all of these forms' (6).

Not surprisingly he runs into some difficulty in imposing his four-fold classification, especially when he finds it necessary to include households with a male head under his category of 'Maternal or Grandmother Family'. It is difficult to evaluate the significance of his scheme since he presents very little in the way of case material, and practically no distribution figures apart from statistics taken from the Jamaica Census, which deals in different categories. His 'rough estimate' of the incidence of different types of domestic group is very unsatisfying, for it is a matter of some importance to know the incidence of each type more precisely when one is dealing with such apparently heterogeneous data.

In British Guiana Negro communities, individual households do appear to exhibit a wide variation in the categories of persons who make up their membership, and a cursory examination of August Town was sufficient to make it quite clear that there was no superficially apparent norm of domestic grouping. Over 300 houses in the village seemed to contain a somewhat bewildering array of occupants, and although one could draw up a list of various 'types' of grouping it seemed necessary to make a comprehensive survey of all households in order to introduce an element of certainty into any discussion of what is 'normal' for this community. Fortes has demonstrated the difficulty of arriving at definitions of normality in domestic groupings in modern Ashanti, and shown how the application of simple statistical techniques can serve to illuminate structural features which are otherwise obscured by the application of blanket terms such as 'matrilocality' and 'patrilocality' (7). The same general method of approach was applied in British Guiana, and indeed it would seem to be the only logical method to adopt under the circumstances and for this particular kind of study (8).

We begin then by considering the composition of the household group in terms of the relationship of its members to the person we have defined as the 'household head'. Our first distinction will be between households with a male head and those with a female head, for these categories form convenient points of reference for a synchronic enumeration and they are broad enough to prevent us making prematurely specific classifications. This avoids for the time being any preconceived notions as to the genesis of household groups, and we take particular care not to introduce terms such as 'matriarchal' or 'patriarchal' at this stage.

For the purposes of classification it has been necessary to attach labels to persons to indicate their conjugal status, and the following terminology which was used in the field has been consistently adopted throughout this book. The terminology has its limitations but taken in conjunction with case histories it does provide a convenient set of working definitions.

1. *Married.*—Legally married.
2. *Common-law married.*—Where a person is living in the same house as their partner without being legally married. This category definitely implies cohabitation.
3. *Single mother or single father.*—Where a person is the biological mother or father of a child or children which he or she recognizes, but has never lived with a member of the opposite sex in a marital or common-law union.

4. *Single.*—Where a person has never had any children and never lived with a member of the opposite sex in a marital or common-law union.
5. *Widower.*
6. *Widow.*
7. *Common-law widower.*
8. *Common-law widow.*
9. *Separated.*
10. *Common-law separated.*
11. *Divorced.*—Only refers to those cases where a divorce has been granted by the courts.

It is realized that some individuals may fall into more than one of the above categories if their whole life history is taken into account, though of course it is the status of the person at the time of the survey which is of primary interest to us here. The term 'spouse' has been used in a rather unorthodox way to include not only marital partners of either sex, but also common-law partners of either sex, so that wherever the term is used no distinction is made between marriage and common-law marriage. The term 'common-law marriage' has been adopted not only because of its wide use in the West Indies by government agencies, but also because it does convey the idea that such a union is almost the same as a marital union apart from the legal and religious sanction. The term 'concubinage' carries more of the suggestion of extra-marital relationship, and will only be used in contexts where its meaning is made quite clear.

In the following tables the membership of household groups in terms of relationship to the head is enumerated in detail for all three villages. In the case of August Town and Perseverance the figures are based on complete censuses of the villages, whilst in Better Hope they are based on a random sample of eighty-four households. For all three villages certain cases have been excluded, including those where a man or woman lives completely alone of course. It must be remembered that these are simple distribution figures of persons standing in a definite relationship to the head of the household and have a limited value in that they cannot tell us anything of the particular reasons for the configuration of any specific household. Tables VIIIa and IXa present a more detailed breakdown of the categories enumerated in Tables VIII and IX.

TABLE VIII

RELATIONSHIP OF MEMBERS TO MALE HEADS OF HOUSEHOLDS

	AUGUST TOWN		PERSEVERANCE		BETTER HOPE	
Category of kin	*No.*	%	*No.*	%	*No.*	%
Spouses ..	157	17.27	81	17.05	47	25.00
Children ..	527	57.97	298	62.74	118	62.76
Grandchildren (mainly daughters' children) ..	123	13.53	50	10.53	9	4.79
Children's spouses	7	0.77	7	1.47	1	0.53
Kin of Head ..	22	2.42	17	3.58	6	3.19
Kin of Head's spouse	50	5.50	18	3.79	6	3.19
Adopted and non-kin ..	23	2.53	4	0.84	1	0.53
TOTALS ..	909	100.00	475	100.00	188	100.00

N.B.—Total No. of households covered by tables:—
August Town, 173; Perseverance, 86; Better Hope, 51.

TABLE IX

RELATIONSHIP OF MEMBERS TO FEMALE HEADS OF HOUSEHOLDS

	AUGUST TOWN		PERSEVERANCE		BETTER HOPE	
Category of kin	*No.*	%	*No.*	%	*No.*	%
Children ..	147	36.39	30	35.71	28	49.12
Grandchildren (mainly daughters' children) ..	158	39.11	37	44.05	21	36.84
Siblings and Siblings' children	61	15.09	8	9.52	3	5.26
Affines	13	3.22	7	8.33	3	5.26
Other miscellaneous (see Table IXa) ..	25	6.19	2	2.38	2	3.50
TOTALS	404	100.00	84	100.00	57	100.00

N.B.—Total No. of households covered by tables:—
August Town, 102; Perseverance, 17; Better Hope, 20.

TABLE VIIIa

RELATIONSHIP OF MEMBERS TO MALE HEADS OF HOUSEHOLDS

	AUGUST TOWN		PERSE-VERANCE		BETTER HOPE	
CATEGORY OF KIN	*No.*	%	*No.*	%	*No.*	%
1. Wife	136	14.96	55	11.58	38	20.21
2. Common-law wife	21	2.31	26	5.47	9	4.79
3. Son of head and spouse						
(*a*) under 18	210	23.10	109	22.95	38	20.21
(*b*) over 18	38	4.18	20	4.21	10	5.32
4. Daughter of head and spouse						
(*a*) under 18	211	23.21	132	27.79	45	23.94
(*b*) over 18 single	22	2.42	14	2.95	8	4.25
(*c*) single mother	16	1.76	5	1.05	2	1.06
(*d*) married	6	0.66	4	0.84	1	0.53
(*e*) C.L. married	1	0.11	1	0.21	0	0.00
(*f*) separated	6	0.66	2	0.42	0	0.00
5. Son of head only	2	0.22	1	0.21	1	0.53
6. Daughter of head only	3	0.33	1	0.21	2	1.06
7. Son of						
(*a*) wife only	3	0.33	0	0.00	3	1.59
(*b*) C.L. wife only	4	0.44	3	0.63	2	1.06
8. Daughter of						
(*a*) wife only	4	0.44	2	0.42	4	2.13
(*b*) C.L. wife only	1	0.11	4	0.84	2	1.06
9. Child of single son	16	1.76	2	0.42	0	0.00
10. Child of single daughter	46	5.06	15	3.15	3	1.59
11. Child of 5	0	0.00	0	0.00	0	0.00
12. Child of 6	3	0.33	3	0.63	0	0.00
13. Child of 7	1	0.11	0	0.00	0	0.00
14. Child of 8	10	1.10	11	2.31	2	1.06
15. Child of married daughter	19	2.09	13	2.73	4	2.13
16. Child of married son	19	2.09	0	0.00	0	0.00
17. Child of C.L.M. daughter	1	0.11	1	0.21	0	0.00
18. Child of C.L.M. son	3	0.33	5	1.05	0	0.00
19. Child of daughter's child	5	0.55	0	0.00	0	0.00
20. Child of son's child	0	0.00	0	0.00	0	0.00
21. Son's wife	4	0.44	0	0.00	0	0.00
22. Son's common-law wife	1	0.11	1	0.21	0	0.00
23. Daughter's husband	1	0.11	3	0.63	1	0.53
24. Daughteı's common-law husband	1	0.11	2	0.42	0	0.00
25. Spouse of 8	0	0.00	1	0.21	0	0.00

TABLE VIIIa—*continued*

CATEGORY OF KIN	AUGUST TOWN No.	AUGUST TOWN %	PERSEVERANCE No.	PERSEVERANCE %	BETTER HOPE No.	BETTER HOPE %
26. Brother	1	0.11	2	0.42	1	0.53
27. Sister	5	0.55	2	0.42	0	0.00
28. Brother's child or grandchild	6	0.66	1	0.21	0	0.00
29. Sister's child or grandchild	5	0.55	9	1.89	2	1.06
30. Wife's brother	2	0.22	2	0.42	0	0.00
31. Common-law wife's brother	1	0.11	0	0.00	0	0.00
32. Wife's sister	6	0.66	7	1.47	0	0.00
33. Common-law wife's sister	1	0.11	0	0.00	0	0.00
34. Child or grandchild of 30 or 31	13	1.43	2	0.42	5	2.66
35. Child or grandchild of 32 or 33	20	2.20	0	0.00	0	0.00
36. Father	1	0.11	1	0.21	0	0.00
37. Mother	2	0.22	2	0.42	2	1.06
38. Wife's father	0	0.00	2	0.42	0	0.00
39. Wife's mother	4	0.44	2	0.42	0	0.00
40. Common-law wife's mother	2	0.22	0	0.00	0	0.00
41. Adopted child	18	1.98	4	0.84	1	0.53
42. Non-kin	5	0.55	0	0.00	0	0.00
43. Other kin of head	2	0.22	0	0.00	1	0.53
44. Other kin of spouse	1	0.11	3	0.63	1	0.53
TOTALS	909	100.00	475	100.00	188	100.00

TABLE IXa

RELATIONSHIP OF MEMBERS TO FEMALE HEADS OF HOUSEHOLDS

CATEGORY OF KIN	AUGUST TOWN No.	AUGUST TOWN %	PERSEVERANCE No.	PERSEVERANCE %	BETTER HOPE No.	BETTER HOPE %
1. Sons						
(*a*) under 18	23	5.70	7	8.33	4	7.00
(*b*) over 18 single	23	5.70	3	3.57	9	15.80
(*c*) single father	5	1.24	1	1.19	0	0.00
(*d*) married	2	0.49	2	2.38	1	1.75
(*e*) C.L. married	0	0.00	1	1.19	0	0.00
(*f*) separated	2	0.49	1	1.19	0	0.00

TABLE IXa—*continued*

CATEGORY OF KIN	AUGUST TOWN		PERSE-VERANCE		BETTER HOPE	
	No.	%	*No.*	%	*No.*	%
2. Daughters						
(*a*) under 18	33	8.17	7	8.33	3	5.26
(*b*) over 18 single	23	5.70	2	2.38	6	10.52
(*c*) single mother ..	22	5.45	3	3.57	3	5.26
(*d*) married	7	1.73	3	3.57	1	1.75
(*e*) C.L. married ..	4	0.99	0	0.00	0	0.00
(*f*) separated	3	0.74	0	0.00	1	1.75
3. Child of single son	7	1.73	0	0.00	1	1.75
4. Child of single daughter	81	20.04	14	16.70	9	15.80
5. Child of married son	10	2.47	8	9.52	0	0.00
6. Child of married daughter ..	28	6.93	9	10.71	3	5.26
7. Child of common-law married son	8	1.98	1	1.19	0	0.00
8. Child of common-law married daughter	10	2.47	0	0.00	0	0.00
9. Child of dead daughter	8	1.98	4	4.76	4	7.01
10. Child of 3	1	0.25	0	0.00	0	0.00
11. Child of 4	4	0.99	1	1.19	0	0.00
12. Child of 9	1	0.25	0	0.00	4	7.01
13. Brother	2	0.49	0	0.00	0	0.00
14. Sister	9	2.23	0	0.00	1	1.75
15. Brother's child or grandchild ..	12	2.97	0	0.00	1	1.75
16. Sister's child or grandchild ..	38	9.40	8	9.52	1	1.75
17. Son's wife	2	0.49	2	2.38	1	1.75
18. Daughter's husband	2	0.49	3	3.57	1	1.75
19. Daughter's common-law husband	4	0.99	0	0.00	0	0.00
20. Son's common-law wife ..	0	0.00	1	1.19	0	0.00
21. Brother's wife	1	0.25	0	0.00	0	0.00
22. Spouse of 15	1	0.25	0	0.00	0	0.00
23. Spouse of 16	2	0.49	1	1.19	0	0.00
24. Spouse of 9	1	0.25	0	0.00	1	1.75
25. Non-kin	5	1.24	0	0.00	0	0.00
26. 'Distant' relative	6	1.48	1	1.19	0	0.00
27. Adopted child	5	1.24	0	0.00	0	0.00
28. Common-law husband	8	1.98	1	1.19	0	0.00
29. Child of 28	1	0.25	0	0.00	2	3.50
TOTALS	404	100.00	84	100.00	57	100.00

COMPOSITION OF HOUSEHOLD GROUPS WITH A MALE HEAD

Tables VIII and VIIIa show the composition of those households with a male head in all three villages. It is immediately apparent that by far the greater number of households with a male head also have the head's wife or common-law wife present, and this confirms the view that all households irrespective of headship tend to be matrifocal. In all three villages there is a uniformity in the percentages of different kinds of kin present in the household, and in each village there is a larger proportion of persons in this type of household who are related to the head's spouse than to the head himself. Apart from a few adopted children, we do not find any members of these households who are not kin of either the head or his spouse, so that we can immediately characterize the household group as a kinship group. There are one or two exceptions where we find persons boarding with the head but these are very marginal cases.

It is also clear that the majority of male household heads in all three villages are married, and even where the head has a common-law wife he is definitely supposed to provide for her and their children, and their relationship cannot be considered as any frivolous arrangement. It implies quite definite reciprocal rights, duties and obligations, and is a socially recognized form of union. Categories 3 to 8 inclusive represent children of the head and his spouse and comprise the largest single category of kin in these households, representing 57.91 per cent of all members (excluding the heads themselves) in August Town, 62.79 per cent in Perseverance and 62.78 per cent in Better Hope. The great majority of these children are the offspring of both the head and his spouse, but the presence of a few children of either the head or his spouse alone shows that couples entering a conjugal union can bring children by other liaisons to live in the household, and they are treated in exactly the same way as the other children. In August Town there is a tendency for these children to be found more frequently in households where the couple are in a common-law union, and this bears out the observation that women only enter common-law unions in this village when they are already mothers. Of the children, relatively few are over 18 years of age, and there are more adult daughters than sons. So far as August Town is concerned, this is correlated with the fact that many young men are away working at the bauxite mines and these have not been included as resident members of the household. In Perseverance young men who make regular seasonal migrations to the sugar estates have been included, and only those who are permanently away or away on extended working trips have been excluded. This balances the numbers somewhat in the case of Perseverance.

In Better Hope the numbers are almost equal, and this reflects the more stable marriage pattern in this village, as well as the fact that there are almost equal opportunities for both young men and young women to find work in Georgetown.

Households with male heads are primarily two generation groups devoted to the rearing of children. They are also predominantly based upon a conjugal union of some kind. Categories 9 to 20 inclusive are the grandchildren of the head and his spouse (with an almost negligible number of great-grandchildren which only represent one case in August Town, where an old man was titular head of a household containing his granddaughter and her husband). These grandchildren are predominantly daughters' children and are found more frequently in August Town than in either Perseverance or Better Hope, being relatively few in the latter village.

Categories 21 to 25 inclusive are children's spouses and in keeping with the rule that a man sets up his own household on entering a conjugal relationship there are very few persons in this category. The figures are not large enough to have any significance for the formulation of a statement as to whether marriage or common-law marriage is *viri-local* or *uxori-local* in cases such as this, and the people themselves have no explicit rule. Where a child's spouse is living in the household in these cases it will usually be for some specific reason. The young couple may be waiting to finish building their own house, or in the case of Perseverance the young husband may be working away for most of the time. In one case in August Town, a daughter's common-law husband was a stranger to the village and the girl had lived with him on the East Coast of Demerara before they both came to settle in August Town. He was in a very precarious position in the household and whenever a quarrel broke out, his common-law wife would threaten him with expulsion. Such quarrels were particularly frequent when there was no work available on the sugar estates and the man would have to sit around all day doing nothing. He had no land in the village and absolutely no means of providing anything for his common-law wife and their child, and on one occasion he resorted to stealing cassava from someone else's farm, only to be discovered and branded as a 'tief-man'. Whenever a quarrel broke out, he would remove himself to a neighbouring yard and sit there until the storm had passed.

Categories 26 to 29 inclusive, and 30 to 35 inclusive, make an interesting comparison, because it is clear that collateral kin of the head's spouse predominate over his own collateral kin and it is particularly children of the spouse's sister that get incorporated into the household. This helps to confirm the fact that the female spouse is the real focus of the group, but it also illustrates a point about the relations between sisters which is discussed more fully in Chapter VII. This is much less true for Perseverance and Better Hope, and in Perseverance there is actually a greater number of the head's collaterals than those of his spouse. However, the figures alone conceal certain important variables. In Perseverance there is one case where a young man and his common-law wife are sharing a house with his sister and her common-law husband, and this one case accounts for a large proportion of the numbers involved in the whole category. An arrangement such as this is a temporary one and were it not for the fact that the two couples cook one pot we should have treated them as two separate households, which in many respects they actually are.

Fathers and mothers of the heads and their spouses are very few, and in these cases there is no doubt that the old persons are not the heads of the households. They have been taken in by their children, who are caring for them, and although they are respected and exercise considerable influence in the household they do not control it.

Adopted children are adopted in the full sense of the term, not being regarded as servants or domestic help. They grow up as children of the person adopting them, and often inherit property in the same way they would if they were natural heirs. Childless couples often adopt one or more children, and in one case in August Town, a Negro couple had adopted East Indian as well as Negro children.

Other kin of head and his spouse are persons not covered by the above categories such as a mother's sister's child or grandchild and the persons listed as non-kin are paying boarders, such as young men working at the near-by Post Office, or in the Perseverance case, three young male school-teachers who were boarding with the head-teacher and his wife.

COMPOSITION OF HOUSEHOLD GROUPS WITH A FEMALE HEAD

Tables IX and IXa show the categories of persons present in households with a female head, excluding the heads themselves, and once again it is clear that these household groups are in fact kin groups, there being very few non-kin present at all. Persons on very short visits were not included, where the period of the visit did not extend beyond a few weeks. Persons away from the villages on short visits of not more than a few weeks were included, as were men working away for short periods of time. Some households in August Town which at first appeared to have a female head, have been included in the male-head group where it was a case of the head being out of the village working, but regularly sending money home to his spouse, and coming back to the village whenever he could. In these cases, the female was only head of the household by virtue of the absence of her spouse at the time of the study. Conjugal relations were maintained, and the couples were definitely not 'separated' in the technical sense of the term.

Households with female heads are predominantly three-generation groups and this can be seen from an examination of the tables. Categories 1 and 2 of Table IXa are children of the head and they comprise 36.58 per cent of all household members (excluding the heads) in August Town, 35.71 per cent in Perseverance and 49.12 per cent in Better Hope. However, unlike the case of households with a male head, they are not the largest single category throughout, and the majority of them are over 18 years of age. They are predominantly daughters. The largest single category is that of grandchildren and great-grandchildren, comprising categories 3 to 12 inclusive in Table IXa. Better Hope is excluded from this generalization, for there are fewer unmarried mothers and fewer women taking care of their daughters' children. The reasons for these variations as between the three villages will be taken up later, but the point which concerns us most at the moment is that in these households the children under 18 years of age are mainly the head's grandchildren or great-grandchildren, or her nieces and nephews. Categories 13 to 16 inclusive are siblings and siblings' children and here again we see quite clearly the predominance of sisters' children, particularly in August Town.

The percentage of spouses of the two descending generations from the head is greater than in the case of households with a male head, and the percentage is highest in Perseverance, where housing is bad, and the age at which persons enter conjugal unions is lower.

At this point, a deficiency in the field-work must be noted which may have resulted in our placing some cases in categories 4 and 6 which should properly be in category 9. It is likely that information concerning the mothers of some children did not include whether they were dead or alive, though it did include whether they were married, common-law married or single.

Category 28 calls for some explanation. In these cases there was no doubt that the woman was head of the household and that the man was in a subordinate position in the household group. In most of the cases, the woman had her grown-up children around her, and had no children in common with the man.

Conclusion

These tables present us with an over-all picture of the situation as it existed in the three villages at the time of the study, and if we so desired we could go on to develop a synchronic classificatory scheme in much more detail. Synchronic in this sense would mean at that point in time at which the field-study was carried out, or the phenomena observed. This is essentially the process followed by the writers who have drawn up lists of family types. The limit to the number of such types would be determined only by the range of variability of our data, and the range of variability is fairly extensive. Thus we could have elementary or nuclear families based on marriage and on common-law marriage; three generation families with a female head; two generation families with a female head; families including collateral kin of either the male head or his spouse; and so on until we had exhausted our range of variations. This procedure would be no more valueless than squeezing all our 'types' into three or four procrustean categories and leaving it at that. In either event we should have left out the vital dimension of time, and it is only by trying to arrange the various types of household grouping along a time axis, that we shall be able to gain a real insight into the nature of the structural principles, which are at work in determining the composition of any particular household group at the time of the field-study. Our synchronic unit then becomes not the arbitrary period of time spent in the field but the period of time represented by the lives of the three generations normally existing at the time of the study. The actual cases we observe represent various stages in the life process of individuals and of household groups and if we allow for factors of change which have taken place in the recent past we should get a clear picture of the normal cyclical growth and decay processes involved. In fact, there has been very little real change during the past fifty years or so in any of the three villages, and such changes as there have been, have not affected the family system to any significant degree. This general type of analysis has been documented by Fortes and the present study confirms his view that structure is to be seen as 'an arrangement of parts brought about by the operation, through a period of time, of principles of social organization which have general validity in a particular society' (9). Our only modification to this view would be that the 'principles of social organization which have general validity', may vary as between certain groups or social classes within the same total society, and account will have to be taken of this new social dimension. Thus in British Guiana, these principles will vary as between different status groups in the colour/class hierarchy, and this has certain repercussions on our three villages in so far as they exhibit a greater or lesser tendency towards the norms of status groups higher than themselves. Thus Better Hope approximates more closely towards the 'middle-class' norms than do August Town and Perseverance. There may exist separate, though overlapping and cross-cutting value systems, and structure will vary correlatively with the intensity of application of these as well as along a time dimension.

In the next chapter we shall deal with the analysis of variation over time, and in Section III we discuss some aspects of the variations to be detected in association with the variability of cultural and class norms.

CHAPTER V

THE TIME FACTOR IN RELATION TO THE STRUCTURE OF THE HOUSEHOLD GROUP

DEVELOPMENTAL SEQUENCE OF THE HOUSEHOLD GROUP

THE real starting point of the development of all household groups is the birth of children, and it is around their care and protection that domestic relations tend to crystallize. Some writers on the West Indies have tended to place the primary emphasis upon the marital relationship, and to classify households according to the type of conjugal union (or absence of it), on which they are 'based' (1). We are approaching the problem from a somewhat different point of view in that we are stressing the functions which all household groups fulfil, and examining the various constellations of relationships which exist within these groups at different stages of their development.

Men build houses, or sometimes rent them, and then bring a woman to live there as a wife or common-law wife. The couple may have children in common already, in which case the formation of a household group had in some senses been anticipated with the birth of their first child. On the other hand, they may have no children when they set up house, but the assumption is that they will have children eventually, and from an analytical point of view one might say that a household group in the real sense of the term has not come into being until this condition has been met. In practice we find very few couples living together without children unless the children are grown up and have dispersed, and a couple who do not produce offspring of their own often adopt children. It is when a household group becomes differentiated by moving into a house on its own that we can see it most clearly, and this is particularly true in a society where it is not considered normal for a young couple to live with their in-laws.

From another point of view, households come into being when sons and daughters break away from their family of orientation, and this is a matter of some importance since we do not get the development of large joint families which include the spouses of the children of the founding couple. There is a tendency for children to be borne by a young woman whilst she is still in her parents' home, and before she has established a real conjugal relationship, and this must be regarded as an important feature of the system. Some of these children may be fathered by a man with whom the girl will set up a household later on, but not necessarily. The fact that such children are not sharply differentiated by any stigma of illegitimacy involving social disabilities is perhaps a crucial feature of the system. We shall deal with these two points later.

Although we have said that the real starting point of the development of household groups is the birth of children, it is much easier for us to observe the point at which a household group actually becomes physically differentiated from other groups by establishing itself in a separate house, and in fact we have taken this as our working definition of what constitutes a household. If we are at pains to point out that this event of moving into a new house is only one stage in a gradual severance of the couple from their families of orientation, and in their establishment of a definite relationship to each other, it is because we wish to dispel the idea that the event is a precipitous one. It is quite remarkable that there is no ritual connected with a couple's setting up a new household together by moving into their own dwelling. One day they are living separately, and the next they are living together, and unless they got married immediately prior to setting up house together, there is no social recognition of the fact. In the case of a couple getting married the ritual is associated only with the fact of their getting married, and once again it is highly significant that there is very little development of the idea of a honeymoon which would stress the fact of the newly married couple's exclusive sexual rights over each other, and their new social relationship as a separate unit.

Practically all houses are built by men prior to, or soon after they enter a conjugal relationship involving common residence. We have taken common residence as our criterion of marriage and common-law marriage, because it almost invariably coincides with marriage anyway, unless the couple are separated or one of them is temporarily away, and because it is only in the context of common residence of some sort that the mutual rights and obligations of a common-law couple become explicit. A man and woman who do not live together and yet have established an enduring relationship involving the birth of several children will have very close ties and mutual expectations, but until they begin to live together these ties will not have the stamp of authenticity, and it is doubtful if much is to be gained by coining a new word for such a relationship. In Perseverance one hears the term 'frenning' which is common in Trinidad also (2), but in August Town it is customary to use the term 'keeper' to indicate both common-law unions involving common residence and those few cases where a man and woman have a well established relationship without living together. The dividing line is difficult to draw precisely, because the building up of such relationships is a gradual process, and moving into a house together is just one point on the line of development. Here we are not dealing specifically with marriage and mating and so we can ignore these considerations for the time being and work on our original assumption that common residence is a basic criterion of an effective conjugal tie.

In a sample of forty-four houses in August Town, selected at random using a table of random numbers, twenty-eight had a male head and sixteen had a female head at the time the survey was made. Of the houses occupied by household groups with a male head, all but one had been built by the head himself. In the odd case the man had inherited the house from his father but had renovated it himself and this involved quite extensive work. All but four of the houses had been built during the past twenty-five years and ten of the twenty-eight had been built since 1940. The value of the forty-four houses in the sample varied from 40 dollars to 1,800 dollars, and the money to build them had been acquired in the following ways in the case of those households with a male head.

Method of acquisition of capital for house building	Number of cases
Working in gold or diamond fields	6
Working in balata fields	1
Working on American bases during the war	2
Working at the bauxite mines	6
Working on sugar estates	5
By farming and particularly rice cultivation	2
By teaching	1
By working as a shop assistant	1
By working as a railway porter	1
By working as an assistant to a land surveyor	1
By burning earth for the Public Works Dept.	1
By working driving cattle from the Rupununi	1

These must not be thought of as mutually exclusive categories of income sources, and in fact informants would indicate the main source of the capital for building their house and then almost invariably add, 'and by working all about'. When it is considered that the process of building a house is often spread over a period of more than a year, it will be realized that income may be obtained from several sources during this time. In one of the above cases a man who was working at the bauxite mines was assisted in financing the building of a new house by his wife who worked as a dressmaker.

Of the sixteen houses with a female head of the household group, seven of the women inherited the house from their husbands or common-law husbands. In five cases the house had been built by the woman's sons, or with the help of her sons. In these cases it is quite likely that the woman inherited a house from her deceased spouse, but that it was broken down to make way for a new house the building of which was financed by a son, or sons. One woman had bought the house she was living in when she returned to her natal village after having lived in her husband's village until he died. One woman was blind and lived alone in a small house given to her by her brother. Two women had financed the building of their houses by their own efforts, but in both cases the houses were not very valuable, one of them being estimated as being worth only $20.00. Of all the houses in the whole sample, only two were more than fifty years old and one of these was the house bought by the woman who had returned to her natal village on the death of her husband.

The picture presented by this sample is fairly clear. The building of houses is financed largely by men, and particularly by men who are taking on the rôle of husband-father. The fact that the building of some houses is financed by men in their rôle as sons tells us something of the strength of the mother-son bond, and we shall have more to say of this later. What we have tried to do so far is establish the fact that the wage-earning activities of men are of primary importance in the establishment of household groups within a separate dwelling. The age at which men do establish these new dwelling groups is usually somewhere in the 30 + age-range, except for Perseverance where it tends to be earlier (3).

It is in the stage of the early development of the household group that we get the greatest incidence of occurrence of the nuclear family as the dwelling group. Out of 184 households with a male head in August Town, sixty-two consist only of the nuclear group of a man, his wife or common-law wife and their own children, and these couples are mostly in the 30–50 years age-range. If we count those households with children of one or both of the conjugal pair by different mates, and those where there is just a couple living together alone, then the total comes up to eighty-four, the majority of which are again in the 30–50 years age-range. This pattern of distribution also holds good for the other two villages.

This helps to demonstrate a fundamentally important fact about the family system as a whole, namely that at some time during her life, almost every woman is in a relationship of dependence with a man to whom she is in the status of wife or common-law wife, and it also helps to demonstrate that nearly every household group goes through the stage of being a nuclear family group at some time during its existence.

We are perfectly aware of the fact that we are in some senses transforming a pattern of synchronic distribution of types of household group into a pattern of distribution along a time axis, but there is some justification for this in that the age of the household head is in fact a point on a time scale, and our observations are backed up by individual life histories. Under actual field conditions it proved extremely difficult to get detailed histories of particular households as opposed to individuals, and it has been felt to be more satisfactory to deal with distributions which could be actually observed and did not depend on the memories of informants, particularly relating to their childhood. In a system such as this, where there is a fair amount of movement from household to household, and accretion and shedding of members of the household group, there tends to be selective remembering concerning the exact constellation of kinsfolk who were members of the household group when the informant was a child. On the other hand, the case histories of individuals and the general comments of informants do not suggest that there was any great difference in the general pattern of domestic life say fifty years ago. It therefore seems justifiable to regard existing households as representing different stages of development though it is less accurate than actually observing a developmental sequence over a period of years. We have tried to present as clear a picture as possible by combining observed distributions with a case-history approach.

To return to our argument, we can see that it is precisely during this period of the early development of the household group that women are tied to the home, bearing children and rearing them, and this is the period when they are most dependent on the support of their spouse, and most subservient to his authority in the home On the other hand, this is also the period during which men spend a considerable amount of time working away from home and they do not take any significant part in the daily life of the household. They rarely play with their children, and they spend a considerable portion of their time outside the home in the company of other men. There are no tasks allotted to a man in his rôle as husband-father beyond seeing that the house is kept in good repair, and providing food and clothing for his spouse and the children.

Even at this early stage of development, the household group may begin to accrete members who do not belong to the nuclear family. One finds juvenile brothers and sisters of the head's spouse, sometimes children of a dead sister, and what is more significant is that it it is usually at this stage that collateral kin of the head himself are incorporated in the group. This helps to bear out our contention that it is at this period of development that the authority of the male head is most pronounced. We might also mention that the relations of spouses at this stage are very little different whether the couple are married or living in a common-law union. Contrary to reports from other parts of the West Indies, where it has been reported that common-law unions are marked by a greater degree of equality between spouses than in a marital union, our data would indicate that if anything, a woman in the status of common-law wife is even more subject to the authority of her partner than in the case of a married woman. This is particularly true if the woman has small children, for if her common-law husband deserts her, she will not be able to claim maintenance for herself as a married woman could, and since she has small children it would be difficult for her to go out and work. Of course, if there are no children to consider, then the case would be different, but there are very few couples living in common-law unions who do not have children.

There are certain cases where a woman who owns her own house, or even lives with her parents, forms liaisons with men who come to live with her, and these are sometimes very unstable, the woman having a high degree of independence. This type of union would perhaps correspond to Henriques 'Keeper family' as opposed to his 'Faithful Concubinage' which corresponds more closely to our common-law marriage (4). We have not felt it necessary to designate this kind of union by a separate term, as it is not of very frequent occurrence, nor does it seem to constitute a generically different type of family. It is really a marginal case of the normal development of household groups and will be treated as such. It may be that in Jamaica or in urban areas of the West Indies generally, it occurs with much greater regularity but there are not enough adequate data to assess this, though if it could be established that the regularity of its occurrence under urban conditions is very high it would perhaps throw interesting light on the whole problem of the relation between development of household groups and other factors. We can only work in terms of the material from our three villages in view of the inadequacy of comparative data.

The incidence of infidelity on the part of women in this early period of their conjugal careers seems to be extremely low, even when their spouses are working away. Once a woman has gone to live with a man she will tend to be faithful to him, and this is particularly true if she has small children. His rights over her sexuality in return for supporting her are socially recognized, though if no children are born the likelihood of infidelity is considerably increased. Men on the other hand are frequently unfaithful, even at this early stage, and if they are working away they will often have another woman and may father a series of 'outside' children, mainly with single girls. Even within the village they may have affairs with other women, and the jealousy of wives and common-law wives often results in their consulting an Obeah man for the purpose of working sorcery against the other woman, or using magical means to recover the undivided attention of their spouse. In the case histories, one rarely comes across a man who has left a wife or common-law wife on account of her infidelity, but there are many cases of women leaving their husbands or common-law husbands because they have too many other women. However, it must be remembered that this may be a rationalization resorted to when other factors have predisposed a couple to break up their union. Infidelity on the part of men tends to be tolerated or not tolerated by the woman according to whether she can afford to dispense with the man's support. A man's infidelity does not break up the important unit of the family, which is the woman and her children. On the other hand, a woman who is unfaithful to her husband or common-law husband runs the risk of losing her claim to his support and of breaking up her relations to her children. In a few cases observed in the field where a woman has had an open affair with another man, her husband or common-law husband has kept the children, perhaps taking them back to his mother's home if they are very small. From this point of view it is quite clear that a woman has far more to lose than a man if she has 'outside' affairs, and consideration for her children militates against her being unfaithful.

As the household endures through time and the children get older, the woman becomes more and more the focus of the group, and she acquires more and more authority in the home. She becomes the mistress of a household group in a much more real sense than she was when her children were small, and her authority derives largely from her status as a mother. When her adult children begin to work it is to her that they give money, not to their father, though they will begin to help with the farm and the rice work, particularly in the period when they are too young to go off to the bauxite mines or work on the sugar estates, or in other wage-earning occupations.

Women who are approaching the menopause (and very few women have children after they are 40 years old) quite often begin to embark on minor economic enterprises of their own. Quite frequently their spouses disapprove of this but unless the family is particularly well-off, in a comparative sense, it is unlikely that their disapproval will carry much weight.

Households with heads in the age range over 45 years begin to take on a more complex character in terms of composition. Daughters' children begin to appear and less frequently, sons' children. Also from now on the number of households with female heads begins to increase, as does the number of widows and common-law widows. This is clearly shown in Tables X to XV, where the distribution of the population of all three villages by age and conjugal condition is shown. (In the case of Better Hope the figures refer to a random sample of eighty-four households.)* The discrepancy between the number of widows and the number of widowers is striking, but this is accounted for by two facts. In the first place the survival rate of women to old age is higher than that for men, as can be seen if the number of persons of either sex over

*Explanatory note.—These tables include several cases which have been rejected from other calculations but this does not affect the distribution significantly. It should also be noted that there is a possibility of error in the case of males in the category of single father, since some men will not acknowledge paternity of their children. However it is doubtful whether this error is very great, and it would only involve a transfer from the category of 'single' to that of 'single father'. In the tables referring to females, it is possible that some of the women listed as single have had abortions, but where a child has actually been born, even if it was a still-birth, they have been listed as mothers. Here again it is in the two categories of 'single' and 'single mother' that the greatest possibility of error arises.

60 years of age is compared. In August Town there are forty-two males over 60 years as compared with one hundred and one females. In the Better Hope sample there are fourteen males compared with nineteen females, whilst in Perseverance there are seventeen males to twenty-two females. This higher survival rate of women as compared with men is a feature of the whole colony, and has been clearly worked out in the 1946 Census Report (5). The other fact to be considered is that a widower is more likely to enter a new conjugal union than is a widow, who usually continues to run her household alone, having no more than odd affairs with other men after her husband dies.

DISTRIBUTION OF POPULATION BY AGE AND CONJUGAL CONDITION

TABLE X

AUGUST TOWN MALES

Age		*S.*	*S.F.*	*Mar.*	*C.L.M.*	*W.*	*C.L.W.*	*Sep.*	*C.L.S.*	*Div.*
0– 1	..	45	0	0	0	0	0	0	0	0
2– 5	..	111	0	0	0	0	0	0	0	0
6–10	..	156	0	0	0	0	0	0	0	0
11–15	..	102	0	0	0	0	0	0	0	0
16–18	..	45	0	0	0	0	0	0	0	0
19–20	..	24	0	0	0	0	0	0	0	0
21–25	..	26	3	2	0	0	0	0	0	0
26–30	..	15	4	8	2	0	0	1	1	0
31–35	..	8	4	9	7	1	0	2	1	0
36–40	..	6	3	20	4	1	0	1	1	0
41–45	..	2	3	27	5	1	0	2	1	0
46–50	..	1	0	22	11	0	0	3	0	0
51–55	..	1	0	22	5	2	0	2	1	0
56–60	..	0	0	12	4	2	1	2	0	0
61–65	..	1	1	7	0	2	0	2	2	0
66–70	..	1	0	15	2	2	0	3	0	0
71–75	..	0	0	5	0	0	0	0	0	0
76–80	..	0	0	4	0	3	0	0	0	0
81–85	..	0	0	1	0	0	0	0	0	0
86–90	..	0	0	0	0	1	0	0	0	0
Totals	..	544	18	154	40	15	1	18	7	0

TABLE XI

AUGUST TOWN FEMALES

Age		*S.*	*S.M.*	*Mar.*	*C.L.M.*	*W.*	*C.L.W.*	*Sep.*	*C.L.S.*	*Div.*
0– 1	..	47	0	0	0	0	0	0	0	0
2– 5	..	122	0	0	0	0	0	0	0	0
6–10	..	137	0	0	0	0	0	0	0	0
11–15	..	102	1	0	0	0	0	0	0	0
16–18	..	47	1	2	0	0	0	0	0	0
19–20	..	22	8	1	0	0	0	0	0	0
21–25	..	25	18	19	5	0	0	0	1	0
26–30	..	10	8	26	7	1	0	1	1	2
31–35	..	4	8	26	7	0	1	1	0	0
36–40	..	3	6	25	6	2	0	3	1	0
41–45	..	3	6	14	5	4	1	2	4	0
46–50	..	4	2	16	7	2	1	0	1	0
51–55	..	3	4	19	2	5	3	2	2	0
56–60	..	1	3	7	2	3	3	0	1	0
61–65	..	1	3	12	0	6	3	1	0	0
66–70	..	2	4	1	0	13	2	0	0	0
71–75	..	1	1	7	1	8	0	1	0	0
76–80	..	1	0	0	0	8	2	0	0	0
81–85	..	1	0	1	0	8	0	0	0	0
86–90	..	0	0	0	0	2	0	0	0	0
91–95	..	0	0	0	0	1	0	0	0	0
Totals	..	536	73	176	42	63	16	11	11	2

TABLE XII

PERSEVERANCE MALES

Age		*S.*	*S.F.*	*Mar.*	*C.L.M.*	*W.*	*C.L.W.*	*Sep.*	*C.L.S.*	*Div.*
0– 1	..	19	0	0	0	0	0	0	0	0
2– 5	..	42	0	0	0	0	0	0	0	0
6–10	..	53	0	0	0	0	0	0	0	0
11–15	..	38	0	0	0	0	0	0	0	0
16–18	..	21	0	0	0	0	0	0	0	0
19–20	..	7	0	0	0	0	0	0	0	0
21–25	..	15	0	1	5	0	0	1	0	0
26–30	..	2	0	10	6	0	0	0	0	0
31–35	..	5	1	10	3	0	0	0	0	0
36–40	..	0	2	5	11	1	0	1	0	0
41–45	..	1	0	8	6	0	0	0	0	0
46–50	..	0	2	11	2	0	0	0	0	0
51–55	..	0	0	5	3	0	1	0	0	0
56–60	..	0	0	6	1	1	1	0	0	0
61–65	..	0	0	4	1	1	0	0	0	0
66–70	..	0	0	3	0	1	1	0	0	0
71–75	..	0	0	1	0	0	0	0	0	0
76–80	..	1	0	3	0	0	0	0	0	0
81–85	..	0	0	1	0	0	0	0	0	0
Totals	..	204	5	68	38	4	3	2	0	0

TABLE XIII

PERSEVERANCE FEMALES

Age		*S.*	*S.M.*	*Mar.*	*C.L.M.*	*W.*	*C.L.W.*	*Sep.*	*C.L.S.*	*Div.*
0– 1	..	23	0	0	0	0	0	0	0	0
2– 5	..	44	0	0	0	0	0	0	0	0
6–10	..	66	0	0	0	0	0	0	0	0
11–15	..	51	0	0	0	0	0	0	0	0
16–18	..	17	0	0	1	0	0	0	0	0
19–20	..	6	4	2	2	0	0	0	0	0
21–25	..	5	7	12	9	0	0	0	0	0
26–30	..	2	0	9	4	0	0	2	0	0
31–35	..	1	2	10	8	0	0	1	0	0
36–40	..	1	0	8	9	1	0	1	0	0
41–45	..	0	0	5	2	0	0	0	1	0
46–50	..	0	0	6	2	1	0	1	0	0
51–55	..	0	0	4	1	2	0	1	1	0
56–60	..	0	0	3	1	0	0	0	0	0
61–65	..	0	0	7	0	1	0	0	0	0
66–70	..	0	0	2	0	1	4	0	0	0
71–75	..	0	0	1	0	4	0	0	0	0
76–80	..	0	0	0	0	1	1	0	0	0
81–85	..	0	0	0	0	0	0	0	0	0
Totals	..	216	13	69	39	11	5	6	2	0

TABLE XIV

BETTER HOPE MALES

Age		*S.*	*S.F.*	*Mar.*	*C.L.M.*	*W.*	*C.L.W.*	*Sep.*	*C.L.S.*	*Div.*
0– 1	..	6	0	0	0	0	0	0	0	0
2– 5	..	15	0	0	0	0	0	0	0	0
6–10	..	18	0	0	0	0	0	0	0	0
11–15	..	16	0	0	0	0	0	0	0	0
16–18	..	10	0	0	0	0	0	0	0	0
19–20	..	6	0	0	0	0	0	0	0	0
21–25	..	6	0	1	0	0	0	0	0	0
26–30	..	10	0	6	1	0	0	0	0	0
31–35	..	0	0	5	0	0	0	0	0	0
36–40	..	2	0	4	0	0	0	1	0	0
41–45	..	1	0	9	3	0	0	1	0	0
46–50	..	0	0	2	2	0	0	0	0	0
51–55	..	0	0	4	1	1	0	0	1	0
56–60	..	0	0	1	2	2	0	0	1	0
61–65	..	0	2	5	0	0	0	0	0	0
66–70	..	0	0	1	0	0	0	0	0	0
71–75	..	0	0	2	0	0	0	0	0	0
76–80	..	0	0	2	0	1	0	1	0	0
81–85	..	0	0	0	0	0	0	0	0	0
Totals	..	90	2	42	9	4	0	3	2	0

TABLE XV

BETTER HOPE FEMALES

Age		*S.*	*S.M.*	*Mar.*	*C.L.M.*	*W.*	*C.L.W.*	*Sep.*	*C.L.S.*	*Div.*
0–1	..	6	0	0	0	0	0	0	0	0
2–5	..	18	0	0	0	0	0	0	0	0
6–10	..	24	0	0	0	0	0	0	0	0
11–15	..	16	0	0	0	0	0	0	0	0
16–18	..	9	2	1	0	0	0	0	0	0
19–20	..	6	1	0	0	0	0	0	0	0
21–25	..	9	1	7	2	0	0	1	0	0
26–30	..	1	1	5	0	0	0	0	0	0
31–35	..	2	2	8	1	0	0	1	0	0
36–40	..	1	3	6	1	0	0	0	0	0
41–45	..	0	0	5	3	0	0	0	0	0
46–50	..	0	0	4	2	2	0	1	0	0
51–55	..	0	0	2	1	3	1	0	0	0
56–60	..	1	0	5	0	2	0	0	0	0
61–65	..	0	2	0	0	2	0	0	1	0
66–70	..	0	1	0	0	2	0	1	0	0
71–75	..	0	0	0	0	2	0	0	0	0
76–80	..	0	0	0	0	3	0	0	0	0
81–85	..	0	0	0	0	4	0	1	0	0
Totals	..	93	13	43	10	20	1	5	1	0

Abbreviations used in these tables are as follows:—
S = single; S.F. or S.M. = Single Father or Mother; Mar. = Legally married. C.L.M. = Common-law married; W. = Widower or Widow; C.L.W. = Common-law widow or widower; Sep. = Separated from legal spouse; C.L.S. = Separated from common-law spouse; Div. = legally divorced.

A woman's elevation in status to titular headship of a household usually comes about through the death of her husband or common-law husband, and from the age of 60 years onwards there are forty-nine female heads of households in August Town as compared with forty-eight male heads. Whether her husband or common-law husband dies or not, a woman with her children, some of whom are adult or adolescent, and established in her own household, is in a very secure position and this seems to be quite irrespective of the type of conjugal union she enjoys. The composition of the household group at this stage of its development is not so complex as has been sometimes suggested, and a careful examination shows that there are quite definite processes of selection involved (6). Daughters' children constitute the largest single addition to the nuclear family, and in many cases they are assimilated to a filial relationship to their maternal grandmother. These daughters will normally live at home with their mothers, particularly if they are young, and during the birth of their first few children. They may go away to work in town or near to one of the larger estates, and in villages such as Queenstown on the Essequibo Coast we find that this migration of young women is the normal thing. In the three villages with which we are dealing, it is not normal and most young women will only leave the village to enter into a conjugal relationship. A girl's first child is often the result of a rather casual affair and if later on she enters a more permanent liaison with a man with whom she eventually goes to live, she may leave her first, or first two or three, children with her mother, who then rears them as if they were her own. In this way many women effectively extend their period of functioning motherhood beyond the point where they are biologically capable of bearing children. If the daughter should die, even if she has gone to live with a man, her children will usually be taken over by her mother, or in later life by the dead woman's sister, particularly if the mother is dead. A woman will also take in her sons' children especially if their own mother has gone to live with another man or has died. However it must not be thought that a woman who goes to live with a man will not take her children by previous lovers to live with her, for in fact she often does.

Unmarried sons stay on as nominal members of their family of orientation even when they begin to go to work away from the village, but although they usually send money home to their mothers or otherwise assist in the maintenance of the household, there is no well-defined place for them in the family group except as sons who are obliged to show deference to their mother. It is mothers who often show jealousy when their sons contemplate breaking away and getting married, and cases occur of women resorting to some form of Obeah practice to try to prevent their sons leaving their home. On the other hand, sons will rarely have an open breach with their mothers and even after they do set up their own household they continue to send money and gifts to them if they can afford it. The tie between mothers and adult daughters is effected more through their common interest in their children and their solidarity as mothers, whereas the mother-son bond finds maximum expression in economic co-operation of some kind. We saw earlier that sons help to build houses for their mothers, and they may also take on the responsibility for the payment of rates on their mother's land if she is left alone without a spouse.

Not all adult daughters bear children whilst they are in their mothers' home, and some are married off quite young, sometimes by means of arranged marriages. Some daughters have only one or two children whilst they are living with their mothers, but a few stay on, bearing their children and eventually inheriting their parents' house without ever entering a conjugal relationship involving common residence at all. In August Town there are sixteen female household heads who had never been in a conjugal relationship involving common residence with a man. In Perseverance there were none.

Not all women who attain old age manage to gather around them a household unit consisting of their children's children and other kin, and some are left alone, but if they have had children at all, they will probably be supported by them. In August Town there are more men living alone than there are women, and this is a reflection of the difficulty men experience in holding a household together on the death of their spouse, or after they separate. As a matter of fact the majority of them are men who are left alone because they are separated, and they may pay a woman to wash for them, and eat with a relative. One or two widowers do manage to keep their household together particularly if one of the daughters is old enough to take care of the smaller children, and in these cases one often finds that the old man is well-loved both by his children, and by his grandchildren when they come along. The tension in the husband-wife relationship has been removed, and the old man becomes the centre of affective ties in a way he would rarely be were his spouse alive. If he lives on until his great-grandchildren are born into the household (which is rare), he not only comes to occupy a place of affection, but in many ways he is himself treated as a child, being chided by his grand-daughters as they would speak to a child. He is also careful not to annoy them by doing anything wrong, but of course his age means that he is expected to be a little perverse sometimes. He will nurse, and play with his great-grandchildren, and they in turn treat him with a marked sense of equality.

It is clear that as soon as a daughter in a nuclear family type household begins to have children she is the potential focus of a new household group, though its emergence as a separate unit may be considerably delayed, and the fact that some of her children may be left behind in her parents' home means that that household unit gets an extension of life as an effective child-rearing group. The functions of motherhood are prolonged for older women, though their sexual functions as wives tend to cease from the menopause onwards. If women are the potential foci of household groups, men are the potential originators of such groups by virtue of their functions as providers, and builders of new houses. (It should be noted that when we refer to men 'building' new houses, in the majority of cases we mean that they finance the building of new houses, and they will almost always have to pay for labour.)

At this stage of the discussion it will be useful to examine a few specific cases of households at different stages of the developmental cycle in order to see how the processes we have described work out in practice.

Case No. 1

John Richmond is 33 years old, his wife Emily is 28 years and they live in a two-roomed mud-thatched house with their three children aged 13 years, 11 years, and 7 years. He divides his time between fishing and working as a cane-cutter on an estate, where he spends the whole week during the cutting season, only coming home at week-ends. He would spend more of his time operating his fishing boat, but he never has enough capital to see him through the periods when his fishing net gets damaged by large fish such a sharks, and he is forced to go to work on the estates in order to accumulate enough capital to enable him to repair the nets and begin operating again.

He and Emily began their relationship in 1935 (it is now 1952) and at that time they were both living in the homes of their respective parents. Their first child was born in 1937 but it died when it was only one month old. In 1938 John bought a piece of land which had belonged to his mother and her siblings jointly, and he built the present house at a total cost of $45.00. In 1939 Gertrude the eldest daughter was born and in 1940 John and Emily began to live together in this house with their daughter Gertrude. In 1941 their son Robert who is now 11 years old was born, and in 1943 and 1945 two more children were born but neither survived infancy. In 1946 Gwendoline who is now 6 years was born, and then followed two still-births in 1949 and 1951.

John and Emily lived together in a common-law union from 1940–4 and then they got married in church.

This case illustrates the way in which a new household may be set up after a couple have begun to have children in common whilst living separately. Both John and Emily were unusually young when they set up house together, and Emily in particular began her period of childbearing at a very early age compared to most women.

Case No. 2

Stella Parris is 21 years old and she is living alone in a one-roomed house whilst her husband is away working at McKenzie City. She has only been married for a few months and the marriage was arranged between her husband and her parents, she only having seen him twice before she married. Her parents are alive and living in the village but she has moved into this small house lent by her mother's mother's brother.

This is a potential nuclear family and represents what is considered to be the ideal form of starting a new household group. The girl was a virgin when she was married and much was made of this during the wedding ceremonies.

Case No. 3

Sybil Brown lives alone in a two-roomed house. She is 24 years old and has been married for 6 years, though her husband works away at Bartica as an electrician at the moment. Her first child was born whilst she was still living with her mother but she married the child's father James Brown the following year and went to live with him. A second child was born the following year but it died when it was 4 years old. James Brown's mother asked that the first child be allowed to go and live with her because she wanted a companion and help around the house and so the child is now being reared by its paternal grandmother. A third child was born to Sybil before the second one had died, but this last child was a very sickly infant and it was cared for by Sybil's mother who has kept the child since then. After the second child died, Sybil was left alone whilst her husband was away but she is expecting another child soon.

Case No. 4

William Jones and Mary Johnson live in a two-roomed thatched house in a common-law union. He is 42 years old and she is 38 and living with them are Ronald Thompson, Mary's first child by another man, who is 25 years old, John, Eunice and James Jones the last three children of William and Mary, who are 17, 15, and 12 years old respectively.

Mary Johnson had her first child when she was only 13 years old and she was living in her mother's home at the time. Her mother didn't approve of Thompson, the father of the child, and so Mary broke off her friendship with him. The following year she became friendly with William Jones and when she became pregnant for him, William moved in to live with Mary and her parents. This was because he had no home of his own, but two years later he managed to build a little house and they moved into it. Besides the four children who now live with them, they have three other daughters, the eldest of whom is married and the other two are living in common-law unions.

This case is in Perseverance and we shall have more to say about Perseverance later on, but it is included here to show how a woman will take her children by previous lovers with her when she moves into her own household.

Case No. 5

Agnes and Matthew Jackson are 51 and 56 years old respectively. Agnes grew with her mother and maternal grandmother as a child but when she was 15 years old she ran away from home and came to the village with Matthew. She did not live with him at first but stayed with an older woman who she used to help in the house. She didn't get her first child until she was 20 years old and when she became pregnant she went to live with Matthew in their own house. They lived together for nearly four years before he married her. She has had nineteen children for her husband in all, but nine of them died and she has difficulty in remembering the order of birth.

Her husband has had several 'outside' children. The first one was born before he took up with Agnes. He never recognized it as his own and it grew up with the name of its mother's husband. After he began to live with Agnes he was still carrying on an affair with a village girl and he had three children by her in all, one of which died. He had another child by a woman in another village where he worked and he contributed to the support of that child.

Agnes raised all her own children herself and, as she says, she never had time for much else because sometimes she would have two children within one year, so rapidly did pregnancies follow each other.

Her eldest daughter who is now 31 years old, got her first child when she was 17 years old and at this time her own mother was still bearing children. The child lived with its mother and maternal grandmother for the first two years of its life and was treated exactly as a child of the older woman. It called her 'Mama' and its own mother by her christian name, 'Julie'. When the child was 2 years old it was sent away to live with its paternal grandparents, but it has always been a frequent visitor in the home of its maternal grandparents and still continues to use the terminology it used during the first two years. It calls its paternal grandparents 'Auntie' and

'Uncle' which happen to be the terms by which they are generally known in the village as a whole. This elder daughter later went to live with another man and they eventually married and now have five children. They live in a house which is quite close to the house of Agnes and Matthew and these children are very frequent visitors in the home of their maternal grandparents, and they play with and mix on terms of absolute equality with Agnes' own younger children. They all call Agnes by the term 'Ma' and call their own mother 'Julie'.

Agnes' second daughter also got her first child whilst she was living at her parents' house and it too was assimilated to a filial relationship with its maternal grandmother. This daughter then went away to live in Georgetown for about four years and during this time she had two children for another man, but they both died. On her return to the village she went to live with the father of her first child and they now have five children including the first one who is now living with them. These children now call their own mother 'Mother' and call their maternal grandmother 'grandma', including the first one which grew with Agnes.

Case No. 6

Richard and Amelia Edwards are 58 and 52 years old respectively and live together in a two-roomed wooden house with twelve of their children and grandchildren. He works for the local authority and sometimes on the sugar estates as a shovel-man and also plants rice of which he has fourteen acres under cultivation this year (1952).

Amelia had one child for another man before she became friendly with Richard, and this daughter, who was born when Amelia was 18 years old, is now married and living at McKenzie City. She was reared by Amelia's mother and never lived with Richard Edwards. Richard himself had two children with two women he met whilst he was working in other parts of the country in his youth but they both died in infancy.

Richard and Amelia became friendly in 1919 and in 1920 their first child was born. At this time Amelia was living with her mother, her father being dead, and Richard was nominally living with his mother and her husband, he being his mother's first child by another man. They continued to live separately until 1927 and during this time Amelia had three more children for Richard and then they moved into a partially completed house where they are now living. The house was finally completed in 1930, but meanwhile they got married, in 1928. They were neighbours even before they became friendly and they built their house close to Amelia's mother's house and to Richard's sister's house, his mother having died by this time.

There are five of their daughters living with them at the present time (Amelia having borne fifteen children in all for Richard, of which eleven are still alive), the youngest being 8 and the eldest 22 years old. All their sons have dispersed, one being common-law married in the village and the other two are working at McKenzie City. Amy is the eldest daughter living at home and she has four children all living with her, and she got these children by three different men. Her last two children are by the same man, and it looks as though there is a good chance of her settling down with him as soon as he can provide a home for her. Joyce, the second daughter living at home, is only 16 and she hasn't had any children yet. However, she has been carrying on a surreptitious affair with a married man and her parents are thinking of sending her to live with an older sister at McKenzie City to preclude the possibility of her getting a child for this man. The next younger sister, Winifred, is only 15 but she already has two children for a young man in the village. The first time she became pregnant her mother gave her a good beating, but it didn't prevent her doing the same thing again and when she gets older she may go and live with this young man, or marry him, if they are still friendly by that time. The two youngest daughters are 12 and 8 years old and they are both going to school. In addition to the grandchildren we have already mentioned, there is another child of one of Amelia's and Richard's married daughters. This daughter left home when she was quite young to go to live in New Amsterdam and she had three children by different fathers before she married. She has kept her first two children with her and Amelia is looking after the third, though the child's mother sends money for its support.

There is no doubt that in this household Amelia is the real power centre. Richard earns money only sporadically and when he does he spends a great deal of it on rum. He is responsible for the rice cultivation, but when it comes to harvest time, the daughters on their own initiative set out to do the cutting when he is negligent and spending his time with his friends. Amelia sometimes goes herself to collect provisions from the farm and she earns money of her own by making and selling cassava bread. She also has her own fowls and ducks. Her sons send her money now and then, and the daughters whose children are living with Amelia all give her money which they receive from the fathers of their children. Amelia is a competent, resourceful woman and she shows no signs of deference or subservience to her husband and quite often berates him for his laziness and shiftless habits.

This case illustrates quite clearly the type of situation one often finds in households where the woman has passed her child-bearing period and consolidated her position as authoritarian mistress of the household. She could get on quite well without her husband, but they maintain a reasonably amicable relationship and don't interfere unduly with each other's sphere of activity and interests. It is unlikely that they would ever separate now, for they have achieved a working relationship where each knows what is expected of the other and makes the best of it. The man is undoubtedly in a marginal position, but if on an odd occasion he were to take any of his friends home with him, his wife would keep out of the way and not obtrude on his party. Actually I never knew him to do this during the year I was in the village.

Case No. 7

Florence Chester is a 52-years-old widow living in her own home with two of her daughters, two grandchildren, three of her sister's sons' children and one adopted boy who she refers to as a 'distant relative's child'.

Florence was married when she was 21 years old and her husband had three children by three different women, two of them after he had married Florence, but when he was working away in other parts of the country. Florence's first three pregnancies resulted in abortions and it was not until she was 24 years old that her first child was born. She subsequently had three more children, her last being born when she was 30 years old. Her husband died in 1939 when she was 39 years old. Florence's sister Ermiline died leaving three boys and Florence took them over and reared them alongside her own. They are all grown up now and have left home but one of them has sent his three children to Florence since his wife is dead.

Florence's own two daughters who are living with her are both adult and the elder of the two has two children for a man who was working close to the village for some time. The younger daughter has a steady job as a servant in a neighbouring village.

In this case we can see how a woman will take over her dead sister's children and rear them as her own, and how they in turn will send their children to her when misfortunes occur. This is also a fairly typical pattern for a female household head at this stage of her life. The next case shows a household that is almost completely at the end of its developmental sequence.

Case No. 8

Margaret McDougall is an 84-years-old widow drawing a government old age pension of $3.00 per month. Her daughter Jane and Jane's son Norman, live with Margaret in her two-roomed cottage.

Margaret was born in 1868 in August Town and she says that her mother was the daughter of a pure Ibo, her father's father was a Congo, and her husband was a Cromanti. Her father's father came direct to British Guiana from Africa, though she never actually knew him.

Her first child was born when she was 18 years old and was still living with her mother, but after the birth of their second child, George McDougall, the children's father, married her and they came to live in their first mud-thatched house on this same lot. The land did not belong to them, and to this day she has to pay 25 cents per month rent to the owner, who lives in the village. This absolves her from having to pay the rates, however. They subsequently had five different houses on this same lot, each old one being broken down as the new one was built, until finally this board house was built in 1918 at a cost of $200.

Margaret had twelve children in all and she now has forty-six grandchildren and at least thirty-two great-grandchildren, many of whom live in the village. However, she doesn't see a great deal of them and she can't by any means remember them all and even has difficulty in recalling all her grandchildren. Many of her great-grandchildren are the children of grandsons and therefore they have no real tie with her, being bound up in their mothers' families rather than their fathers'.

Her daughter Jane, who lives with her, is 44 years old and she lived for some years in a common-law union with a man, bearing three children for him before they separated, and he subsequently married another woman. The eldest of Jane's children works away at Kwakwani and the youngest was taken by its father. Jane's middle child lives with her and he is 15 years old and already helps her with the farm. Jane herself is a hard worker and besides running a farm she works on the sugar estates as a labourer. When her mother dies she will become head of the household in her own right and will probably build up her own group around her.

During her lifetime Margaret McDougall has reared many children both her own and those of her daughters but they are all grown up and dispersed now except Jane her youngest daughter, and the household is really at the end of its cycle of growth and decay, it being only a matter of time before its final dissolution with the death of Margaret. The new household with Jane as head will have grown out of the old one in a sense, but Jane has had her own history as a mother and it is really more correct to think of the two as overlapping in time than as being continuous.

In these eight cases selected from the field-records we have been able to see some of the ways in which actual households are constituted and some of the life experiences of their members and it would be possible to include all kinds of variations from the general pattern to illustrate special points, but this would fill several volumes. What we have done is to pick some key stages in the developmental cycle to show that our abstract principles do work out empirically in a very clear way.

THE LIFE-CYCLE OF THE INDIVIDUAL

In order to round out our description of the family system and the developmental sequence of the household group, we may now consider the development and life experiences of the individuals who go to make up the household group. This is merely introducing a new perspective, and it must be emphasized that we are primarily interested in the way in which individuals fit into the social structure rather than in their development as personalities in the psychological sense. We shall therefore concentrate on the way in which individuals come to exercise claims and responsibilities, and have these exercised against them. It should also be mentioned that our neglect of the extremely interesting aspects of customs connected with childbirth, and the various rituals involved in *rites-de-passage*, is deliberate, and we shall only have space to outline those which seem most relevant to our field of interest in this book.

Birth

In days gone by childbirth was exclusively a village affair, and older women acted as midwives ('Nanas' or 'grannies'), practising with a moderate degree of skill, a good deal of empirical knowledge, and using a great many magical and supernatural aids. Today, the villages are served by trained midwives, and infant welfare and maternity clinics offer both ante-natal and post-natal care. A government health visitor pays periodic visits to expectant mothers, and to mothers with infants. Many village women go into hospital to have their babies but the majority still bear them in their own homes. Under normal circumstances a woman bears her child in the house in which she is living, though a few married or common-law married women go back to their mother's home for the actual birth. More usually the woman's mother comes to her house to take over the responsibility for the running of the household during the confinement. Women carry on with their normal work right up to the onset of labour pains, and I have seen women in an advanced stage of pregnancy going off to cut firewood in the bush as usual.

As soon as the labour pains start, the woman is confined in the bedroom, and she usually lies on the floor where rice bags, covered with a sheet or with clean flour bags, have been spread. The older women who are present quite often sprinkle rum around the room as an offering to the spirits of the dead 'house-people', and this is done even in the presence of the government midwife who always refers to such practices as 'superstitious nonsense'. No men are allowed in the room during the confinement, and most of the women present will be close consanguineous kin of the woman, or neighbours. If the woman is married and on good terms with her mother-in-law, then she will probably be present to help.

During labour the woman is given thyme-leaf tea to drink and the 'grannies' would assist the birth by manipulation, and by pressing the abdomen. Oil was also introduced into the vagina, but these practices have diminished considerably under the influence of the trained midwives. During one account of childbirth given by a woman, the informant said that the woman in labour often shouts and struggles and calls for her mother, or her husband. If she calls for her husband the older women tell her to call on God, and don't bother with her husband. This statement is an interesting example of the differential attitude to male spouses on the part of younger and older women (7). The importance of the father of the child in the whole affair is clearly shown in the custom of giving the woman a piece of his sweaty clothing to smell if the delivery becomes very difficult. This symbolizes very clearly the recognition of the father in relation both to the mother and child, despite the maternal bias, and it should be noted that this recognition is quite independent of whether the couple are married or not.

After delivery both the child and the mother are bathed in warm water in which both rum and silver money have been placed. The cord is severed and the *placenta* is buried in the house-yard with the cord uppermost. Salt may be sprinkled on it, supposedly to prevent the mother becoming pregnant again too quickly. Very often a coconut tree is planted over the spot where the cord is buried and this gives the new born individual a point of territorial reference. The symbolism of umbilical-cord burial is freely used, and I have heard a woman refer to her husband's fondness for drinking and staying out of the home by saying, 'His navel-string is buried on the public road'. Hot stout mixed with ground black pepper, or ginger tea, is often given to the mother after she has given birth, and this potion may be drunk every morning for nine days.

For nine days after delivery both mother and child are confined to the bedroom in which birth took place. The windows and all cracks etc. are blocked up, and visitors are strictly limited. It is increasingly common for mothers to come out of the room after only one or two days, but under no circumstances is the child brought out before the ninth day, lest it catch 'cold' and die. On the ninth day the child is dressed in its very best clothes, brought out into the sun and carried around the village to all friends and relatives of the parents. It is the mother's duty to carry the child to its paternal grandparents first. As the child is presented to its kinsfolk and neighbours they customarily place a silver coin in its hand (8).

The custom of giving 'day-names' to children has practically died out, but an old woman in August Town gave the following as the customary names given to children according to the day of the week on which they are born. The Ashanti day-names as given by the *Dictionary of the Asante and Fante Language* are added for comparison (9). The August Town names are spelled as my informant spelled them.

	AUGUST TOWN DAY-NAMES		ASHANTI DAY-NAMES	
Day of birth	*Male*	*Female*	*Male*	*Female*
Sunday ..	Quashie	Quashba	Kwasi	Akosuwa (= Akwasiba)
Monday ..	Juba	Koto	Kwadwo	A'dwowa
Tuesday ..	Kwamna	Bani	Kwabena	Abenaa
Wednesday ..	Kwakoo	Kuba	Kwaku	Akuwa
Thursday ..	Yao	Yabba	Yaw	Yaa (Yawa)
Friday ..	Cuffy	Feba	Kofi	Afuwa
Saturday ..	Hamba	Kwami	Kwame	Amma

All village children are christened in church irrespective of the marital status of the parents, or whether they are church members or not. A woman who is unmarried will usually ask a friend who is a church member to take her child to church for her, but this is the only difference to be detected in the baptism of legitimate and illegitimate children. Two persons, one of either sex, are asked to stand as god-parents and one always endeavours to choose god-parents who are slightly better off than the child's own parents (10). To this end, school teachers are often in great demand as god-parents. After the baptismal ceremony, a party may be held (known locally as a *Condel*) to which friends and relatives of the parents are invited. This follows the traditional pattern of village parties, but the child takes no particular part in the proceedings, and may not even be mentioned unless speeches are made congratulating the parents on the christening of their child.

Breast feeding is the general rule with all rural mothers and the child is fed whenever it cries or is thought to be hungry, though a few mothers have now adopted the feeding schedules recommended by the Infant Welfare Clinics. Almost from birth, the infant's diet is supplemented with thin gruels and various infusions known as 'tea'. Starches such as arrowroot starch, or finely mashed potato, are mixed with warm water and fed to the infant from a bottle. Bottle feeding is not widely used as a substitute for breast feeding, but merely as a supplement when the infant seems hungry. Children are weaned at 9 to 12 months as in other parts of the West Indies, and the process is a fairly abrupt one. The nipples may be smeared with bitter aloes or animal dung to make them distasteful to the child, or alternatively the child may be sent away from the mother for a few days (11). To stop the flow of milk women resort to various forms of sympathetic magic such as dropping a little of the milk into an ants' nest, or hanging a piece of cork on a string around the neck.

Let us now go back and consider more carefully the significant events in the first year of life. Even before the child is born difficulties may have arisen over the question of its paternity, and if it is a girl's first pregnancy then she may quite easily have had trouble in effecting her change of status to that of a mother. The question of recognition of paternity is an important one, not because it will affect the jural status of the new-born in any major way, but because it is a social norm of great importance that every individual must have both a mother and father. There is always recognition of a *genitor*, and no individual was ever encountered during the whole of the field-work who could not name a father. Even the most promiscuous young woman has a pretty good idea of the person who is most likely to be the father of her child, and even if the man refuses to recognize paternity, and the girl does not ask the court to establish it, there is still an overwhelming tendency for a father to be assigned to the child by public gossip. In any case, where a child is born to an unmarried woman, the name of the father is omitted from the official register of births even where the man clearly recognizes paternity. In a few marginal cases, the father himself may go to register the birth of the child and insist that his name is entered, but this is extremely rare (12). Where paternity is recognized then the child is almost always known by the father's surname. In a few cases the child takes the mother's surname, but even in these cases when the child gets older it will have a father assigned to it even if it never sees him, or knows very little about him, or is not even sure of his name. In short, it is inconceivable that a child should be fatherless, no matter how vague the father-figure may be, and in the overwhelming majority of cases the father is known and recognized by the whole community, even if he does not support the child and does not live in the village. By the time the child has reached school age, its father has generally been established, and his name, in the form of the child's surname, is entered in the school register in all but a very few cases. The importance of this cannot be stressed too much, for we must never lose sight of the emphasis which is placed on paternity, and the fact that the social norm is for every individual to have a father-figure.

The parturient woman is normally surrounded by her own family particularly her mother, maternal aunts, sisters, etc., as well as neighbours, but if she is married or living in a common-law union she generally gives birth in her own home, and only in a minority of cases does she actually go back to her mother's home. None the less, it is significant that the child is born into a situation where the principal actors are his maternal kinsfolk. The importance of the paternal interest in birth is clearly shown by the various customs which assign the father a definite place in the proceedings. His mother may be present to help, particularly if the conjugal bond is well established. A piece of his sweaty clothing is used if the delivery is a difficult one. He should be the first to be told of the birth and the sex of the child, etc., and it is to his parents that the child should first be carried when it is brought out for the ninth-day ceremonies. Even elements of the complex generally known as the *couvade* are not entirely absent, for it is often said that the father may get toothache or pains at this time, and if he does 'he is helping the mother to bear the pain'. This is hearsay evidence and no father was ever observed to react in this way.

There is a considerable body of evidence to suggest that the eight days confinement of the mother and child after birth, and the subsequent emergence on the ninth day is of Ashanti origin, but the custom also 'works' in a very real way in its contemporary setting. The ceremony of carrying the child around the village to be given gifts of money is a means of establishing its social 'birth' and starting off a whole series of relationships which will grow in importance as the years go by, and of course the whole complex could be analysed according to van Gennep's schema, with the seclusion of the mother and child as his *rites de séparation* and *de marge*, and the nine-day ceremony as his *rite d'aggrégation* (13).

The christening and baptismal ceremony completes the social 'placing' of the child and the acquisition of god-parents ties him into the wider community of the village. Christening is not only a family affair, for it brings the child into the life of the church which is homologous with the life of the widest social system in which he is likely to participate, and it is essentially a public ritual.

Childhood

During the early stages of its life, a child has considerable freedom and experiences few restraints. It is fed when it is hungry and although it wears nappies of some sort during most of the first nine months or so, it is given no toilet training until it is about 2 years old, and rarely punished for messing the floor of the house until it is big enough to use the latrine at about 5 years of age. The young child is never far away from its mother or mother-substitutes, and we have already mentioned the manner in which the maternal grandmother sometimes takes over the mother rôle. Contact with the father is usually limited to receiving small presents, on the one hand, and regarding his presence as the signal for silence and restraint on the other. Many children grow up without even seeing their father, but this does not mean that they never experience the idea of a father-figure. To begin with there is the general social acceptance of the ideal that every individual has both a mother and a father. We have already seen that almost every woman lives with a man at some period of her life and usually this is when her children are small. Even if she does not live with a man she will almost inevitably have semi-permanent liaisons with one, or several, during this period. If the biological father of a child lives in the same village, then the child will be sent to visit his home now and again, or will at least know him as an individual.

At the age of six, all children are sent to school, and here the child is caught up in an almost perfect model of the 'ideal' family pattern. All schools are presided over by a headmaster who is the ultimate source of discipline and authority. In the lower classes of the school, the child is taught by women teachers. It is beyond the scope of this study to enter into a discussion of the educational system as exemplified by the village schools, but it is vitally important to bear in mind the fact that there is this institutionalized educational system which performs so many functions. Apart from indoctrinating the pupils with the values of the total social system and teaching them its culture, it acts as a sort of age-grading system and provides a reference of social maturation (14). The strict authoritarian attitudes of the male teachers with the marked accent upon physical punishment and beating, provides a sharp contrast to the absence of a strong father-figure in the family system. Observation during the field-work leads to the conclusion that fathers beat their children very infrequently and certainly much less frequently than do mothers and mother-substitutes. Despite this fact, adults always contend that the younger generation is 'lawless' because they are not punished in the same way that they (the adults) were when they were small.

Miss Kerr contends that the normal pattern in the West Indies is for the father to be a fantasy figure, and if the father is not there then the child feels unjustly treated, and may even go so far as having guilty feelings over having got rid of him (15). The important thing, however, is that there is a father-figure and that for the majority of children he is a very real person.

Sex distinction in the sense of differential activities for boys and girls is accentuated from about 8 or 9 years onwards, and at about this age children begin to sleep on different mats according to sex and age differences. Girls begin to participate more fully in the activities of the women, and to take part in the household tasks, whilst boys are given odd jobs helping with livestock, in the gardens and rice-fields, etc. Of course they are still attending school and any work they do is because they are under parental control and obedience is obligatory. There is no question of their being 'paid' in the way that children are often paid for doing odd jobs for their parents in England or North America. At this stage of development, boys and girls still play together, particularly in the traditional semi-formalized or formalized children's games, but the growing awareness of their differential sex rôles is exemplified in the growing reserve with which they tend to treat each other. Boys take great care that their sisters shall not step over them whilst they are lying on their sleeping mats, since they believe that this will make them stupid or harm them in some way. Girls begin to develop a sense of modesty much earlier than boys, and they take care to bathe or dress in private whereas boys will bathe openly until they are 12 or 13 years old. Boys at this age or even a little older begin to show antagonism towards girls by 'pulling their breasts' and then running away.

The idea of male antagonism towards women is highly developed, and is reflected in the Que-que songs, many of which narrate the sexual hostility of a man (16).

Sanko lick he lova pon the dam—De gal a holla murder.
Bip-bap police a come—de gal a holla murder.
Sanko hol the gal 'pon she breast—De gal a holla murder. etc.

or

Anyway Sanko meet you—lick you down,
Anyway, anyway—lick am down.
Don ka a dam top an all—lick am down.

The above two fragments are typical of this type of song, but in fact inter-sexual relations rarely, if ever, approach this type of aggressiveness. Rape is virtually unknown, and in those cases where it is alleged, it usually appears that the girl has consented to intercourse and later built up a fantasy of being attacked, particularly if she feels she may be discovered. In practice, men usually approach girls by 'begging' for 'a lil', rather than aggressively taking the initiative. This type of institutionalized aggression fantasy may of course represent a reaction formation to the close dependence relationship to the mother-figure, but sex antagonism of this type also has other functions as Nadel has pointed out, and there are many ways in which this antagonism is expressed in Guianese Negro society (17).

The age at which children leave school is usually around 15 years, but some children begin to stay away earlier than this, in order to do jobs around the home or on the farm.

Adolescence, Courtship and Marriage

As Miss Kerr has pointed out for Jamaica (18) it is an outstanding fact that the transition from childhood to adult status is almost imperceptible, and is marked neither by initiation rites nor by a period of participation in what might be termed an 'adolescent culture' (19). For the growing girl, the onset of menstruation and her gradual incorporation into the domestic tasks forms a focus for her maturity, and once she starts to have children her transition to the status of 'mother' is well under way, though not necessarily complete. For the boy there are no such well marked physiological changes to punctuate the progress of his maturity, and it is interesting to note that one often finds it extremely difficult to ascertain the ages of men from either their deportment or their behaviour until they become really old. Once a boy has become enmeshed in the wage-earning system he is in a sense 'mature', and 'becoming a father' is of far less importance than is the fact of 'becoming a mother'. For a young man, the tie to his mother which involves him in contributing money to her support is not easily broken, and he may go on living with her even when he has fathered several children. It is interesting to note that many young men decide to get married after having been away from the village for some time, and whilst it might be argued that they are able to earn money outside the village and thus begin to think of setting up a household, it is also worth bearing in mind the fact that leaving the village in search of work has something in the nature of an initiatory experience about it. From August Town the majority of young men go off to the bauxite mines as soon as they are about 18 or 19 years old, and there they are free to feel grown up and responsible for themselves. When they come back to the village at holiday times they are easily distinguishable with their berets, sun glasses, long coats and narrow bottomed trousers: the hall-marks of the smart young city man, or the 'saga boy' of the local dialect. They clearly recognize their earning power, and hence their spending power, to be a mark of attraction to the girls, and when an auction sale was held at the Congregational Church in August Town after the harvest festival, it was the young men from McKenzie and Kwakwani who happened to be in the village at the time who took the leading part in the buying, often giving their purchases to their girl friends who were watching on. The dances which are held in the village schools also provide opportunity for the young men to demonstrate their generosity by buying cakes, ice-cream and drinks for their sweethearts, and the girls are highly critical of any signs of meanness or 'cheapness' in the young men who are competing for their favours.

There can be very little doubt of the fact that the majority of young women are eager to marry and set up their own household, but at the same time they expect a prospective husband to be able to support them, and the fact that they are able to work themselves for cash wages (except in Perseverance) and enjoy a sense of security in their mother's home, means that they can easily postpone marriage. Young men are far less eager to marry or set up house, for it means that they have to provide a house, as well as support for a wife and family, and in any case a young man feels a duty towards his mother whom he is in all probability helping to support. If young men are reluctant to marry, they are certainly not reluctant to have affairs with young women, and they form attachments which often result in pregnancy. In this eventuality it does not by any means follow that the man will be expected to marry the girl. He will certainly be expected to support the child if he is able, and he may continue his attachment to the girl, and other children may be born. Once he has accepted responsibility for the child he has some sort of a tie with its mother and the relationship may endure until they can set up house together, probably in a common-law relationship. On the other hand, the pregnancy itself may precipitate an estrangement, particularly if the man denies paternity and the girl has to apply to the court for an affiliation order. In this way a young woman may bear several children for different men until she finally finds a partner with whom she establishes a lasting relationship. It should be borne in mind that a woman has claims for financial support for her children on all the men for whom she has borne children, and if she attempted to procure abortions before her first child was born she is much less likely to attempt to do so afterwards. After a young woman has begun to have illegitimate children she does not suddenly become less eager to marry, but she is likely to realize that she can only achieve this end by means of establishing a quasi-marital union first. The type of marriage entered into by a young childless woman is different in that it is often mediated through her kinsfolk and those of the young man, and certainly involves the man in making formal approaches to the girl's parents (20). In such cases the idea of romantic love may play some part in the relationship of the young couple, but the main consideration is the man's ability to take care of the girl, and provide her with a home. In both marital and common-law unions, men expect their spouses not to work for wages, for since the man has accepted responsibility for a spouse and her children, it is a reflection on his ability to fulfil the responsibility if she then continues to work. There are cases of course where the woman does still take jobs, and at rice harvest time it is recognized that any woman can work for money without her spouse feeling ashamed, but apart from this, the principle is very generally recognized. When a married or common-law married woman does work for her own money, it is generally a sign of her attitude of independence, and not of her desire to contribute to the joint income of the house, and thus permit a higher standard of living for the household group as a unit, as is often the case in higher status groups. The insistence of the man on his spouse not working outside the home must be regarded as an attempt on his part to stress the basis of his authority as the provider for the group, and in this respect it is highly significant.

Entering a conjugal union does not mean that ties with the parents are broken, though inevitably they are considerably weakened. The whole ceremonial of marriage including the Que-que serves to emphasize the new relationships created by the marriage, but the full effect of the ritual is only seen in those cases where persons marry before having lived together in a common-law union. Even in these cases the separation of the spouses from their respective families is not so complete as in many societies, and even if one of them has to go off to live in another village, the visits to their mother will be frequent. Moving into a house together is the main event in the development of any conjugal union for it is only at this stage of such a relationship that the responsibility of the man and the dependence of the woman become unequivocal. He has accepted the rôle of husband and the duties that go with it, and she has accepted the obligations that flow from having someone to 'mind' her. Previously she accepted the control of her mother, and father perhaps, but there is a clear social recognition that ideally she now comes under the control of her husband. The fact that such control is not embodied in a clear-cut set of rules, legally prescribed and enforced by strong sanctions, is important. A mother never completely relinquishes her claims on her children, and between spouses there is a recognition of each other's duty towards their respective mothers. The balancing of the conflicting obligations to the spouse and to the mother is a difficult matter and a man is always suspicious of his spouse's alliance with her mother, particularly where the couple are still childless.

Not all persons enter conjugal unions involving common residence, and there is sometimes a persistence of a sibling group as a co-residential unit. In one such household in August Town, two brothers and two sisters aged 65 and 49 years, and 70 and 57 years respectively, lived together as a household. Both the sisters had children and the household was enlarged by the addition of the following persons.

Daughter of sister No. 1 (70 years), aged 33 years.
Daughter of a dead sister, aged 23 years.
Three children of a sister's daughter, aged 9, 7 and 5 years.

The two sisters functioned as the effective heads of the household, and the younger of the brothers was extremely sickly, did not work, and was consequently almost wholly dependent on his two sisters. The other brother was recognized as the nominal head of the household, but he had a house of his own which he used as a dormitory and this he regarded as his own house as opposed to the family house in which he only had a joint interest.

This type of situation is not common, and there would normally be a tendency for such a unit to break up into several households once the mother of the group of siblings had died.

Old Age

Old age does not automatically confer honour and elicit respect, for the increase in years does not bring an increase in responsibility, in the number of offices held, or in the exercise of leadership. A majority of men manage to consolidate their position as head of their household group and although their wives become the effective managers of the household, they continue to run the farm, manage the stock and perhaps work for cash wages as well. Unless a man becomes sick and weak he continues to work no matter how old he is, and one sees men of 80 years of age going off to their fields every day. On the whole men die at an earlier age than women as we saw earlier, and if a man's spouse pre-deceases him, then it is likely that he will enter another union (21). For a widower the task of keeping an existing household together is a difficult one, and in the few cases where it is accomplished there is usually a daughter, a sister or a grand-daughter who stays on as the real manager of the household. Some men live alone even when they are very old, a few are sent to the poor-house in Georgetown, and occasionally an old man who has been deserted by his children is taken in by non-relatives when he becomes ill. Men do not look forward to old age, and they often express their fear that their children will ignore them. Their interest in sexual intercourse continues and the fear of impotence is strongly felt. This cannot be regarded merely as a 'biological drive', but must be seen as a means of expression of the desire to assert masculinity. From puberty to death, men are preoccupied with proving their potency and men who have never fathered a child will often claim responsibility for a pregnancy when it is very unlikely to be true. For a man to be the *genitor* of many children, or to 'have children all about' is a matter for pride rather than shame, for it proves that he is a 'man', strong and virile.

For women the situation is far different. As a woman gets older her position as the focus of a household group is consolidated and she is respected as a mother and a grandmother. It is very unlikely that she will be neglected in her old age or infirmity, and not many women are left to be cared for by strangers or sent to the poor-house in Georgetown, as men sometimes are.

CHAPTER VI

THE NORMS OF DOMESTIC GROUPING

We have now examined most of the principal features of domestic organization and the structure of the household group, and the purpose of this chapter is to gather together some of the main threads of our argument, and to examine some of its implications.

It will be recalled that we have been dealing almost exclusively with Negro families which belong to the category of 'village families' in the narrower sense of the term. These families belong to what is usually termed the 'lower-class'. We have neglected the families of persons in the higher status group, such as school teachers, for the most part, and we shall have to take up this question of 'class' differences in the final section of the work.

The fundamental importance of the relationship which we shall term 'matri-filiation' has been amply demonstrated, and it is around mothers that all forms of domestic grouping seem to be ordered. The primacy of the mother-child relationship has been reported for practically all Negro societies in the New World, and our findings do not substantially conflict with these reports, except that we would point out that this is a relationship of fundamental importance in any society. What throws it into high relief in the West Indies is the fact that males are marginal in many ways to the whole complex of domestic relations, particularly in their rôles as husband-fathers. Though the male head of the household occupies an important position as the nominally dominant person, responsible for, and with well-defined rights over, the other members of the household, and particularly his spouse and children, we find that in fact his authority is undeveloped, and that his spouse becomes the real power-centre of the domestic group. This is true even in Perseverance where there is a much greater dependence of women on the earning capacity of men, and far fewer cases of women achieving complete control of household groups. It is not only with their spouses and their own children that men lack real authority, for unlike a matrilineal system they do not exercise responsibilities in relation to their sisters, and their sisters' children. It is within their own families of procreation, and towards their mothers, that men's fields of responsibility lie. There does not arise any question of the society having to find a solution to what Richards has called 'the matrilineal puzzle'. As she says, 'in most societies authority over a household, or a group of households, is usually in the hands of men, not women, as are also the most important political offices' (1). In the sector of Guianese society with which we are dealing, men have very little authority either over household groups, or in other spheres of political and economic life. Women on the other hand have a clearly defined status as mothers, and it is by virtue of this status that they exercise authority and leadership within the household group.

Motherhood is not only a matter of biological relationship in this context, for we are dealing here with a situation where a woman who is the mistress of a household often stands in the social relationship of 'mother', to children who are not her own offspring. When a daughter bears a child whilst she is living in the household controlled by her mother, the child frequently grows up calling its maternal grandmother by the term 'Mama', and its own mother by her christian name. This is particularly true when the grandmother has small children of her own towards whom the child adopts a sibling relationship. Were this not to be so, and the child were to adopt a different attitude towards the grandmother more compatible with the normal grandchild-grandparent attitude, there would be a serious confusion of authority within the group. The older woman could hardly act as disciplinarian to one set of children and as an indulgent grandmother towards another set living within the same household. Conflicts would arise between the older woman and her adult daughter over the treatment of the younger woman's children and this problem is solved by assimilating the children to a filial relationship to the dominant female. This process is to be observed not only in households with a male head but in those with a female head as well. Even where the grandchild does not live in the same house as its maternal grandmother, the same phenomenon sometimes occurs if the grandmother has small children of her own, for the children will play with each other on terms of equality approximating a sibling relationship, and the same situation will exist. One of the factors contributing to such a situation is the complete absence of any well defined pattern of mutual rights, duties and obligations between uncles and aunts on the one hand, and nephews and nieces on the other, so that there is no precise structuring of these relationships in regard to politico-legal or property factors.

All children who live with their grandmother do not call her 'Mama' and we must be careful to emphasize the fact that there is a normal grandchild-grandparent relationship which is one of affectionate indulgence, and a kind of equality. A grandmother, in particular, will often identify herself with her grandchildren and take their part in quarrels they have with their own mother. When a young girl has been forbidden to go to a dance by her mother, she will often appeal to her grandmother for support in her pleas. It is commonly said that grandparents spoil their grandchildren, and old men certainly display far greater affection for their grandchildren than they ever do towards their own children.

The determining factor in whether grandmothers adopt the rôle of mother or of grandmother towards their grandchildren seems to be inherent in the relative position of mother and adult daughter in any particular case. A daughter who is married but still living with her mother whilst her husband is away working, has a well defined social status in her own right as a married person and her relationship to her mother will be less one of subservience and dependence than one of friendly co-operation. However there is always the danger of quarrelling under such circumstances, and it is significant that the great majority of married women will move into their own households whether their husband is with them or not. Thus a young girl of 21 years who married in August Town, moved into a small rented house to live alone until her husband could send for her to go to McKenzie City. This was a clear recognition of the fact that as a married woman she was now entitled to be mistress of her own household, though she would probably have been a great deal happier staying on with her mother, or in this case the aunt with whom she had grown.

Where two women who are both in the status of 'mother' live in the same household there is always the possibility of conflict inherent in the situation, since being a mother ideally implies having control of a household, and this would be particularly marked if the older woman is herself under the nominal authority of a male partner. The fact that the distribution figures in tables VIIIa and IXa show a larger proportion of child-bearing daughters in the households with a female head would seem to have a special significance if looked at from the point of view of the status of the household head (2). We have seen that in the household with a male head, although the spouse of the head is undoubtedly the focus of domestic relations and 'mistress' of the house, she is still nominally under the authority of her husband or common-law husband. She is a mother with a close emotional tie to her children and with considerable authority over them, but at the same time she is a wife, dependent to a large extent on her husband's earnings, and owing him the duty of a wife. If her daughter becomes pregnant whilst living at home it means that the daughter is approximating to the status of her mother. She too will become a mother, and it is common in the case of illegitimate first pregnancies at least, for the daughter to be beaten and driven out of the house. This occurs both where the mistress of the house is married or living in a common-law union, and where the woman is sole head of the household, but it would appear to happen more frequently in the former case. The girl is often told 'If you want to play a big woman go find yourself a man'. At least one function of this beating and temporary expulsion is to emphasize the subordinate position of the pregnant daughter, though of course other factors are also involved. Where the girl's mother is sole head of the household, her position is less equivocal than where she is subject to the authority of a spouse, and she can tolerate more easily the new status of her daughter.

In both cases, however, there will be the tendency for the older woman to continue to maintain her rôle as mother by placing both the new mother and her child in the one category of children of the mistress of the house. As the older woman gets further away from the menopause and her own children mature, the situation changes and she comes to take her place in society as a grandmother. Her relations to her spouse are changing, and she is much less subject to his authority. Grandchildren who have been left with her whilst their mother has gone away will probably continue to treat her as a mother, but as they get older they are quite aware of the fact of their exact biological relationship to her. However this does not alter their relationship within the field of domestic relations. If the children move away from their grandmother's house with their own mother, they may continue to call the older woman 'Mama' particularly if they see her frequently, and if she has young children of her own. However the terminology is quite likely to change, and certainly the nature of the relationship changes as the child's own mother begins to perform the mother rôle more completely.

This assimilation of a child to a filial relationship to the maternal grandmother (and less frequently to the paternal grandmother) is quite clearly a function of the status of the child-bearing daughter in her mother's home, and of the considerable authority of older women in the household group. It must be borne in mind too that the child's own mother may be away from the home working for a considerable portion of the time. Women always nurse their own children and it would be only in exceptional circumstances that a grandmother would breast feed her grandchild. In any case it is only in a small number of cases that a woman is still bearing children at the same time as her daughter.

It should be quite clear by this time from our descriptions, that the family, or the household group as we have preferred to call it, is primarily a child-rearing unit, and that child-rearing is a task allotted primarily to women standing in the relationship of mother to the child. It is necessary that there should be a division of labour by sex, and that men should provide a large measure of the economic support for the women and children. It is a matter of some theoretical importance to know why there should be a family consisting of a man, a woman and their children as an ideal type of child-rearing unit at all, but this is a question we cannot take up here. Given the fact that there is institutionalized social fatherhood and motherhood, with non-incestuous marriage of some kind as the basis of distinct family units, we are interested in knowing, firstly, the kind of form taken by these family units in terms of their internal relationships, and secondly, their relationship to other structures in the society. The latter is, in this case, really another way of asking why the family system takes that particular form. We need not concern ourselves unduly with the fact that the domestic unit meets certain 'needs' such as the need for shelter, for sexual satisfaction or for nourishment, for these are 'givens' as far as we are concerned. It is the way in which these needs are satisfied that interests us as sociolgists.

If we view the internal relationships of the family system as power or authority relationships, we can see that there are certain fairly well defined statuses involved. We began by discussing headship of the domestic unit and we tried to sort out the criteria by which headship was defined, or legitimated. We discovered that husband-fathers are ideally heads of households, and that the majority of household groups come into being when a man builds a house and enters a conjugal relationship with a woman who is either the mother or the potential mother of his children. The ideal pattern is for a man to marry the woman before they live together and before they have children, and this is the ideal of the total society, not only the sector of it with which we are dealing. His authority as head of the household is embodied in his status as a husband-father and at this stage of the development of the household group it is not seriously challenged. The woman also has a well defined status as a spouse, particularly if she is legally married, and this is recognized to be both complementary to and inferior to that of her spouse, for he is 'responsible' for her in the sense that he must support her economically. As soon as children are taken into account, we can see that they are subordinate to the authority of both their parents, but their most significant relationship is to their mother. It is their mother who directly feeds and clothes them and with whom they develop strong affective relationships. If their father does not live in the same household group, then he has literally no rights over the children in the majority of cases. Children derive practically nothing that is of importance from their fathers. They do not inherit property of a kind that is crucial in affording them the means of livelihood (though they do inherit land and sometimes houses from both their parents); they do not acquire membership in any group primarily on the basis of patri-filiation and they do not suffer if they never even see their father. It is for this reason that it is uncommon for children to be provided with a 'social' father who may be different from their biological father. Every individual must have a father of course, but it is not crucial to have a father with whom one has a concrete and definite social relationship. Within the field of activities of the household group the husband-father associates with the other members of the household with varying degrees of intensity at varying stages of his career. By and large his association with other members of the group is infrequent. He does not lead them in productive activities, and all the occupational tasks of family members in the external system tend to be undertaken independently. This carries over into leisure activities and ritual occasions. When the household group is first established, frequency of association between the spouses is at its peak. They co-operate in the establishment of the home; they spend a good deal of their leisure time together and they are often seen going together to dances, parties etc. This level of inter-action is not maintained, and in any case both spouses have important ties involving close association with other persons. The woman with her mother, sisters and other women, and the man with friends who are members of his occupational and leisure activity cliques. As soon as the woman becomes a mother she virtually ceases to go out with her spouse, and the relationship between the spouses contracts to one of performing reciprocal services such as cooking and washing clothes on the one hand, and providing cash, food and clothes on the other, and of course there are reciprocal sexual obligations involved. The status and authority structure does not change significantly, but there comes to be a redistribution of power within the system. The coalition of mother and children tends to harden *vis-a-vis* the husband-father, and whilst the woman remains technically inferior in status to her spouse, she comes to exercise power within the group, which encroaches on his authority. The conversion of a common-law marriage into a legal marriage often serves to validate this new power distribution and the care with which men address their legal wives as 'Mistress' is illuminating in this respect. The diminution in the amount of power attaching to the authority of the husband-father is keenly felt by males, and they are always complaining of the lack of consideration shown to them by their spouses. The fact that they so frequently contract liaisons with other women must be viewed in relation to this fact. The power of the wife-mother is often buttressed by the accretion of extra members of the household group, who are frequently her kinsfolk. The incompatibility between the ideal status of husband-father and the reality of the power distribution as between he and his spouse often leads to separation. In such cases, males almost invariably rationalize the separation by saying that their spouse was too 'quarrelsome', too wicked or too rude, whilst women complain that their spouse was too fond of other women. The fact that a woman's power in the household group derives from her status as a mother and her relationship to her children, is correlated with the fact that women extend their period of effective motherhood by taking over their daughters' children or adopting other children when their own period of child-bearing is over. The widespread desire to have children and the opposition to birth-control, is connected, at least to some extent, with the social importance and prestige of the mother rôle.

If we are to maintain that the pattern of domestic relations we have outlined constitutes a system, then there must be a set of sanctions which operate to maintain it in some sort of equilibrium. Authority itself constitutes a form of control of social interaction and the interal power distribution of the household group is a self-regulating mechanism in many ways. When we speak of the norms of domestic grouping and organization we must distinguish various types of norm and the way in which they are established (3). In the first place we have mentioned the ideal pattern of domestic organization, and there is no doubt that the norm in this sense is that which is common to the total Guianese structure. It is a feature of the primary value system of Guianese society that the ideal family type is that consisting of a man and woman, unrelated by kinship, and married according to the rites of the Christian Church, who share one dwelling with their own offspring. No one would dispute this as the ideal pattern and the person wishing to improve his status by advancing in the class hierarchy (e.g. by becoming a school-teacher) would certainly try to conform to this pattern in setting up a household group. However, the value system is differentiated with respect to the social sub-system with which we are dealing and it becomes both permissive and expected that persons will deviate from the ideal in certain fairly specific ways. The actual deviations from the ideal we can discover by examining the type of norm which is an average, or numerically defined mode, and this we have attempted to do by our analysis of distribution of types and their development over time. However, it must also be recognized that the permissible deviations from the ideal pattern within the sub-system must themselves be governed by a differential ideal pattern and in fact we find that this is the case. There is a moral system within a moral system so to speak, and although the over-all moral system is accepted as being 'right' for the sub-group, at the same time people will say that because they are black people they do things in a different way. It does not mean that because a couple live together without being married that their union is not a socially sanctioned one or that they are under no moral obligation to behave in certain fairly definitely conceived ways. There are 'moral sentiments' which are held by individuals and which are presumably homologous with the social value system, being its individually internalized personality counterpart. For the anthropologist to attempt to state what these are is a somewhat ambitious undertaking. In our Guianese villages one gets the impression that it would be quite immoral for any person to show open disrespect to his mother, but this is merely an inference. There is no overt expression of this moral norm, nor are there any easily recognizable symbols of its generality. The most one can say is that one never observed anyone showing disrespect to their own mother.

Generally speaking, the sanctions ensuring conformity to the ideal patterns, within the limits of permissiveness of the sub-system, are either diffuse ones such as the effect of public opinion and local gossip, fear of magical reprisals, etc., or more importantly, they derive directly from the processes of interaction in the system itself (4).

We still have not answered the question of why the husband-father should tend to be so peripheral to the complex of intra-household relationships and in order to do this adequately we shall have to engage in a series of comparisons with other societies which will take up part of the final section of the work. At the present stage two fundamental considerations present themselves. One is that our analysis so far has represented the male household head as a provider for his household group, and not as the leader of a unit of production in the way that a typical peasant farmer tends to be. He sells his labour for wages and this tends to be regarded as his most important source of income. Homans has described the American middle-class family as a group in which the authority of the husband-father tends to diminish because of the lack of common tasks in which he can exercise leadership for the group (5). However, the nuclear family in the American middle-class has certain important functions which the Negro Guianese rural family lacks, particularly in defining the social status of its members, and in this respect the husband-father is an important member of the group because of his participation in the status-defining occupational system (6). In Guiana, where one of the main criteria of status is the fact of skin colour, and where there is relatively little occupational differentiation of a status-defining nature in the rural Negro groups, the husband-father does not perform this important function for the other members of the group. As we move out of the very lowest social strata, males do tend to perform this function, but this is a matter we must take up in the final chapters.

CHAPTER VII

THE KINSHIP SYSTEM AND MARRIAGE

THE concentration of attention upon the household group has been necessary in order to gain a thorough knowledge of kinship and affinal relations at the level of the co-residential household group, but we must be conscious of the fact that each village is a close-packed community living on a very small piece of land. This means that households are not spatially isolated as in many peasant communities, where the household itself tends to be a locus of more extensive social intercourse (1). Whilst there is a fair amount of reciprocal home visiting, particularly by women, there are other places and other occasions for social intercourse.

However, living together and growing up together are important foci for the ordering of kinship relations, and the importance of women as the nucleus of affective ties within the household is projected into the wider kinship system. Radcliffe-Brown has said that '. . . we have to recognize that in many systems the structural unit consists of a woman and her children'. 'It is by the position of this structural unit in the total kinship structure that we can define the contrast between mother-right and father-right. In true mother-right the unit group of mother and children is completely incorporated, jurally or legally, in the group of the woman's brothers and sisters. In true father-right the unit group is incorporated for jural purposes in a group consisting of brothers with their wives and children' (2). In the system with which we are dealing, the structural unit clearly consists of a woman and her children, and the difficulty lies not so much in determining where this unit is embedded for jural purposes as in seeing where males fit in relation to it at any particular time. It would perhaps be more correct to say that the significant structural unit is not so much a woman and her children as a woman, her daughters and their young children, for this would then high-light the fact that men do not exercise jural authority over their sisters and sisters' children, nor does the unit of a woman and her children become attached to a male combination of father and sons, in the status of wife and children. In short we are dealing with neither true mother-right nor father-right. We have already established the fact that a woman with her children accepts the authority of a male or males during the crucial period of her life when she is bearing children, but that the tendency is for women to assert their autonomy in their status as mothers, deriving their authority from their control over their children even when they are adult. There is no 'matrilineal' system involved, and the configuration of domestic groups varies according to the differential application of the principles of the autonomy of a short (no more than three generation) matri-line, and the autonomy of a co-residential elementary family with nominal control by the husband-father. The latter is the 'ideal type' of the system, and it is by reference to it that the formal pattern of the kinship system is constructed. The system is bi-lateral, or cognatic, and descent is normally recognized to a depth of three generations. That is, to the extent of a contemporaneously-living three-generation group. The significant lines of descent have been experienced by ego sometime during his lifetime. If ego's grandparents died before he was born, or whilst he was very young he will either know nothing of them or be very uncertain about them. If he knew his grandparents then it is unlikely that he will know very much about their parents.

Whilst the kinship system is a shallow one, it has a fairly wide lateral extension, but it is not a symmetrical concentric system except in a very generalized way. The lateral range of reckoning depends once again on experiential factors, and is related to an ascending and descending recognition of sibling groups. In the descending generation from a sibling group special emphasis is laid on being 'two sisters' children' and this is a commonly employed kinship term without any comparable designation for 'two brothers' children', or a cross-cousin relationship. These relationships are recognized, but the term 'two sisters' children' derives from a very interesting feature of the system, which we have characterized as the focal position of women of the parental generation in the household group. A woman is recognized to have authority over her daughter's children, and can punish or reward them, utilize their services and so on, but she does not have parallel rights over her son's children, for as the saying goes, 'they are another woman's children', meaning that it is to their own mother that they have the primary tie, which brings them within the sphere of influence of some other matri-focal unit. Since this is so, it is clear that two brothers' children, or cross-cousins, do not come within the range of the same matri-focal unit of the maternal grandmother, but belong to different units. It is this fact which gives the whole system a shift towards the female side in both ascending and descending lateral reckoning. This state of affairs is very different from a matrilineal system where the primary emphasis is upon the brother-sister relationship and not the child-mother-grandmother relationship. In a matrilineal system the legal bond is between brother and sister and mother's brother and sister's son, and it is difficult to imagine how the Guianese system could be derived from this any more than from any other system. In modern Ashanti the change seems to be in the direction of a shift from the mother's-brother—sister's-son relationship to the father-son relationship with its main expression in a modification of the rules of transmission of property. In British Guiana there is no comparable record of a shift of property rights, nor is there any retention of a matri-line of the Ashanti type (3.) The essential feature of the Guianese system is the minimal importance of men in any descent line, including the elementary family. Of course this does not mean that relationships are not traced through men; they most certainly are, but the full range of possible ties through fathers is not exploited to the same extent as it is through mothers.

Let us now try to take all possible relationships from ego and examine each one and try to assess its significance. With the reckoning of relationship in so many different lines it is practically impossible to schematize the system into a diagram and so this purely descriptive device has to be employed.

Ego's own generation

In ego's own generation the most important relatives are full siblings, or uterine siblings with different fathers. Even within this group there is one major differentiation and other possible ones. Sisters have a closer bond than do brothers, or brothers and sisters, and this is due primarily to their identification with the mother as women and mothers. Sisters render each other mutual help with their children, and when the mother of two sisters is dead they take responsibility for each other's children in the event of serious trouble or death. As we might expect, the relationship of sisters is not uniformly one of co-operation, reciprocal help and amity. There is a certain amount of competition and latent hostility between sisters which is co-existent with their co-operation. Sisters quarrel with each other, and even fight, and cases crop up in court where two sisters living close to each other become involved in brawls and find themselves prosecuted for using obscene language or disturbing the peace. Such cases are infrequent, and would hardly occur whilst the mother of the two sisters is alive, for then their relationship to each other is quite definitely conditioned by their common subordination to their mother. In the folk-lore, one finds stories in the 'Nancy' (4) story series which refer to a woman with two daughters, one of whom she likes and one whom she doesn't like. The two daughters are set to compete against each other in some way and the disliked one emerges as the better of the two. The following is an example.

> There were two girls, one bin name Bucky an one bin name Klajo. Their mother na bin like Bucky—only Klajo she does like—so every time Bucky goes upstairs she does drive down Bucky and tell she fu go wash de dutty wares. So one day she went at a river and dropped the silver spoon, an she went an say 'Ma de silver spoon los'. She say 'you best go an caranker for it'. She go, she go an fine de place an she meet two head a fight, an she turn to the head an say 'Good afternoon me grandpuppa', and the head say 'Good afternoon me daughter'. The head say 'Go good an come back good'. She go, she see two lion a fight an she turn to one an say 'Good afternoon me grandpuppa' and the lion say 'Good afternoon me grandmother'. She go again, she see two tiger fight. She tell the tiger de same ting an the tiger tell she back. And then she go an see an ole lady an she turn to this ole lady an say 'Good afternoon grandmother' and this lady say 'Good afternoon me daughter'. She say 'How far you goin?' She say, 'I los me mother's silver spoon an she tell me to go an caranker for it'. And de lady call she in an she go in. She say 'Daughter, me got one grain rice, an you must cook it, an if you see a cat comin, you must give it this food an break it back with a stick'. Dis gal tek it an cook it an gie it to the cat an then gie it water to drink. An the cat return back and turn to this same ole lady comin. 'Me daughter please can look me head, it got pimpler'. An the gal look the old lady head an tek out the pimpler. She say—'Me got one fowl-shit bed an one good bed. Which one you goin sleep on?' The girl say it is the fowl-shit bed she does sleep pon. When day clean the old lady say she got two egg, one wha say 'tek me', and one wha say 'na tek me'. Take the one wha say 'tek me'. When she go to turn, she bus de egg, an she bus the silver spoon from the egg. She bus, she bus she self pure gold 'pon she skin. She go, and when she tell she mother she foun the silver spoon, she mother chase out de nex' gal, an tell she she mus go and caranker too. When she go

she see two head a fight an she say 'Oh my lord, ah never see two head a fight yet'. She go an she see two lion a fight an she say de same ting. De lion say 'Go bad, an come back bad to me'. She go again an see two tiger a fight an she say de same words, an the tiger tell she 'Go bad an come back bad to me'. She go an she see the ole lady sit down an she ent tell the lady 'good afternoon', and the lady call she. She say 'Wha you a call me for?' an she went over. She say 'Gal, me got one grain rice, an you must cook it, an if you see a cat comin you must give it this food to eat, an break it back with a stick'. She say 'One grain rice can't-cook'. She say 'Well a got this two grain rice, you mus cook it'. She say 'Two grain rice can't cook', an she say 'A got this half cup rice' an she took it an cook, an the rice run all over the pot, trow away till it done cook. An then she saw the cat, give it of that food, and broke the cat back. Then the lady come in an draggin, an she say, 'look me head got plenty pimpler'. She say, 'Who goin look you head for pimpler', and she ent look. The old lady say, 'A got a good bed and a bad bed, which are you going sleep on?' She say 'De good bed, na, the good bed. Who goin sleep pon bad bed?' She sleep on it till nex mornin. When day clean, the ole lady turn to she an say, 'I got two egg in the pen. One wha say "Tek me" an one wha say "na tek me", an tek de one wha say "na tek me". An she tek de one wha say 'na tek me'. When she meet out, she bus, an she bus pure tar, an when she bus the nex' one, out jump lion an tiger an eat she up. Story done.

This story illustrates many other points apart from the latent rivalry between sisters in relation to the mother, and serves particularly to point the moral that obedience, politeness and unselfishness are rewarded, whereas bad manners and covetousness are eventually punished. The interesting terminological usages where the lion calls her his 'grandmother' and tiger and the old lady refer to her as 'daughter' are not repetitions of normal usages. A young person would rarely refer to an older one as 'grandpuppa' or 'grandmother' as a polite form of address, though they might, and the older person would almost invariably address the younger as 'child' or 'my child'. However, in the story the terms of address are quite compatible with the type of relationship existing between kin under certain circumstances and it is interesting to find 'grandmother' actually used where 'granddaughter' might be more appropriate, for these two are terms denoting a relationship of equality. This story is reproduced exactly as it was recorded from a 16-years-old girl who was telling it to a group of younger children. Any discrepancies and lack of consistency were there as the story was told.

Between brothers there is rarely any such mutual assistance, though occasionally one does find brothers farming together, or assisting each other in time of need. Between brother and sister there is a bond of friendship, but no real sense of mutual responsibility. One rarely finds a young man interfering in his sister's love affairs, or taking her side in any quarrel with one of her lovers. Despite this, the sibling group is an important one, and all siblings have equivalent rights to inheritance of property, land often being passed undivided as 'children's property'. This is discussed more fully elsewhere, where we show that the holding of undivided rights in property is often only a method of delaying the resolution of individual ownership for a while (5). Quarrels may arise between siblings over property, but such quarrels are infrequent and of very limited severity. They are very sharply contrasted with the quarrels which arise between the children of the wealthy shopkeepers over the inheritance. Where a certain amount of land is held jointly by a sibling group, there may be the development of a greater solidarity within the group in the sense that the eldest brother will often allocate pieces of land to the children of the members of the group when they wish to start farming, or to build a house. This is not common though, and few men are willing to accept the jurisdiction of their elder brothers in this way, preferring to accumulate their own collection of parcels of land, and allow whoever is using it to acquire ownership of the joint property.

Half-siblings by the same father but with different mothers normally belong to two quite different and often mutually antagonistic matri-focal units. This naturally conditions their relationship to each other and only in a minority of cases do you find any close tie between half-siblings of different mothers. A man's 'outside' children do not rank equally with his legitimate children as far as a share in his property at his death is concerned. Ideally they should be given something, but this is usually left to the widow or the surviving legitimate heirs. A widow will often give preference to her own children, by different men, who have grown in the dead man's household and this may cause a certain amount of friction. However, the right of the widow to dispose of the property as she sees fit is unquestioned in the last resort.

The most important factor in shaping the sibling relationship is the fact of growing together in the same household. This is the real social sibling tie, and children who have grown together in a household can all expect a share in the inheritance of the household head, and his wife or common-law wife. It is often said that an illegitimate child who grows with his grandparents is in many ways better off than anyone. He is likely to get a share in his grandparents' property, in his own mother's property, and has at least a chance of a share in his *genitor's* property. Living together means common allegiance to the same female of the ascending generation, but living in a household, whilst strengthening one's ties to the members of that household does not sever completely the other ties of consanguinity, particularly within the village. The tie to your own mother is always important to some extent even if you don't live with her, and your siblings by the same mother are always your friends even if you live in different villages.

The sibling relationship shades over into the cousin relationship with very little break, particularly when ego is young. We have already seen that two sisters' children are particularly close because of their common attachment to their maternal grandmother, and this is the closest to the sibling relationship. Other first cousins are always on easy and friendly terms and there is more intimacy between cousins of opposite sex, than there is between full siblings of opposite sex. Marriage or sexual intercourse is prohibited within this degree of relationship, but marriage does take place occasionally, though the couple will have to leave the village at least for the wedding, and there will be a good deal of opposition from the older generation. At the lateral range of second cousins within the same generation, the relationship will be of less importance than a neighbour relationship. Whilst marriage or intercourse is formally forbidden between second cousins because they are felt to be 'too close,' it would not be impossible for such a marriage to take place within the village. Beyond second cousins, kin relations merge into local relations and it is at the point of 'cousin' that the two are articulated.

The term 'cousin' as a form of address is used for anyone including strangers to the village, and this is the key to an understanding of its importance. Whether the term 'coz' was derived from Elizabethan English or not is of secondary importance (6). What is important is the fact that it designates the point at which local relations and kin relations become fused and cease to be differentiated, and hence it is a position of structural importance.

First ascending generation from ego

There is no need to recapitulate our remarks concerning intra-household relationships here, but something has to be said about the relations of parents to children who do not live with them. This pattern of divided residence occurs most frequently in the case of fathers and their 'illegitimate' children. A young woman who bears a child whilst living with her family of orientation without being married to, or living with, the father of the child, has complete rights over the child, or at least shares rights over the child with her parents, particularly her mother. The father has no rights over the child, but he has a very definite obligation to support it and the courts will issue a maintenence order on reasonable evidence of paternity, rightly giving the benefit of the doubt to the mother. Children of unmarried parents have to be registered like any other children, but the name of the father is almost invariably omitted from the official registration record. However, the child takes the *genitor's* name unless he has denied paternity and the courts have upheld his denial. In practice most children do take the name of their *genitor* though they may have been known by their mother's name when they were very small. It is when they go to school that the matter becomes crystallized, for their names then have to be registered in the school records. Sometimes mothers do not press the fathers of their children for maintenance, and fathers often contribute to the support of their children without being taken to court. The derivation of the surname from the *genitor* is obviously an important social recognition of paternity and it serves to distinguish half-siblings even though they grow up together.

As soon as a child is old enough it is sent to visit its father, and some kind of relationship will be established. The father will give small presents to his child, and although the child will normally be very shy and reserved under these circumstances, it is a well established custom for it to be able to go and ask for small gifts. Of course if the father does not live in the same village, then the child may never know him at all. A great deal depends on the father's proximity and on the fact of his having 'recognized' his child.

Food taboos are commonly found in rural Guiana, and when such taboos occur, persons will say of the taboo food (which is usually skin-fish, goat, sheep or pumpkin), 'it is me kinna'. Eating the taboo food will allegedly result in severe rashes or leprosy. In some areas it is asserted that one's 'kinna' is inherited from one's *genitor*, and although there was not total agreement on this by informants it does show that symbolic ways are found of expressing the importance of the relationship of a child to its *genitor* (7). Also, the fact that when a child grows up in the household of its mother's spouse, this man not being its *genitor*, there is no suppression of the fact that it has a different father, must be regarded as highly significant. Even in England when a child is adopted or acquires a *pater* who is not its *genitor* it often remains unaware of the facts of its birth. In the situation with which we are dealing **social** fatherhood is itself not highly developed and it is instructive to find that it is hardly ever considered necessary to suppress the fact of actual biological fatherhood, but on the contrary it is from him that you acquire not only your name but also in many cases your 'kinna', or food taboos.

Aunts and uncles (i.e. brothers and sisters of mother and father), are important relatives, and are treated with the same deference afforded to one's own parents. Again it is necessary to stress the female bias and point out that mother's sisters are usually the closest relatives, with mother's brothers and father's siblings ranking lower in order of importance to ego. There is no fixed pattern of rights, duties and obligations towards aunts and uncles, but the tendency is for mother's sisters to be closely identified with the mother, and ego often ranks as 'house people' in his mother's sister's house. The spouses of mother's and father's siblings are also referred to as 'aunt' and 'uncle'.

Second ascending generation from ego

Terms of address and relationships to grandparents vary according to the context in which they operate. This is to be seen most clearly in ego's relation to his maternal grandmother where it sometimes happens that he will refer to her, and regard her, as a mother, using the term 'Mama' as a form of address (8).

The normal relationship between grandparents and grandchildren is one of affection and easy familiarity, though the maternal grandmother always tends to be a figure of authority to be respected. A grandfather may function in the rôle of father to ego, just as a grandmother may act as mother, but the relationship is always much more vague and ill-defined in such cases. Since the functions of fathers in relation to **any** children are very limited, the child does not need to adopt a set of specific responses to a particular male whom it calls 'father'.

The relationships between ego and his paternal grandparents are usually limited to occasional courtesy visits and the giving of small presents. A great deal depends upon the relationship between ego's mother and his paternal grandparents. If they live near by then it is quite likely that friendly relations will develop but there is rarely that close identification that is found with the maternal grandmother, unless of course ego grows in the household of his paternal grandparents as sometimes happens.

Relations with grandparents' siblings and their descendants tend to come in the category of 'distant relatives' or 'we are family'. The terms 'great-aunt' and 'great-uncle' are sometimes used, and 'cousin' is a term used to cover both ascending and descending generation relatives, as well as those in ego's own generation. If pressed to be specific, persons will indicate relationship by the use of such phrases as 'my mother is to call her aunt' which show clearly that ego's relationship to alter is a derivative of his parents' relationship. Such relationships lie outside the bounds of the close kinship unit, and are only stressed for special purposes which may arise.

Throughout our discussion of kinship ties we have had to refer again and again to the importance of the unit comprising a woman, her daughters and their children. Although we have stressed the fact that this unit rarely becomes completely differentiated as a functional whole, we have to regard it as an important focus of social relations. If we view the total kinship system as a network of ties extending over the whole village community it will be an irregular network with gaps here and there, but within it one will be able to discern a regular motif where the ties of a woman, her daughters and their children are more closely knit than any other relationships. The closeness of these bonds, which are really constituted by virtue of the fact of motherhood, obtrude time and again as determinants of the form taken by household groups. Men are less closely bound up with any kin groups than are women, but it is of course a matter of degree, and not an assertion that they are not tied into the kinship system. What we have been saying so far about kinship refers particularly to August Town, though the general principles apply equally to Perseverance and Better Hope. In Better Hope there is a slight shrinkage of the range of kinship ties, whilst in Perseverance men are relatively more integrated into the pattern.

TERMINOLOGY

The analysis of kinship terminology becomes quite complicated when one comes to consider a situation where there is a comparative lack of precision in the patterning of kinship relations, and where terms which are familiar to the investigator are used in ways which differ to some degree from the accepted usage of the same words in this country. We have already touched upon the main relationships which are recognized, and indicated briefly the terms of address and reference associated with them, but a consideration of actual usage will throw more light on the situation.

The widespread use of 'fond names' or nick-names is rarely recorded in the West Indies, but it is important and should not be overlooked. Almost every villager is endowed with a fond name, by which he or she is often better known than by their real name, a fact which can cause considerable confusion to persons carrying out surveys or censuses, or even in cases where individuals have to be traced for more important purposes. Many of these names seem to be African in origin, whilst others are more topical, or may be simple distortions of the real name. In many cases the fond name is a compound of a kinship term and the person's christian name. The use of fond names as terms of address quite clearly implies a certain latitude in the relationship, and a fond name could only be used by persons standing in certain relationships to the person being addressed. Schneider suggests that the use of kinship terms as a form of address imposes on the situation a kind of constraint imposing conformity to the social definition of the relationship, since the kinship term stands for the way in which each person should behave towards the other (9). He goes on to say that the employment of a personal name as a form of address, permits the relationship wider latitude. However this may be, observation makes it clear that the use of fond names may express either friendliness and a sense of equality, or disrespect, depending on who uses the name, and sometimes on which name is used, since one individual may possess several. Kinship terms are most frequently used in addressing persons of ascending generations. 'Ma', 'Mama', 'Mother', 'Pa', 'Papa', 'Daddy' or 'Father' are the most common specific kinship terms used in address, for these are the kinship relations with the greatest degree of social specificity. Children do not use 'fond-names' in addressing their parents. In the 'fond-names' themselves, we find older persons acquiring names which are compounds such as 'Uncle Rocca', 'Auntie Big', 'Papa Dick', 'Nana', etc., which are essentially respect terms generalized as 'fond-names' and used by the whole village. Such terms label their bearers as being of an older generation and do not express specified kinship relations.

One of the most interesting examples of 'distorted' kinship terminology is found in situations where there is a co-residential group consisting of a woman, her daughter and her daughter's children. We have already dealt with the relationships involved in a group of this kind, and mentioned that the tendency is for the children to call the maternal grandmother 'Mama' (10). The child's own mother can never be regarded as a full sibling in a case like this, and the conflict is resolved by the child adopting a reference term such as 'sister' or 'auntie' or sometimes just using the mother's christian name, but not her 'fond-name'. The use of the term 'sister' is interesting because it is not normally used as a term of address between siblings, unless they are widely separated in age, when a younger sibling may then use it. The use of these terms is a very clear indication of the position of the biological mother in this triadic relationship, and shows that there is no question of her assuming absolute equality with her child, despite its assimilation to a filial relationship to the maternal grandmother.

In a referential context, exact kinship terms may be used more frequently, but it is interesting to note that latent hostilities between proximal generations may be expressed by the use of the mother's or father's 'fond-name' in certain situations where this might be unthinkable as a term of address. Between husband and wife, adherence to formal terms, both in address and reference, is the rule, for this is the one relationship which requires constant reaffirmation owing to the tensions inherent in it. We said earlier, in citing Schneider, that the use of personal names allows a greater latitude in behaviour than the use of formal terms which tend to define relationships more precisely, but the corollary of this is that where the relationships are extremely well defined, there can be permitted a greater latitude in behaviour and it is not so essential to use specific terms of address which will define the situation. Thus in a household group, siblings or quasi-siblings never use the terms 'brother' or 'sister' in address, and rarely in reference.

THE FUNCTION OF KINSHIP TIES

A discussion of the kinship system should properly be left until we have considered the political aspects of village structure and the system of social stratification, for whilst it is possible to discuss kinship as an extension from the nuclear relationships of the elementary family, it is necessary to bear in mind the fact that the degree to which kinship and affinal ties are ramified to provide a system of social categorization will depend to a large extent on the nature of the economic and political system. We may anticipate a later discussion by stating that the main lines of differentiation in the total social system are those of 'colour' and 'class', and that the major part of the population of our villages is 'black' (low status) and 'lower-class'. In this sense each village is primarily a local solidary sub-group with a minimum of internal status differentiation amongst its Negro inhabitants. This is an inadequate statement of the position, but it will do for the time being. This being the case, taken in conjunction with the fact that in the economic system it is the ability to earn cash wages which is the most important single consideration, it becomes clear that kinship only performs the function of providing a basis for status ascription in a very limited sense. Of course being born a Negro is in itself a derivative of a kinship tie, but the kinship unit which is significant from this point of view is the whole Negro section of the population of the country which forms an almost completely endogamous group. The word 'almost' is important for it is a feature of the 'middle-class' kinship system that marrying across the colour lines is a mechanism of upward social mobility and colour status is exchangeable with achieved status within this social stratum, at least to some extent. It is beyond the scope of this study to deal with this aspect of the matter but it has been reported in some detail for Trinidad (11) and Jamaica (12).

Of course, for any individual the initial ascribed status is a kinship status as a member of a particular family, or more significantly as the child of a particular woman. However, the absence of significant ranking as between families means that the primary status determinants for any individual spring from the position of his family of orientation as a village family and as part of the Negro group. At this level, membership of these groups is a status determinant which completely over-rides the membership of a particular family or household group.

Where political control is largely imposed from above, or vested in the persons arbitrarily chosen by the Local Government Board, there is no inheritance of positions of importance. In August Town it would seem that the office of overseer was tending to become hereditary, as the position of headman may have been in the past. However, even during the course of one year's field-work two overseers were discharged at the suggestion of the Board because of their alleged inefficiency. Church offices too are usually filled by teachers or persons who have proved their competence at conducting meetings, keeping minutes, etc., in the 'proper' way, and are not passed on from father to son, mother to daughter, etc. They tend however to be kept within the group that constitutes the village, particularly in the case of August Town Congregational Church.

If kinship is not utilized as the basis for segmentation and the transmission of political office, what then is it used for, and how? The lateral range of kinship recognition is fairly wide, and August Town is often spoken of as being 'all one family'. However, this is merely a recognition that any person can trace a multitude of ties to other members of the village, particularly since village endogamy is the rule, but there is no provision for a systematic ordering of all local relationships on a kinship basis in the sense that everyone is placed in a kinship category of some kind. The term 'we are family' can be used to cover any type of relationship within the range of kinship recognition.

Kinship in its aspect of lateral extension then comes to be a mechanism of integration of the solidary sub-group. If anything, it works to inhibit internal rank differentiation by binding a large number of cognates into an extensive network of kinship ties which are conceived as relations of equality as implied in the term 'we are family to each other'. The order of kinship ties at this level are very little different from the ties springing from territorial co-residential patterns, and the term 'all August Town is one family' illustrates the coincidence of the two orders of relationships. Kinship ties do cross the boundaries of the village because of the fact that village endogamy is not complete, but they extend for the most part into communities of a similar kind, having the same general position in the total social system.

WITCHCRAFT BELIEFS

At this point a brief reference to a widely held belief is introduced since it throws some light on the kind of relationships we have been discussing.

The witchcraft beliefs of the coastal Negro population concentrate on the conception of the 'old hag' who can magically shed her skin at night, and fly forth in the form of a ball of fire to suck the blood of her victims. Although the terms 'old hag' implies femininity, in fact witches may be of either sex, and the terms 'suck man' or 'suck woman' (meaning to suck blood) are frequently used. The victim gradually weakens through loss of blood and dies, and it is particularly children or pregnant women who are liable to attack. The quality of being 'old hag' is referred to as having 'fire' and may be acquired in several ways, the most common of which is having the 'fire' passed on in the form of a trinket or coin which the person is asked to 'keep' for someone else who is already a witch. Alternatively the 'fire' may be acquired by a person who has attempted to get riches by means of obeah (black magic), and whose plans have gone awry, being given 'fire' instead. In short the acquisition of 'fire' is usually involuntary, and it is handed on as soon as possible to someone who is close to you, and probably a member of your own family.

People who 'suck' can be detected by their downcast furtive glances and their red-rimmed eyes, as well as by more formal means such as their inability to walk across a white chalk line drawn across the road, or to pick silver money out of a pail of water. If salt is sprinkled on the skin of a person who has gone out 'to suck' then when he returns he will be unable to get back into it and will cry 'skin, skin, you no know me? Skin, skin you no know me?' The defence against attacks by 'old hag' consists in placing a manicole broom (13) or a knife blade over the door of the house, or in making a chalk mark  which the 'old hag' cannot cross. One house had this sign chalked on the door and it was reputed to be to keep away 'old hag'.

It is not intended to discuss the origins or distribution of these beliefs though it may be noted that they are substantially the same as those reported for other parts of the West Indies (14), and bear marked resemblances to the *Obayifo* beliefs of the Ashanti (15).

The persons generally reputed to 'suck' have no over-riding common characteristic in real life. They may be men or women, young or old, ugly or normal, but they may quite well be 'peculiar' in a series of apparently unconnected ways. A man or woman who is secretive and unfriendly, or ill-tempered and ill-mannered may be singled out. A person who is mean and selfish or who is suspected of making a lot of money which he keeps secret and does not spend in entertaining others; a person who lives alone and has few friends; or a person who is a stranger to the village. All these may be singled out for accusation. Accusations are rarely made publicly, for a person so accused can take his accusers to court and claim damages for slander, but there have been occasions when a person has been attacked by a body of accusers and severely beaten, though not, to my knowledge, in any of the three villages studied. The accusations usually take the form of gossip which is generated by his tendency to deviance from the normal ways of behaving as a member of the village community (16). In this respect witchcraft accusations may be no more than a means of making explicit the social disapproval of persons who repeatedly and continuously show signs of deviance. The rumours alleging witchcraft do not normally interfere with a person's continued membership of the group for they rarely result in any action being taken against the offender and their very vagueness is an indication of the fact that witchcraft is not a 'problem' in these villages. The fact that witches normally attack children and pregnant women, may be related to the high infant mortality rate and malnutrition on the one hand, and the perils involved in pregnancy and childbirth on the other.

The whole complex of witchcraft beliefs forms an interesting contrast to that reported for the Nupe by Nadel (17). He argues that the fact that all witches are women and that these female witches attack men, dominate them and threaten their authority, is bound up with the economic position of women as the controllers of the market complex. There is a similarity in the position of women in British Guiana in that they enjoy positions of economic independence and power, particularly when their sons are old enough to work and send them money, and at this stage of their lives they very definitely threaten men's authority, particularly in household affairs. However, the witchcraft beliefs do not follow the same pattern at all. It would be ridiculous to suggest that the name 'old hag' constitutes a female symbol for all witches regardless of sex, and in any case the majority of victims are children and pregnant women. We cannot therefore arrive at such neat conclusions for the British Guiana case, and we do not have a sufficiently large series of actual cases to sort out the basically significant factors in what appears to be a rather heterogeneous complex. The most we can do is to offer a very tentative hypothesis which may be useful as a guide to further research, but no more.

Two main facts are significant. The first is that witchcraft of this kind only operates within the local territorial unit, and the second is that the main object of attack is the mother and child, i.e. the 'motherhood' complex. It would be compatible with the structural fact that the village is taken as the widest effective 'kinship' unit in a symbolic sense, that witchcraft would operate within this range, but the fact that the mother-child unit is singled out for attack cannot be simply correlated with inter-sex hostilities as in the case of Nupe. The two main threats to the mother-child relationship come from the dominance of the mother's mother on the one hand, and from the dominance of the husband-father on the other. If it is true that the status of 'mother' is an important and desirable one in the social system, then it is not surprising that young women should experience anxiety concerning their performance of the rôle, and particularly when they are so likely to have to surrender a good deal of their authority to their own mothers. Inter-generational conflict between women is almost completely suppressed in real life situations, and its main focus would centre around the relationship of both women to the children of the younger one.

If this is the 'type case' of an 'old hag' attack it is certainly not the only one, and there seems to be a definite tendency for the belief to become generalized so that it can be made to fit almost any anxiety situation. Thus in some villages, particularly on the West Coast of Demerara, one hears of men being attacked by 'old hag' and in these cases the situation is almost completely reversed and would more nearly fit the Nupe pattern. However, men's antagonism to women is expressed in a number of other ways which are more nearly on a fully conscious level. Men are perpetually complaining about the way women exploit you if given half a chance. It is said that a wife or common-law wife will steal all your things and give them to her mother. John Campbell complained that his wife left him only a few months after they were married, taking all the furniture and household effects with her back to her mother. On top of this she went to the police and falsely accused him of hitting her with a hammer, thereby trying to get him jailed. Later when he became ill, he consulted an obeah-man who told him that his wife and her mother were working obeah against him, and to this cause he also attributes his failure to be selected for the American farm labour scheme.

Thus the belief in 'old hag' once established (and its form is almost certainly derived from West Africa) can spill over into all kinds of situations, especially since it is not highly institutionalized as in some other societies.

MARRIAGE AND MATING

So far we have considered marriage and common-law marriage only in their relation to domestic structure and the growth processes of the household group. Within the limits of our frame of reference we have been able to treat them as being equivalent in so far as they both result in a man and woman living together within one household, and performing their mutually reciprocal rôles as spouses. Even within this frame of reference we have had to simplify our descriptions somewhat in order to make our exposition clear, but it now remains to take up the question of the differences between the two types of union at this level of organization—i.e. of the domestic unit itself. In addition we shall examine marriage and common-law marriage within the context of the village as a unit, and also from the point of view of their respective functions in the social system of British Guiana as a whole. It is important to realize at the outset that there are these three perspectives from which we can view the question of mating, and the kind of answers we can expect to our questions will be related to our frame of reference. Before embarking on this scheme of analysis, a description of the preliminaries to, and the ritual associated with, marriage, will be given, and it should be borne in mind that our analytic referents are implicit in the descriptions to a very large extent.

Marriage is an important occasion no matter when it occurs, for it marks the passage of a couple into a legally and religiously sanctioned union, which is in conformity with the ideal values of the whole society. This is equally true even if the couple have lived together previously, though one does find cases where couples who have lived together for many years get married quietly in their own homes or in Georgetown. During the course of the field-work there was no opportunity to observe the wedding of a couple who were transforming a long-established common-law union into a legal marriage, but from the statements of informants it is clear that such weddings are often celebrated with a good deal of ceremony, particularly if the couple have plenty of close relatives in the village.

Courtship and Engagement

The first category of marriages to be considered are those contracted between young men and women, particularly before either of them have had any children. This applies more to the girl than to the man, for a childless girl is much more likely to have a marriage contracted for her than a girl who already has even one child. In such cases courtship follows a quite definite pattern, and here one often finds the girl's father taking a prominent part. A young man looking for a wife will usually go back to his own part of the country to find one, even if he is working at the bauxite mines, or even farther afield in some other part of the West Indies. In one case a young man who was working in Curaçao wrote to his parents asking them to find a suitable girl for him to marry, and the parents 'courted' a girl on his behalf; he returned, married her and took her back with him to Curaçao. In another case the father of a young girl was approached by a friend of his from another village a little way up the coast, who said that he would like his son to marry the girl. The girl's father consulted his wife and they agreed to let the girl decide. However, her father made it quite clear that if she didn't do as he wished she could expect little help in the future, so she finally agreed, and by all accounts the young couple have been very happily married for a considerable number of years now.

Although such arranged marriages do occur, it is more usual for a young man to meet a girl and take a liking to her, after which he will also write to her parents. These letters are usually characterized by exaggerated statements of the young man's assets and his ability to provide for the girl, as well as his statements of how much he loves her. If the girl likes the young man and her parents agree to the match a formal engagement will be arranged. It should be noted that a man intending to marry a girl who has already borne him a child will not go through the procedure of 'writing' for a girl, nor of 'engaging' her. The following is a description of an engagement party attended in one of the villages:—

> The young couple involved met at McKenzie City, where the young man was working, and where the girl had been staying with a relative. The girl's father was dead and so the engagement party was held in the house of her mother's brother. The young man was from another village about six miles away, and he had brought with him a party of relatives and friends from his own village. The most important of these was the woman with whom he had grown—his aunt. In all there were about thirty people present in this small, two-roomed house, and the formal part of the proceedings began with a speech from one of the more voluble village men, who was related to the girl through his grandparents and her great-grandparents. He spoke a great deal about love and devotion and the binding obligation of engagement, which he compared to the wedding vows. He was followed by the boy's aunt who spoke with more brevity and realism, stressing the fact that the young couple must not take this as an excuse for relaxing their behaviour, but must wait patiently for the next stage, which they did not intend to rush. She stressed how fortunate it was that the couple were both from the same district, and how gratifying it was that they had

> returned home to pledge their troth. The couple had been sitting side by side at the head of the table during the speeches, and the young man's aunt now produced a gold ring engraved with the girl's initials, and a gold bracelet and placed them in a saucer prior to placing them on the girl. The couple kissed and the girl then rose and walked around the room to show the engagement presents to every person present. Food was now brought out and placed on the table, and the man who had spoken first, who was acting as a sort of master of ceremonies, declared the table 'open'. Rum and wine were served throughout the whole proceedings. Many of the young men present had comments to make on the number of gifts with which the young man had 'engaged' the girl. They boasted that they would never engage a girl with less than a ring, a bracelet, a gold necklace and a brooch, the ring and bracelet being the absolute minimum one could offer.

Informants state that the usual procedure is for the presents to be circulated amongst the guests on the saucer before the presentation, and the guests place money in the saucer as a gift to the young couple. It is also customary for the young man to provide rum, whilst the girl's family provide the food. Engagement parties are always held in the home of the girl or her close kinsfolk.

A ceremony such as the one described above is a well defined procedure, and it can be expected that marriage will follow in the not too distant future, usually in less than a year. It is essential that both sets of kin participate in a ceremony of this kind and the fact that the match has reached this stage is a good indication that the wedding will go through without any trouble. It is interesting to note that the woman spokesman laid stress upon the fact that the couple were both from the same district, for this is a constantly recurrent theme, and in August Town at least, the preferred marriage is between two persons from the same village.

Not every young couple will go through the procedure of engagement, particularly if they and their parents are very poor, and it has already been noted that this is an unlikely procedure if the couple already have a child. Preparations for a wedding begin months in advance, for there are a large number of items to be assembled before the actual event. The family of the bride have to bear the greatest financial burden of the ceremonies involved, but the bridegroom has also to prepare a home for his future wife, which involves finding furniture of some kind as well as a house. In Perseverance many people said that a young man would first provide a home for a girl and then start thinking of marriage as he accumulated a little more money. So far as August Town is concerned it is extremely rare for a childless girl to go and live in a common-law union with a man, and she would consider this more shameful than having a child without being married.

It is difficult to assess exactly how the expenses of a wedding ceremony are divided up, but certainly the bridegroom has to buy the wedding ring, provide rum, buy himself a new suit and pay all the church fees. The bride's parents have to provide her wedding dress, and see that she has an adequate complement of bridesmaids and flower girls. A description of the various ceremonies will give a better indication of the expenses likely to be involved.

Que-que dances

The Que-que dance appears to be primarily a Berbice custom, and it is held on the night, or several successive nights, prior to the church ceremony (18). Although one does find Que-que being held in other parts of the colony, the general lack of any kind of ritual and the fact that the dances are usually just accompaniments to popular songs or 'shanties', suggests that the Berbicians' contention that it has spread outside Berbice in the last few years is probably true.

An old man living in Stanleytown, near New Amsterdam, claimed to have special knowledge of the origin of Que-que dancing. He was estimated to be about 95 years old at the time of the study, and although I was unable to interview him personally before he died, a reliable informant obtained the following information. The old man was born at a village which is just a few miles from August Town, and he claims that Que-que dancing is a 'direct' Ibo custom which was kept up even during slavery times. In those days it was reserved as a special ceremony to be performed only when an undoubted virgin girl was to be married, preferably to a young man who was also known to be virtuous (19). The biggest Que-ques were kept for the daughters of headmen or 'drivers', individuals who apparently had a great deal of authority, although slaves themselves, and commanded a good deal of respect in the slave community on the plantations. For a week before the marriage the girl had to stay inside the bedroom of her parents' house and must not be seen or go outside at all. The dance would be performed every night for a week or even two weeks before the marriage, and on the last night the ceremony known as 'buying the bride' could be attended only by the members of the two families, and no strangers should be present. This, explained the old man, was a very 'sacred' thing, and to be witnessed by the family members only. On the last night there would be feasting, but no rum-drinking. He was particularly insistent that rum-drinking has degraded the whole ceremony, and contended that in the past only pure clear rain water was drunk. The dance itself was the same kind of circle dance that survives today (which will be described presently) but it was formerly called 'Mayan' or to 'mash mayan'.

On the morning after the consummation of the marriage, the bridegroom came out of the bedroom and sang 'If you don't believe, come in come see', whereupon the members of both families would enter to inspect the blood on the sheet of the marriage bed, and present the new bride with gifts. On this day when they saw the new bride the visitors were enjoined to preserve sexual abstinence. During the first night of the marriage, guards would be posted around the house to prevent the young couple from being disturbed.

This was the only story concerning the history of Que-que dancing which it was possible to obtain and it is presented for what it is worth. Old 'Zwacky' who told the story is dead now, and it is doubtful whether there is anyone else left alive who could dispute or corroborate it.

A contemporary Que-que dance has a definite form, but it is capable of a good deal of modification in individual cases, though the idea of keeping up a celebration on the night before the wedding is still strictly adhered to by most people in August Town, and it does form an important and integral part of the whole cycle of marriage celebrations.

It has been stated previously that the ideal marriage is between two persons from the same village, and the families of both the bride and the bridegroom are expected to hold a Que-que so that there will be two households in which the celebrations are taking place. One room in the house is cleared of all furniture except a few chairs or benches around the walls and at about 10 p.m., when the company has begun to assemble, the dancing starts inside the house. A circle of people, mostly older women, but quite often including one or two middle-aged men, begin to dance around following each other in a slow stamping dance. The opening song which is always sung is as follows, and we will suppose that this is a Que-que being held in the home of a bride called 'Clarice' whose father, the head of the household, is known as 'Buddy Willie' (20).

Goo night eh, Goo night eh,
Awe come fu tell you goo night, eh.
Goo night Buddy Willie, Goo night Buddy Willie,
Awe come fu tell you goo night eh.
Six an ten dem walk a dam,
Dem a talk poor Clarice name, eh.
Goo night Buddy Willie, me come fu tell you goo night eh.

Normally one person stands in the middle of the circle and sings the words whilst the rest of the people respond with the chorus lines, which are lines one and two in the above song. The tone of the opening song quite definitely implies that the group of dancers are going to dance Que-que for the girl and her family, and the reference to the people who 'walk a dam' (meaning the paths on top of the drainage dams) talking the bride's name, is to emphasize that this group are going to defend her reputation in the singing.

It is said that in the past an endeavour would be made to hold the two Que-ques in two houses close together, so that songs could be used in a kind of battle between the two families, each side criticizing the other and boasting of its own virtues. This does not appear to be a very important aspect of the Que-que today, though there are certainly songs which defend the good name of the bride-to-be. Practically all the songs have a highly erotic content, and a Que-que is an occasion for free reference to sex, and the more scandalous the songs are the more they are enjoyed. The liberal quantities of rum which the head of the household is supposed to provide help to eliminate any restraint, and if the singers feel that they are not being given sufficient rum they can raise a song specially designed to 'shame' the host into giving them more.

Some of the songs contain words which people no longer understand, but they are still preserved in the songs. The following is an example:—

Weero, weero, weero, bambara
Na me one a weero bambara (Chorus lines)
Tek me han an a knock me Kumboro,
Bo Boy Brown dem a whorin family.
So dem seh me a whorin family
Weero, weero, weero, bambara.
Awe weero today, an awe weero tommorow
Awe weero a front side, weero a back side.

No one seems to know what 'weero bambara' means but the very words themselves evoke a spontaneous enthusiasm for the dance and they are sung with great vigour. That *Bambara* is the name of a West African tribe is a fact completely unknown in the village.

Favourite songs are those referring to the female genitalia or boasting of the sexual prowess and aggressiveness of men. One or two songs emphasize the economic value of a woman's sexual attractiveness as in the chorus line 'Its me livin gal, its me livin'. One song which is frequently sung has reference to 'nation', meaning tribal or racial group and the words are as follows:—

Nation, a weh you nation
Nation, a weh dem deh. (Chorus line)
Nation, a wha kine a nation?
Nation, a Kissi Nation.
Nation, come shout me you nation.
Nation, me go beat you nation.
Nation, a briga* nation
Nation, a Fula nation
Nation, a royal nation
Nation, come meet wid me nation.

The dancing and singing go on without break for quite long periods and then another person will take over the lead, and the dancers may have a short rest. Young childless women very rarely take part in the dancing and singing, but there are always boys and young men joining the circle and they are periodically driven out by an older man or woman.

Outside the house in the yard, there may be a local string band playing dance music for the younger people who prefer calypsoes and jive to Que-que, and there will always be groups of men sitting around talking and drinking rum. Older informants say that in the past there would be African drumming and dancing and the Cromanti, or the Congo, would have their own drumbeats and dances. This has died out completely now in August Town, but in a few villages in other parts of the country Congo dancing and drumming is still held as a pre-marriage ceremony.

At about midnight to one o'clock, a party of people from the bridegroom's Que-que house come over to the house of the bride's Que-que, and the bridegroom comes with them. They come singing and dancing into the yard, and up the steps into the house. Meanwhile the bride has been hidden, usually in the bedroom, under a sheet. The groom's party sing, 'Search am, go find am,' over and over again, dancing through the house looking for the bride.

**Briga* means fussy or particular.

Eventually they find her, and she is brought out resisting with a cloth covering her head and face. She is placed on a chair which is held aloft by a group of young men, and then 'the auction' begins. In the very few Que-ques I have seen where this little ceremony took place, there did not seem to be any special person who would act as auctioneer. The men in the room began making bids for the bride, bidding small amounts of money, cigarettes, fowls or rum. The groom always won, usually offering one bottle of rum, and the bride was then carried back into the bedroom. The groom was then seized and held up on the chair, and the family of the bride allowed to buy him. It would appear that this latter part of the ceremony is not so important, for there doesn't seem to be any fixed ritual connected with buying the groom, and I have never seen the bride's family go over to the groom's house to 'buy' him. One gets the impression that this extra bit of ceremony involving the 'buying' of the groom has been fitted in to show the equality of the claims of both families. After this ceremony the Que-que begins to break up, and if there is rum and food left, the visitors who have come a long way for the wedding next day, plus a few special friends, will be fed and go on drinking and talking. By three or four o'clock in the morning everyone will be asleep, and soon the women of the household and the bride herself will have to be up preparing for the wedding ceremonies.

We have said that the Que-que dances are held by the families of both the bride's and groom's families, but in fact what happens is that there are sometimes more than two Que-ques held, depending on the relationship between the parents of the bride or bridegroom or the persons with whom the bride or bridegroom grew up.

> John Rodney and Virginia Watson became engaged about a year ago and he has a regular job on a sugar estate. The wedding had been arranged, and then postponed in order to allow everyone involved to accumulate enough money. John is the son of Wilma Jeffries and Frank Rodney, and his father and mother had never lived together, he himself having grown with his mother. However, his father had always contributed to his support when he was small, and decided to keep a Que-que for his son's wedding. His mother also kept a Que-que in her own house. Virginia was in a similar position. Her father and mother had never lived together and Virginia herself had been reared by her maternal grandmother, having been left with her when her own mother married. In this case Que-ques were kept both by Virginia's maternal grandmother and by her father, her own mother being present at the former Que-que house.

It is quite clear that in this case, the number of Que-ques held and the persons by whom they were held was a reflection of the various kinship ties involved, and of the relations between the household heads in their own right, and all felt constrained to play a part in the marriage of the couple. This aspect of the Que-que, namely where, and by whom it is kept is of interest and importance from the point of view of kinship relations and of the claims and obligations which arise from close family ties and intra-household relations. The content of the Que-que ritual and the Que-que songs, and their meaning, is a different order of problem which cannot be dealt with at length here. When a couple who have been living together for many years get married, Que-que is still kept, but in this case it is likely that the parents of the bride and groom will be dead. In this case the couple will keep Que-que in their own house, and some of the siblings of the pair may also hold a Que-que in their house or houses. If we were to think of Que-que as being a ritual connected only with the transfer of status of the bride and groom from that of son and daughter, to that of man and wife, this would be inexplicable, but we shall see later that Que-que has other functions when viewed from a different frame of reference, and in this context it will become clear why elderly couples who have lived together for a long time should also keep up this ritual.

The wedding

Weddings are always celebrated in church, and the banns are published in the normal way on three successive Sundays preceding the wedding. The actual church ceremony receives the least amount of social emphasis and is attended only by the principal participants, (bride, bridegroom, best man, the person who is giving away the bride, the maid or matron of honour, the bridesmaids, page-boys and flower girls), plus some of the closest kin of the couple and a large number of the village women. The dresses and suits of the principal participants enumerated above must all be new and of a uniform pattern, and a great deal of money is spent on these items of dress. Shoes, stockings, gloves etc., must be bought for the occasion, and there can be no question of a simple ceremony from this point of view. The participants and the principal guests must all be conveyed to church by car even if it is only a matter of 200 yards or so. It was mentioned that the wedding ceremony is attended by a large number of women, and in fact men rarely turn up at the church to watch a wedding. That is considered to be an affair of primary interest to women, not to men. Of course males closely related to the couple will attend, and male guests who have come from other villages will also be at church, but so far as the general village public is concerned a church wedding is women's business. They go to admire the dresses, or perhaps more usually to criticize them, as women will anywhere.

After the church ceremony the wedding party, consisting of the principal participants, the close kin, and the invited guests, embark upon a tour of the houses where 'tables' have been prepared. These are usually the same houses where Que-que has been kept, but not necessarily so. Any close relative such as an aunt or uncle, brother or sister, as well as the parents may prepare a 'table'. A 'table' is nothing more than a feast at which curried fowl or meat, or chow-mein, and cake and possibly ice-cream are served. There will always be rum for the men, and probably wine and soft drinks for the women. The 'table' has to be 'opened' by speeches which are very stereotyped and stress the sanctity and indissolubility of marriage, as well as the mutual obligations of the pair. There is rarely any reference to the newly acquired sexual rights involved, as there is in England by way of salacious remarks about the forthcoming wedding-night.

The rounds of the various 'tables' and the feasting are very much a private affair restricted to members of the family and invited guests, but later in the evening a dance may be held if the families of the couple can afford it. Even if the dance is not held in the school, where anyone would feel free to attend, it may be held in a house and any villager would feel at liberty to look in on this part of the festivities.

As with the Que-que dances, we can see that where, and by whom, the 'tables' are prepared is an important index to the kinship and domestic group ties involved. In the actual church ceremony maximum emphasis is placed on the conspicuous display of lavish preparations, and the whole pattern is based upon European upper-class weddings, even to the point of sometimes wearing top hats. But it is the women in particular who are concerned with this, and all the village women will be interested in a wedding whereas men will only express a passing interest unless they themselves are directly involved in some way or another. There is no significant difference in the ceremonies described, and the attitudes of the participants, whether the wedding takes place in a Congregational, Anglican, Methodist or any other kind of church.

Marriage in its relation to the household group

Legal marriage is the only type of union officially sanctioned by the Guiana government and by the Church, and theoretically all children born outside legal marriage are illegitimate. Despite this fact we have stressed the almost complete absence of any social disabilities incurred by the illegitimate child, and we are inclined to agree with a writer describing the law of the *Bavili* of the French Congo, who says that, 'birth sanctifies the child' (21). According to village custom it is not even the legitimacy of a child's birth which determines inheritance, but rather the fact of growing up in a certain household, or having a recognized physical father. The main relevance of legal marriage is the manner in which it defines relations between spouses. In fact we can say that 'illegitimacy' in Guianese Negro villages is not a quality of the status of the child, but simply a function of the relationship between the parents. In defining relations between spouses, it is legal marriage which gives a woman legal claims to the support of her husband, and a legal claim to his property if he dies intestate. It is doubtful whether such considerations are very important in motivating persons towards getting married, rather than living in common-law unions. A woman in a common-law union may feel less secure, particularly in the early stages of the union when she is most dependent on the man, but there is no difference in the customary rights and duties of the couple towards each other whether they are married or not. The insecurity is only in terms of what would happen if the man were to turn the woman out of his house. This is largely off-set by the fact that the woman in a common-law union knows that no matter what happens the man will always be forced by the courts to maintain his children. In certain types of common-law union the man lives in the woman's house, and in these cases the position is exactly reversed. It is the man who is in a very insecure position and his insecurity as a member of the household has nothing to do with the type of conjugal union, but is a function of the authority of the woman in her own household. There are a few cases like this where the man has actually married the woman, but his position is no different.

When common-law unions which have been in existence for some time are transformed into legal unions by the couple getting married certain interesting occurrences may result. It has been remarked from other parts of the West Indies that so-called welfare workers who have arranged mass-weddings of couples living in common-law unions have often been dismayed to find that their protégés sometimes separated shortly after their weddings, despite the fact that they had previously been living together harmoniously for many years (22).

In conversations men are always pointing out that you live happily with a woman for years, but as soon as you marry her she ceases to be considerate and takes liberties which she would never have done previously. Invariably they end up by saying that, 'a good living is better than a bad marriage'. Getting married seems to upset the pattern of mutual expectations which have been worked out between common-law couples, but more particularly it tends to emphasize the independence of the woman. After marriage she is entitled to be called 'Mistress' even by her husband, and this lends weight to her authority within the home (23). There is of course absolutely no change in the social position of the man after he is married, nor is there any real change in the rights, duties and obligations involved in the relationship of the conjugal pair. It is precisely because of this that marriage is a somewhat meaningless transition looked at from the point of view of internal domestic relations. Its real significance is as an act of conformity to the 'respectable' values, but because it alters the status of the woman in the church, and in the community, it at the same time tends to disturb the equilibrium of the internal domestic relations, and the disturbance is along the path which is normally taken by changes in relations between spouses; namely towards a greater degree of independence on the part of the woman. In the majority of cases a new equilibrium is reached without a complete disruption of the relationship, but because it is a change concentrated at one point in time there is always the possibility of it causing complete disruption. It would be interesting to follow up a large number of cases where a common-law union has been transformed into a marriage, and see if there is any correlation between the size and elaborateness of the wedding, and the possibility of the subsequent separation of the couple. Throughout the West Indies one always hears of separations following the most elaborate weddings of this nature.

Marriage in its relation to the village community

Within the village a distinction is made between women who are married and those who are living in common-law unions. The former are referred to as 'Mistress' whilst the latter are not entitled to this form of address, and are usually referred to as 'Miss', or the descriptive term 'Kept Miss' is used. One also refers to 'his wife' and 'her husband', or 'his or her keeper'. In Perseverance there is much less distinction drawn, and informants will often refer to common-law couples as husband and wife, unless pressed to make a distinction. No real stigma attaches to living in a common-law union as opposed to being married, but marriage confers a different status on the woman. It is very important to be clear on the fact that it is the status of the woman and not of the man which is involved here. It is the woman who acquires a wedding ring and the right to be called 'Mistress', not the man, and since there are no sanctions against living in a common-law union which would be a social handicap to the man there is no difference in his social status in one type of union or the other. As soon as we shift our attention from the ordinary villager to the school-teachers, and then to the Guianese middle-class, there is a very marked difference in the way the male partner to a marriage is regarded. For this group very strong sanctions operate against their entering common-law unions at all, and in the case of a school-teacher, to live with a woman without marrying her would be impossible unless the man gave up his post. Of course this does not preclude teachers from having concubines whom they visit regularly and who may be wholly maintained by them. Since most teachers tend to marry young, these are often extra-marital affairs. Cases have also been known of school-girls becoming pregnant by one of their teachers, and there is provision in the regulations of the Education Department for the dismissal of the teacher in such a case, provided a complaint is made, and the facts established after due inquiry.

Outside the school-teacher/government-employee group in the villages no such sanctions operate, and the occurrence of common-law marriage is not confined to any special group. Wealth in itself is not a determining factor, for one finds cases where the wealthiest villagers may be living in a common-law union. Once the system has social tolerance within a given group it is accepted as normal for that group. In this case the group is what we might term the 'lower-class'. Within the village the question of choice between marriage and common-law marriage is entirely a matter for the couple involved, except in the case of young childless women, when the views of the woman's kin, and to some extent of public opinion generally, will have considerable influence. Marriage is thought of as a 'respectable' institution, and as a middle and upper-class pattern. It is upheld by the church which is one of the most powerful vehicles of middle and upper-class morality, but the church usually presents its views in the form of a condemnation of the lower-class pattern. Because it is a middle and upper-class pattern it is sometimes regarded as being wrong for the lower-class by villagers themselves. Even married persons will often say 'marriage is not for awe black people.' Thus common-law marriage becomes a symbol of class differentiation, and is in a sense legitimatized within that group, taking 'legitimate' in this context to be an expression of normal or expected behaviour.

At the same time the village is integrated into the larger society and shares part of the common value system, and marriage before the law, and before the church, is an important part of that value system. These values have to be reinforced even within the lower-class village group. In August Town there is a very interesting custom which merits mention here.

A small group of people, comprising several families related by blood, are referred to as *Nyame*. *Nyame* is the Ashanti word for Sky-God, but in August Town this meaning of the word is quite unknown (24). *Nyame* in August Town are reputedly characterized by the fact they have small heads, poor taste in dress, cease sexual activity at a relatively early age, and by the fact that their girls marry as virgins, or are supposed to. This is the stereotyped explanation of *Nyame* characteristics. When a young *Nyame* man marries he will try to find a virgin girl, ideally. On the morning after the wedding night the family of the groom led by his mother go to the bridal chamber and inspect the sheet for signs of blood. If it is found there is rejoicing, and a song is sung; 'If you think I lie—come in come see.' The boy's mother makes a presentation to the bride, usually of a gold chain or some such piece of jewellery. If there are no signs of blood, there may be quite a row, and the present is not given. The derivation of this custom would be difficult to assess, since it is a common practice of Mohammedan tribes in Africa, but is also reminiscent of old Dutch customs. In any case it seems clear that within the village context this small group has become 'specialized' in maintaining the force of the value of marriage and pre-marital chastity. The fact that the majority of villagers regard this custom as being 'nasty' or 'common', and even look down on *Nyame* as a 'low nation', does not alter the fact. On the occasion when a *Nyame* ceremony of this kind was witnessed, the kin of the bride who were present at the house the morning when the sheet was inspected, began shouting, '*Nyame* for ever', to which a number of bystanders began to reply 'Big Driver people for ever'—Big Driver being the semi-mythical ancestor of the largest tribal group in the village, who refer to themselves as 'mixed Ibo and Cromanti'.

Marriage in relation to the wider society

We have already stated that common-law marriage is exclusively a lower-class custom within the whole community of British Guiana, and it is from this point of view that it becomes most explicable. The question of being able to afford, or not being able to afford, to get married is a false dichotomy when the whole complex of social facts is taken into consideration. Such considerations may operate at a certain empirical level, but the matter can be viewed in much the same way that Durkheim treated suicide (25). His argument was that the significance of suicide as a social fact will be obscured if an attempt is made to understand it only by reference to the particular precipitating circumstances in each case. The same argument applies in this case and common-law marriage is a social fact of the same kind. Particular reasons for choosing common-law as against legal marriage are important at certain levels of analysis, but in its total social context common-law marriage is a feature of the total social system. It is confined to the lower-class and is part of the lower-class cultural tradition, and its function is not clear merely at the level of village organization. Simple explanations in terms of economic causation will not suffice because they are not borne out by the field material. Whilst it is true that there is a primary correlation between wealth differences and the colour/class system, this is in many ways a derivative rather than a causal relationship, and within the lower-class itself wealth is only a partial determinant of the type of union entered into.

Factors influencing selection of a conjugal partner

The range of kinship ties within which marriage, or sexual relations, are considered to be incestuous is ill-defined. I never heard the word 'incest' used, nor any other word which would have approximately the same meaning. Instead persons would refer to any suspected or imagined sexual relations between close kin as 'nasty' or 'common' or 'low'. No distinction was made between incest proper and adultery with the spouse of a kinsman, and both would be referred to in the same way. We have already spoken of the categories of kin that are regarded as being too close to marry or have sexual relations and we may take it as a rough guide that the range of prohibition extends as far as second cousins. Whilst there is this circle of kinsfolk between whom inter-marriage is, at the least, frowned upon, the preferred marriage or common-law marriage is within the village. In tables XVI and XVII samples of extant

TABLE XVI

COMPARISON OF NUMBERS OF ENDOGAMOUS AND EXOGAMOUS UNIONS

TYPE OF UNION	AUGUST TOWN	PERSE-VERANCE	BETTER HOPE
1. *a.* Legal marriages contracted between villagers	93	47	14
b. Common-law marriages contracted between villagers	13	27	3
Total No. endogamous unions.. ..	106	74	17
2. *a.* Legal marriages where man is from outside the village	13	9	11
b. Common-law marriages where man is from outside the village	9	1	1
3. *a.* Legal marriages where woman is from outside the village	13	9	9
b. Common-law marriages where woman is from outside the village	4	4	3
Total No. exogamous unions ..	39	23	24
4. *a.* Legal marriages where both partners are from outside the village	7	2	6
b. Common-law marriages where both partners are from outside the village ..	1	1	2
Total No. of unions in samples ..	153	100	49

unions between persons actually living in the villages at the time of the study are analysed. A distinction is made between persons who 'belong' to the village, by virtue of having been born there, or of having lived there since childhood, and persons who are from 'outside'. The latter have usually established a home in the village by virtue of their marriage or, of course, the marriage itself may have been a means of their becoming integrated into the community. Where we speak of persons being from outside, but from same area, we mean that they are from another community on the Essequibo Coast, the West Coast of Berbice or the West Coast of Demerara. In the case of Better Hope, Georgetown was included in the 'same district' as well as the communities on the West Coast of Demerara.

TABLE XVII

EXOGAMOUS UNIONS WHERE PARTNER IS FROM THE SAME DISTRICT

TYPE OF UNION	AUGUST TOWN	PERSE-VERANCE	BETTER HOPE
1. *a.* Legal marriages where man is from outside the village but from the same district	2	6	7
b. Common-law marriages where man is from outside the village but from the same district	3	1	0
2. *a.* Legal marriages where woman is from outside the village but from the same district	9	9	6
b. Common-law marriages where woman is from outside the village but from the same district	2	3	2
Totals	16	19	15

Before we discuss these tables one point must be made clear. The tables show a large preponderance of legal marriages over common-law marriages, but it must be remembered that a common-law marriage does not exist according to our definition unless the couple actually live together. A marriage exists when the couple are legally married, and not 'separated', so that where a woman lives with her parents and her husband is working away, she is still counted as being married. Where a woman lives with her parents and has several children for a man with whom she has never lived, she is not in a common-law union, though she may have a quite definite semi-conjugal relationship with the man. Since we are not comparing the incidence of legal and common-law unions here, we need not concern ourselves with this problem, though it should be noted that the figures in the tables would need weighting for such a comparison.

The significant fact to be derived from these tables is that practice conforms reasonably closely to the stated ideal that one should endeavour to marry a person from the same village as oneself. In Better Hope the greater number of exogamic unions is in keeping with the greater degree of status and occupational differentiation as well as with the fact that there is less local solidarity than in the other two villages. Better Hope is less 'isolated' as a social group, and consequently its inhabitants have a wider range of regular social contacts with persons living in the surrounding district.

As a very rough device for confirming the fact that persons do tend to enter conjugal unions with fellow villagers more frequently than with 'outsiders', we may look at the tables in terms of the choice made by the partners to the unions. Each person in the samples of unions has had to make a choice as to whether they will enter a union with a fellow villager or with an outsider. Since we are looking at the matter from the point of view of the persons from the villages we are studying, we can ignore the choice made by the 'outsiders' involved in the union.

In the categories 1 (*a*) and 1 (*b*) of Table XVI both partners to each union are villagers and therefore each one has chosen to enter a union with a fellow villager. Therefore we have to double the numbers of unions to arrive at the number of choices made. For the exogamous unions only one partner to the union is a villager, and therefore the numbers of unions represent the numbers of choices made by villagers to enter a union with an 'outsider'. Such a procedure does not give an accurate indication of the regularity of choices for the three villages, for obviously there are no data on the persons who enter unions and go to live outside the village. We can allow for this in a very approximate way by doubling the number of choices to marry an 'outsider' which are represented in the samples. This would presume that for every 'outsider' who comes to live in the village in a conjugal union with a villager, there is a villager who has gone to live with a partner outside the village. There is no indication that permanent emigration from the villages is greater than immigration to them, over a long time-span, though this may be less true for Better Hope.

A comparison of the figures obtained after carrying out the foregoing adjustments is presented below in Table XVIII. We must emphasize that this is merely a rough guide, and not an accurate statistical computation for which more detailed information regarding movements out of the villages would be necessary.

TABLE XVIII

SELECTION OF A CONJUGAL PARTNER

VILLAGE	NO. OF PERSONS CHOOSING A FELLOW VILLAGER		NO. OF PERSONS CHOOSING AN OUTSIDER	
	No.	%	*No.*	%
August Town	212	73	78	27
Perseverance	148	76	46	24
Better Hope	34	42	48	58

From Table XVI it can be seen that men do not enter unions with outsiders any more frequently than do women, at least, not to any significant extent. Table XVII shows that in the unions with 'outsiders' the person is frequently from the same district.

Selection of a conjugal partner may be thought of as being correlated with status factors. In the first place the vast majority of unions are endogamous to the Negro group, except in the middle-class, where choice of a lighter coloured partner becomes a means of assisting upward mobility. In Perseverance and August Town there is both a cultural and a status differentiation setting off the main village group against other groups in the total social system, and militating against an exchange of marriage partners. Since hierarchical mobility is extremely restricted and property considerations relatively unimportant, there is no preoccupation with weighing either of these factors when choosing a conjugal partner. The choice of a person who is both well known and has a similar background is then quite logical.

Exchange of marriage partners between similar villages which are undifferentiated as regards rank might take on some importance as one method of integrating such villages into a wider system. In British Guiana, kinship ties of this kind would be relatively unimportant in a political sense since the framework of political control is maintained in other ways. Choice of a conjugal partner can be restricted to the local group because there is neither a functional necessity, nor any particular incentive, for it to be otherwise.

Village endogamy results in a proliferation of intra-village kinship ties which actually militate against internal status differentiation between families, and it thus contributes to the solidarity of the group and its unitary character in the total social system. In Better Hope the trend is towards a weakening of local solidarity and a participation in a more extensive system with its own internal rank system and a wider range of occupational specialization, and this is reflected in the wider range of choice of conjugal partners, though even here there is very little marriage across the main colour and class lines.

The emphasis which is placed upon the desirability of marrying within the village is explicable if it is seen in relation to the total social structure of the colony and the place of the lower-class Negro group within it. For a person born in one of our villages, the village represents one of his main points of social reference; it is the place to which he 'belongs', and in which he feels secure. Since the majority of villagers are not concerned with improving their social status through marriage they do not seek a partner who could help them improve that status. If they enter a union with someone from another part of the colony they will perforce have to form new and difficult relationships with strange persons, an experience which can be avoided by marrying someone whose family and background they know already. If one marries a fellow villager then one can also be in close contact with one's own family of orientation and especially one's mother.

CONCLUSION

In this chapter we have dealt with the system of kinship and marriage (both legal and common-law), and we have tried to show how relations of kinship and affinity are related to other aspects of the social system. The importance of matri-filiation has been shown to manifest itself in the whole complex of kinship ties, and the unit of mother and children has been fixed in its proper structural position.

The importance of viewing kinship relations, local relations, marriage and common-law marriage as part of a total complex within the wider social structure of the whole colony is apparent and we shall develop this theme further in Section III.

SECTION III

CHAPTER VIII

THE FAMILY SYSTEM IN THE CONTEXT OF GUIANESE SOCIETY

IN the remaining section of this study we shall attempt to place the family system in a much wider setting and try to show its relation to certain factors which are not at all apparent if we restrict our field of vision to the village alone. To this end we shall be particularly concerned with examining the position of the village in the total system of social stratification in the colony. It is beyond the scope of this study to enter into a detailed discussion of the sociology of the whole of Guianese society, but from a methodological point of view it is unprofitable to attempt to isolate the village from the rest of the society. The principal reason for this is that the village as such does not form anything like a self-contained system, and the family system must be viewed in its relations to other structures which are not clearly discernible within the village context. We are fortunate in being able to draw upon a recent study of social stratification in Trinidad which gives us considerable insight into the general features of the Guianese system, since the two colonies are very similar in many respects, and we shall supplement this with our own observations (1).

THE COLOUR/CLASS SYSTEM

The population of British Guiana consists of at least five ethnic groups which are popularly supposed to be capable of distinction on the basis of physical appearance and which are ultimately referable to a 'national' homeland. African Negroes, East Indians, Amerindians, Chinese and Europeans are regarded as distinct races. There are also several other recognized ethnic groups such as the Portuguese, and various kinds of 'mixed' types, generally referred to as 'Coloured' in some contexts, but capable of more precise description in others. Without doing too much violence to the facts, we may speak of seven main ethnically defined segments of the population; Europeans, Negroes, East Indians, Amerindians, Chinese, Portuguese, and Coloured. It must be borne in mind that 'Coloured' is a term employed for a variety of purposes, and from an ethnic point of view it is merely a residual category. There are also a few Syrians in the colony, but they are a very minor group and can be ignored.

The 1946 census of British Guiana gives the numbers and proportions of the main ethnic groups as follows:

TABLE XIX

PROPORTION OF VARIOUS RACES IN BRITISH GUIANA

ETHNIC GROUP	NUMBER	%
East Indian	163,434	43.51
African	143,385	38.17
Mixed	37,685	10.03
Amerindian	16,322	4.35
Portuguese	8,543	2.27
Chinese	3,567	0.95
European (not Portuguese)	2,480	0.66
Asiatic (mainly Syrian)	236	0.06
Not stated	49	—
Totals	375,701	100.00

The category 'mixed' includes all inter-mixtures of African and European and African and Asiatic races. The census report makes the very interesting observation that although the 'mixed' group should theoretically increase more rapidly than any other, in practice it does not, but tends to remain a fairly stable proportion of the total population. This would be explicable if one were to regard ethnic group affiliation as being predominantly a socially rather than a biologically defined phenomenon, for then we would expect an imprecisely defined group such as this to remain fairly constant since it also happens to be both a higher status group, and to some extent a functionally specialized group as well (2).

For the purposes of the following discussion of the colour/class system it is most convenient to leave out of account the East Indian, Chinese, Amerindian and Portuguese segments for the time being and they will only be referred to for specific comment.

a. Cooking arrangements. A typical "fireside"

b. Boys carrying food to the rice fields during the harvest season. They are walking up the main "middle-walk" dam

PLATE V

a. The village office. This is by no means typical for in the majority of villages they are more spacious than this

b. Cleaning the main drainage trench. The sluice gate or "koker" can be seen in the background

The whole system of social stratification in British Guiana, and indeed in the greater part of the British West Indies, is organized around the inter-play of two main status-determining factors. On the one hand inherited biological characteristics, and in particular skin colour, hair formation and facial structure, are taken as criteria for the evaluation of social status, and where a combination of the three characteristics approaches a 'European' configuration (white skin, straight or softly waving hair, straight nose, thin lips, etc.) it is given positive or high evaluation; where the combination approaches a 'Negro' configuration (black skin, hard curly hair, flat nose, thick lips, etc.) it is given a negative or low evaluation. This, of course, is placing emphasis on status ascription, and birth comes to be the point at which status is acquired along this axis of the value system (3). On the other hand occupational differentiation is closely correlated with status differentiation and where there is mobility through various ranked jobs in the occupational sphere there is a certain amount of mobility within the system of social stratification. Parsons has pointed out that the functional prerequisites of a system of instrumental activities involve a differential distribution of facilities and responsibilities, and this is invariably accompanied by a differential distribution of rewards, and hence some system of social stratification (4). This means in effect, that for any social system to 'work' there has to be some sort of leadership or managerial functions allotted to certain individuals, and these individuals will therefore have to be given greater privileges, or wealth, or esteem. This distribution of functions and rewards gives rise to some system of ranking in every society. However, the system of differential distribution of rewards can be organized around various types of value orientation, but as soon as an ethnic differentiation is introduced into the system there seems to be a tendency for this line of differentiation to align itself with others. Certainly, in the West Indies, ethnic and class distinctions do not coincide, but they are very closely correlated. It is at the extremes of the range of ethnic variation that the ascriptive criteria of status are most marked and the least equivocal. Thus discussions of the West Indian colour/class system tend to concentrate upon the middle of the range, where 'whiteness' and 'blackness' become mixed both biologically and socially. There is a very real sense in which the 'coloured' or racially mixed section of the population is the 'middle-class', *vis-a-vis* either the white or the black groups which are the 'upper' and 'lower' classes respectively. This is the simplest and most rudimentary way of looking at the colour/class system, and it is not difficult to see how such a system had its genesis in a slave society where miscegenation created a biologically and socially intermediate group. One factor is of some importance here, and that is, that whereas both the 'black' and the 'white' groups display and feel a certain sense of solidarity, the intermediate coloured group does not. It is in this intermediate group that the evaluation of 'whiteness' and 'blackness' takes on most significance and where there is the greatest anxiety over status placement, as well as the greatest factionalism and clique differentiation. When Henriques talks of a white bias in Jamaican society one supposes that he is thinking particularly of the middle-class emphasis upon an attempt to identifiy with the values of the upper-class, and upper-class culture (5).

The model of a simple three-class structure correlated with a division of the population into three ethnic groups—black, white and coloured—is clearly unrealistic from an empirical point of view, there being many highly visible cases of individuals who do not 'fit'. Guianese themselves vary in their description of the stratification system depending on the context in which they are speaking. At one time they will assert that there is this differentiation into three layers based on indices of colour, and at another time they will point to certain individual Negroes who are high in the status scale as evidence of the fact that there is no exclusive racial criteria of class placement. In other words if we were to look at the situation within the actor frame of reference as Leach does in his study of Kachin social structure we could build two 'ideal models' and assert that 'reality' lies somewhere in between (6). On the one hand we have the model of a three-class hierarchy based on colour, and on the other we have the model of a class system based upon achieved status. In any specific situation for **the middle-class**, we should probably find that status was defined by a combination of ascribed and achieved characteristics. It would not be profitable to push the analysis too far along these lines, for the method denies the validity of establishing objective criteria of class differentiation, and it is our contention that there is an internal differentiation of Guianese society which is of great functional significance and which can only be expressed adequately in terms of an objective analysis. This is not to deny the utility of Leach's method, nor to imply that there is a rigidity in the 'real' situation which corresponds with the abstractions we use to describe the forces which are at work in that situation.

From the actor's point of view there are two polar values of status distinction which we may term 'whiteness' and 'blackness', and the evaluations of these polarities are shared to some extent by all Guianese. This is a conceptualization of status differentiation which cuts across the whole of Guianese society, and no matter how concerned we are in depicting the 'actual' situation, it is necessary to isolate this shared value for analytical purposes. This is what Braithwaite refers to as the 'ascriptive base' of Trinidadian society, but in attempting to demonstrate the objective division of Trinidad society into three classes and show precisely how this is correlated with ethnic divisions, he neglects the implications of the 'black'-'white' polarity, and of the inevitable and even necessary ambiguity inhering in the 'actual' situation (7).

Hierarchical ranking at all levels of Guianese society is **to some extent** in terms of the black-white dichotomy. At the extreme ends of the scale there is a consolidation around the polar definitions so that it is possible to refer to the 'white group' and to the 'Negro group'. Both groups are aware of their identity as differentiated elements in Guianese society, and both are sharply separated off from each other, and from the 'coloured middle-class'. We must stress at this point, the fact that the concepts, 'black' and 'white' are social concepts and correspond not to biological phenomena but to social facts. Blackness and whiteness are symbolized by different cultural complexes, of which we would rate language, marriage customs and dress as the most important elements. This means that there can be a disparity between an individual's physical characteristics and his class affiliation, and the possibility of acquiring culture means that there is the possibility of limited mobility within the system. However, mobility is also dependent upon movement in the occupational sphere, and this means that there is another important correlate of cultural differentiation.

Since the white group is the apex of the social pyramid and extremely close to the cluster of positively evaluated elements (many of which really lie outside the colony in the metropolitan centre, as Braithwaite has pointed out) it forms the most isolated and internally solidary sub-group. Numerically small, and culturally homogeneous (at least within the colony, although its members may come from widely differing backgrounds, and of course it has its own system of distinctions largely referable to the class system of Britain) its members participate almost solely at the executive, managerial and administrative levels of the occupational structure. There is virtually no inter-marriage with other groups and it preserves its social distinction *vis-a-vis* the rest of the population by means of an intricate, and usually covert mythology of racial purity and superiority. But it is equally true that the black group retains a good deal of social solidarity, not so much as a large cohesive group extending all over the colony as in small territorial clusters, such as our three villages. Once again this solidarity is maintained by an elaborate mythology, this time of inferiority. In both cases there is emphasis placed on conformity to the standards of the group and this is the crucial element from our point of view.

We may summarize the above rather discursive and inadequate discussion by saying that there is a shared scale of colour-values couched in terms of a polar distinction of black and white, and that it is around the polar distinctions that real social classes crystallize. These social classes form functionally differentiated groups within the total social system, and they each have a distinct sub-culture, whilst sharing common cultural elements corresponding to their unity as a total social system. We shall not attempt to analyse the position of the middle-class since it does not directly concern us here, but we would be very sceptical of representing this entity as a cohesive social group in the same way as we would represent the white and black. Nor would we stress the existence of a pan-Guiana black group, but would rather tend to see the situation in terms of a series of local communities each with its own internal solidarity as a separate group. These communities may themselves be culturally differentiated one from another and in the urban areas the number of sub-groups may be very great indeed. What enables us to visualize the socially black group as a group, is the fact that it is functionally and culturally differentiated in the total social system; a fact which is clearly visible in the economic occupational system.

We may now turn to an examination of this internal functional differentiation of the total system, and this requires at least a cursory examination of the economic reference points of the system. There can be no doubt that the economy of the coastlands is organized around the plantation cultivation of sugar and it is this sector of the economy which has had the longest historical continuity. Bauxite mining and rice cultivation have developed as the other main sectors. Imports of manufactured consumer goods, and food, are balanced against exports of sugar, bauxite and rice, and these economic exchanges across the boundary of the system are essential to the maintenance of internal economic balance, and result in it being extremely sensitive to fluctuation in world markets. The proper functioning of the economy depends upon its internal organization as well as on its external exchanges, and administrative control and responsibility is, in the main, concentrated in the hands of the 'European' group. This is most obviously true in the case of the sugar industry which generally recruits its managerial class from Britain. The bauxite industry is controlled by American and Canadian interests, and its higher administrative, executive, and technical staff is recruited outside the colony. The rice industry is less obviously controlled by Europeans but its main marketing organization is sponsored by the government and the large development schemes for the industry are to be carried out under the *aegis* of a Development Corporation financed to a large extent by British capital and administered by a high-level staff of upper-class executives. The director of this Corporation is a light coloured Guianese of exceptional ability who is almost completely identified with the white group, despite being technically a coloured Guianese. Negroes provide a good deal of the labour for the bauxite industry, and for the sugar estates, particularly during the cane-cutting season, and they also produce a certain amount of rice on a small scale, which is fed into the rice industry. At the bauxite mines they are employed principally in the lower grades as unskilled, semi-skilled and skilled workers, but there is undoubtedly a wider range of possibility of rising in the occupational scale in this industry, because of the greater job differentiation in a highly mechanized enterprise. In the sugar industry the bulk of Negro workers are field labourers, but there are a few highly skilled technical jobs, such as that of sugar-boiler, in which the Negroes have a virtual monopoly. In the rice industry it is broadly true to say that Negroes only come into the picture as small-scale growers, and they have not participated in the increasing mechanization of cultivation, nor do they own or operate mills or large plantations. It is the East Indians who are the most forceful element and who use the industry as a means of accumulating wealth, and establishing higher status for themselves within their own community.

Apart from these three industries where the Negro's rôle is that of a relatively low status wage-earner, there is a whole range of business organization concerned with the import/export trade, internal distribution of consumer goods, banking, insurance, etc., where Negro participation is practically non-existent. In the higher levels of this organization, European dominance is evident since most of the big firms and the banks are controlled by British, Canadian or American companies. However, there are many businesses owned and controlled by Portuguese, Chinese and Indians, and in the country districts the retail businesses are almost exclusively run by members of these three groups.

The complex system of marketing and exchange whereby farm produce of one kind and another is distributed, requires no over-all organization or differentiation of occupational rôles. Amongst Negroes it is almost exclusively women who participate in the marketing process, and some women are extremely industrious as 'hucksters', or agents, working between the grower and the seller. However, this function is as often fulfilled by East Indians as it is by Negro women.

In our grossly over-simplified picture of the economic reference points of the system, positions of effective over-all control tend to be occupied by the members of the highest status group, whilst the middle range of functions such as office jobs in businesses concerned with administering the economy, are filled by Coloured persons, Chinese and Portuguese. Chinese, Portuguese and Indians operate independent businesses which are not involved in large-scale control activities and which can be run with a minimum of internal organization. Negroes only come into the picture at the lowest level where they work as wage labourers, selling their labour where and when they can, and being wholly unconcerned with the accumulation and control of capital. (Apart from village land and houses.)

It is in the field of the professions, and in the bureaucracy that Negroes come to occupy high status positions. In professions such as medicine, law, teaching, and nursing there is a tendency for Negroes and Coloured persons to predominate, but in law and medicine one finds representatives of all the racial groups. (Except Amerindians of course.) Law and medicine are both professional occupations with peculiar characteristics. To begin with they require a long period of education which usually involves a close contact with the culture of the European group and hence they carry high prestige on that account as well as on account of their intrinsic nature as personal services. Also, they are not occupations in an organization with a hierarchy of control, and there is therefore no conflict involved. It is interesting to note that where an organization does exist, as in the case of the Public Hospital, then top executive control is generally vested in the hands of a European or a very light coloured doctor.

In the bureaucratic machine of the Colonial Government it is quite clear that the open policy of recruitment and promotion on the basis of merit can only work properly when there is some uniformity in the motivations of employees, regardless of race. The fact is that the majority of the top-ranking posts are filled by Englishmen, or by white Guianese, or light coloured persons, and this fact cannot be wholly attributed to the Machiavellian designs of the European group who are plotting to exclude any non-European from any position of power. It is quite clearly one of the major functions of the bureaucracy to safeguard the integration and stability of the social system. It has therefore to assign positions of control and power to those who are prepared to do this. But it is equally true to say that it is extremely difficult for a person who has many of the physical characteristics of the group most lowly evaluated on the colour scale to assume such a position of control. It must be borne in mind that the scale of colour values is shared by all the groups comprising Guianese society, whether they consciously and logically subscribe to it or not. This means that the Negro official is positively denigrated by his own race, and one of the most frequently heard remarks amongst Negro villagers is to the effect that it will be a bad day for British Guiana is ever the colony is 'ruled' by a Negro Governor. Under these circumstances it is not difficult to see why the majority of upwardly mobile Negro civil servants, or politicians for that matter, should be either negatively motivated to aspiring to the highest controlling positions, or aspire only under the impetus of an emotional opposition to the European group. During the recent short period when the People's Progressive Party held power it was striking that the leaders sought to retain their identity with the 'masses' by pursuing a vigorous campaign of opposition to the European group. The whole function of the bureaucracy was transformed from one of system integration, to one of open conflict, and the swift action taken against an alleged 'communist' plot was one way of preserving the bureaucracy from a threatened disorganization, and restoring the values on which stability and integration rest. The very fact that 'reform' came to be couched in terms of a vigorous denial of the legitimacy of the position of the Europeans is an indication that colour values predominated, and that this was merely an inverted application of them. The problem is much more complex than this of course, for the leaders of the P.P.P. were seeking a legitimatization of their position on completely different grounds to that of the existing authority system and in this sense the whole movement was a truly revolutionary one. Of course this is only one aspect of the complex of factors involved in any self-government movements in British Guiana, and we have not even attempted to analyse the full working of the political system or its historical background. Our object at the moment is merely to discuss the way in which functional differentiation of the social system is related to the system of social stratification, and we had got as far as saying that the conflicts involved in acceptance of the colour/class hierarchy, combined with the acceptance of a degree of upward mobility for the members of the Negro group, tends to be resolved by such members accepting statuses which are highly valued but do not involve participation in high-level control of either the economy or the bureaucracy. This is of course not true of all Negroes and there are many cases of persons who are able to adjust to the situation and who successfully hold positions of responsibility in the government.

The church as a social organization has never seriously laid claim to any real political control, and religion has tended to be organized upon sectarian lines with no dominant organization. The Anglican Church is the 'official church' but it has no monopoly of control or of state support. On the whole the churches have never come into serious conflict with the government (apart from one or two minor episodes prior to 1836), and they have resolved any conflict between christian doctrine and social practice by projecting the Kingdom of Heaven into the future (8). There is some contrast with the position of the Roman Catholic church in some Latin American countries where the church seems to act as the focus of stable political structure, thus enabling rapid changes of government to take place without fatally disrupting the over-all system of political control.

If our rough analysis of the correspondence between the system of social stratification and the functional differentiation of the system is correct, it follows that the Negroes, considered as a group, occupy low status, and that where mobility is possible it tends to be channelled in very definite directions which are away from control functions and towards a concentration on the maintenance of the ascriptively based hierarchical system. Paradoxical as this may seem there is a sense in which every Negro who has achieved high social status, is taken to be the exception that proves the rule. Upwardly mobile Negroes tend to validate their new status by ensuring that their children will fit the position by ascriptive criteria, and this is possible by seeking a lighter coloured spouse.

Portuguese, Chinese and East Indians all came to British Guiana after the foundations of the colour-class system had been laid, and all are in a sense marginal to it. Originally brought in to replace the Negroes as estate labourers, the Portuguese and Chinese were able to take over economic functions particularly in the field of distribution, which, if entered by Negroes, would have necessitated a reorganization of the social structure to allow for a differentiation of the Negro group on the basis of some individuals having control over comparatively large economic resources. Although the East Indians were always regarded as the lowest status group in the whole community, they never fitted completely into the ascriptive status hierarchy based on colour. Owing to the fact that they could maintain a certain degree of social separation, and at the same time retain a system of stratification within their own group, they have tended to be assimilated into the total social system at all levels of differentiation, with the possible exception of the top control positions. Whilst the majority of Indians are still estate labourers, there is a significant minority who are assuming control of land, business enterprises, and political organizations. For the purposes of this study we need only treat the fact that they appear at all levels of the social hierarchy, and that their fluidity in relation to the colour scale has on the whole enabled them to stress achievement criteria more than the Negroes have been able to do.

We must finally say a word about the differential ranking of local communities. Our study is not concerned with an analysis of the urban centres, but there is clearly a difference between a highly differentiated urban centre and a small rural community. In the urban centre all levels of the hierarchical ranking are represented, and territorial contiguity coupled with more intensive social interaction means that the cultural norms of all groups represented within the city tend to converge to some extent. Although relative positions in the status hierarchy may be maintained there is a greater range of occupations open even within the Negro type occupational band, and there is therefore a larger proportion of Negroes who approximate to middle-class cultural standards. At the same time the city produces its own extremely low status groups concentrated in localized communities where different sub-cultures tend to develop. There is also a very noticeable tendency for the difficulty involved in keeping the various sub-groups isolated to result in the development of a system of sanctions against 'deviance'. What is often referred to as 'anomie' or anomic tendencies, begins to appear when the sub-groups with their subcultures are drawn together in an urban situation. Juvenile delinquency, crime and drunkenness appear, and mechanisms of social control relative to the primary social system are brought into play. Each sub-group retains its own mechanisms of social control which are extra-legal in terms of the institutionalized control system of police, courts etc. Thus obeah continues to flourish in the city, and in the upper-class group social sanctions peculiar to itself are prevalent. The repatriation of persons who do not conform to the standards of the European group is one of the most obvious.

Outside the urban areas there is some ranking of the rural communities, but it would be extremely difficult to draw up a scale of relative positions such as that given by Braithwaite for Trinidad (9). So much depends on the reference point from which the scale is drawn, and it is doubtful whether there would be over-all agreement on such ranking in British Guiana. The ethnic, class and cultural characteristics of a rural community determine its rank order in accordance with the general value system. The nearer the community is to Georgetown or a large sugar estate, the more likely it is to have a diverse ethnic and class structure and the less culturally differentiated it is likely to be from other communities in the same area. This is a very loose statement and cannot be taken to imply any scale such as that posited by Redfield for Yucatan (10).

It is within this framework of the colour/class system that we have to view the internal differentiation of the villages, and it would seem that the most important features to bear in mind are the countervailing tendencies of the values which stress status placement on the basis of achieved criteria and those which stress ascribed status on the basis of 'race' or biological characteristics. These are not the only values involved for there are such differential factors as whether an individual is town or country born, but they are the paramount ones.

The argument we have presented so far can be further elucidated by reference to Durkheim's distinction between 'organic' and 'mechanical' solidarity (11). In the case of British Guiana we could take it that we have a state of affairs where both organic and mechanical solidarity co-exist. The hereditary factors of 'race' are used as a basis for ascribing functions within the social system, but at the same time there is quite clearly a sense in which this process can no longer operate adequately and specialization of function has to break away from the hereditary base, and competence in performing the functions must be taken into account. Historically, the segments which go to make up the total population of the colony were brought together almost solely on the basis of their respective functions in the economy; the economy of plantation cultivation. As this economy breaks down or becomes more diversified, the number of functions increases, and although there is the tendency for special ethnic groups to appropriate special functions, such as the Portuguese domination of the retail trade, so long as the social system continues to become more differentiated and evidences an increasing division of labour, so the ethnic basis of specialization begins to disappear.

It is clear from the evidence presented here that the process of specialization of functions has not become completely divorced from an hereditary ethnic basis by any means, and one of the most noticeable features of our village populations is their relative uniformity of function in the occupational system of the total social system. This is a matter of degree of course, and we must now take up the question of just how much, and in what way, the village populations are themselves differentiated internally.

THE LOCAL COMMUNITY AND INTERNAL DIFFERENTIATION

All three villages, August Town, Perseverance and Better Hope constitute well defined local communities with a very definite sense of unity and distinction from other communities, which is partly related to their distinction as territorial entities, but is much more far-reaching than this. In discussing the stratification of the total social system we pointed out that apart from the criteria of ethnic ascription and occupational achievement, other value judgements enter into the picture, such as place of residence and the distinction between rural and urban dwellers, and all these factors combine to place the majority of our village inhabitants at the very bottom of the status scale. However, this is a macroscopic view, and we shall now examine each village more closely, using our general description of the over-all system as a back-cloth against which to place all the various elements. We shall deal with August Town first, and in greatest detail.

August Town

August Town expresses its corporate identity in two forms which we take to be of the greatest significance. It regards itself as a 'black people's village' and as being 'all one family'.

Neither of these statements is literally true, but they are both made frequently, without any reservations whatsoever. There is no other recognized symbol of village unity, with the possible exception of the village council, but this latter is much more a poorly developed political institution than a cultural symbol which is meaningful to all the villagers. The church and the school are both village institutions (the Congregational church and school particularly), but membership is divided between two churches and two schools, and we find no development either in church offices or in local saints or deities that would lead us to regard these bodies as symbols of local solidarity. It is precisely because the churches only function as associational groupings within the social system of the local community that it is possible for there to be no development of them as symbols of local solidarity, and we shall see that they are much more related in a symbolic way to social units wider than the village group. Occasional inter-village cricket matches are played by the schools against other schools on the coast, and there is an annual schools sports day on which August Town schools compete against all the other schools on the coast, but as two separate schools and not as a village team. In the Congregational church there are occasional 'rallies of the tribes', when each church of the Congregational body competes with the others to see how much money they can raise for their own particular church (12). There is a little ceremony in which each church team brings up its total collection to the platform and the amount is announced. The church with the largest collection is the 'winner'. These expressions of inter-village rivalry are much more concerned with rivalry between special interest groups from each village.

The village council is poorly developed as a representative institution, and one could not regard it as a symbol of village unity except in a very rudimentary way. It meets to review rate collection and discuss matters almost solely concerned with drainage and irrigation, the protection of village lands from stray animals, and the proper management of village lands. Representations to the central government on any matter are much more likely to be made through a local member of the Legislative Assembly, than through the Village Chairman acting in his capacity as Village Chairman. Council meetings are not attended by members of the public, who show very little interest in the actual activities of the council as such.

The 'wake' which is held on the death of any member of the

village (with certain exceptions discussed below), is an important ritual with a great deal of significance to the present discussion. The wake serves as an expression of local solidarity whatever other functions it may have, and the ideal thing is for every household to be represented at every wake by at least one of its members. Even if families are not on speaking terms they will forget their differences when there is a death, and probably attend each other's wakes. It is even more obligatory to attend if the dead person is 'family' to you, but still the wake is open to anyone, and it is a village as well as a family affair. In this respect it seems important to ask who does not attend rather than who does attend, and immediately we ask this question we get some quite interesting answers. The majority of school-teachers do not attend wakes regularly unless the dead person was a particularly prominent villager or a relative of theirs. Even if they do attend they stay on the periphery of the crowd and would hardly go inside the house. The few East Indians in the village, the Portuguese store-keeper, a Chinese shopkeeper, and a mixed Portuguese-Negro shop-keeper do not normally attend wakes, nor do a few other non-Negroes in the village. When a Negro Roman Catholic in the village died, the Portuguese store-keeper, who is the leading Catholic in the village, persuaded the dead woman's husband that he should not keep a wake. A few people did gather at the house, but there was no hymn singing and very little drinking. We find then, that the wake is a good index to the group which considers itself to be of the village in the real sense. The fact that I attended every wake held during my stay in August Town was remembered long after I left the village and was regarded as a good sign of the degree to which I had identified myself with the village as a whole. The wake serves to relate the individual both to his family and kinship group and to the village community, and the ritual itself expresses these relationships.

Now let us return to the statement 'this is a black people's village'. The sense of all being black is a mechanism of solidarity in certain ways, and for 'blackness', as a shared physical attribute having a definite status value in the social system of British Guiana as a whole, to be tied to the local concept of 'village', makes it even more important. What interests us for the moment though is the 'blackness' part of the formula, and we can consider it in relation to another regularly repeated phrase 'we black people can never progress; we don't trust each other and we don't work together'. In this context 'blackness' is used as a relative concept to distinguish the members of the village from Indians, Chinese, Portuguese and Europeans, and it implies a relative position in a hierarchy of colour values, and a relative position in a multi-racial society. This relative position is nearly always expressed in terms which show its distance from the white group. Anyone who doesn't conform to the local customs is 'playing white people' or 'playing great'. To be born in the village community is to be ascribed status as a member of 'a black people's village' as well as of a particular family group. The accent upon not being able to 'progress' is really symbolic of the social distance which must exist between the various social strata for the system to continue in its present form.

Social stratification in the village is largely in terms of cultural differences combined with occupational status; the school-teacher group, with one or two government employees, forming the village 'upper-class'. The school-teachers even if they are born in the village and work their way through the stage of being a pupil teacher, soon begin to feel themselves different from other people and usually break away from their families and set up a separate household. There were one or two persons in the village who had been pupil teachers and had never been confirmed in their appointments. In one such case the person was still occasionally referred to as 'teach' but he had quite definitely been completely assimilated into the village as a whole, rather than into the teacher group. An old retired school-teacher living in the village would always be referred to as 'teach', and he mixed very little in the village affairs, but was not included in the present day teacher clique. On the other hand a retired head-teacher who remained prominent in political affairs would always be included if he were in the village. The hall-mark of the school-teacher is that he wears a jacket and a tie almost all the time, except when he is relaxing at home, and he speaks a more 'grammatical' form of English than the local dialect. Above all these are the symbols of his status, but of course they are not the only ones, and a person who merely speaks 'grammatical' English and wears a coat and tie does not thereby automatically qualify for higher status group membership. The school-teacher approximates more closely than anyone else in the village to the 'white' standards of behaviour, and he is also a specialist in passing on the values of the total social system. Both the church and the school have this function, and the school-teachers are active in both organizations. Women teachers are in a somewhat different position as might be expected in view of the different rôles of women in the social system. Unless a teacher of the female sex is married to a male teacher she is unlikely to become a member of the teacher clique, though she will quite definitely mark herself off in some way from the other women in the village. One way in which she does this is by not having children and not marrying, which may of course be only a by-product of the fact that she is unable to find a partner who will satisfy her desire for prestige, coupled with the fact that she is relatively financially independent. Women teachers play an important part in some of the associational groups such as church groups, youth clubs and women's clubs.

(*The Business group*)

The important thing about social stratification in the village is that it is not based on wealth *qua* wealth. Although the teacher group, and the other few persons who come into the socially superior position of the teacher group, enjoy a steady income and are therefore more economically secure on the whole, they are by no means the wealthiest persons in the village. Most of the wealthy persons are not black, and they are predominantly shopkeepers. The biggest shops and the store are owned by mixed Negro-Chinese, Portuguese, mixed Negro-Portuguese, and mixed Negro-White persons. Some of the largest shopkeepers also own the largest amounts of land. The few Negroes who run shops in the village only run very small cake-shops selling cake, bread, soft drinks and sweets, and the weekly turnovers of these businesses are very small, profits rarely exceeding about ten dollars per week, and usually considerably less. The shops and the ethnic classification of their owners are shown below.

Type of shop	*Race of owner*
Store—selling cloth, manufactured clothing, shoes, farm implements, etc.	Portuguese
Store—as above	East Indian
Rum shop and grocery	Negro-Chinese
Rum shop and grocery	Negro-Chinese
Grocery	Negro-Chinese
Grocery	Negro-Portuguese
Grocery	Negro-Chinese
Butcher	Negro-Portuguese
Cakeshop	Chinese

Type of shop	*Race of owner*	
Cakeshop	Coloured	Persons of indeterminate Negro-white and Negro-Portuguese descent
Cakeshop	Coloured	
Cakeshop	Coloured	
Cakeshop	Coloured	
Cakeshop	Negro	
Cakeshop	Negro	
Cakeshop	Negro	
Cakeshop	Negro	
Cycle-repair shop	Negro-Portuguese	
Tailor	Negro-Portuguese	

It would appear that there is a very positive correlation between economic success and differentiation on the basis of racial distinction, or at least differentiation in terms of skin colour. The people who go into business and are successful, and who accumulate wealth, are marginal to the concept of village solidarity in terms of 'blackness'. A constant complaint is that if you are black, other people in the village don't like to see you doing well financially. In the market held early on Monday mornings in the village most of the persons selling are East Indians, and when it comes to disposing of fowls or small livestock, villagers will normally sell them to an Indian rather than to a fellow villager who is a huckster. In other words there appears to be a positive suppression of internal differentiation on the basis of wealth or economic achievement. Achievement for a Negro is in terms of occupational status, and for all advancement to higher status than that of village school-teacher the individual has to leave the village and usually cuts himself, or herself, off quite effectively from the village group.

In many respects the development of internal differentiation on the basis of wealth would be in conflict with the position of the village as a 'black people's village' within the larger framework of the colour/class system of the country as a whole. The major ascription of status in the total social system on the basis of skin colour means that the whole village shares this status, and internal differentiation on the basis of wealth alone would mean that there would be the possibility of considerable mobility on the basis of criteria which conflict with ascriptive status. In many ways the little mobility that does exist depends upon approximating to the colour group above you by taking on some of the cultural symbols connected with the

a. Village string band

b. Apprentices working in the blacksmith's shop. The hand-operated bellows keeps the charcoal at the requisite temperature

Plate VII

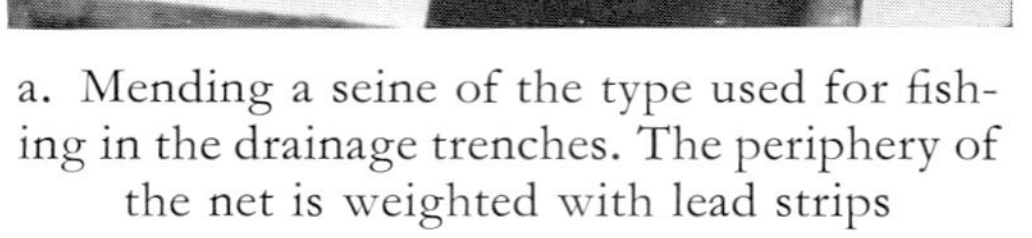

a. Mending a seine of the type used for fishing in the drainage trenches. The periphery of the net is weighted with lead strips

b. Drummers playing for a *Cumfa* dance. The word *Cumfa* is probably derived from the Ashanti word *Akomfo* meaning priest

Plate VIII

very highest group in the whole system, the Europeans. Local solidarity is extremely dependent upon colour values, and since values of economic achievement would clash with these they tend to be suppressed by the community as a whole. To spend money has much more social approval than to accumulate money, and giving lavish parties is a common practice.

Whilst the successful shopkeepers are marginal to the main section of the village in terms of skin colour, they are not sharply differentiated from it in terms of hierarchical status. The majority of them have kinship ties with Negro villagers and they share the same speech patterns, often live in common-law unions, and do not necessarily spend money on items of display furnishings for their houses. Some do of course, and the wealthier ones may send their children to be educated in Georgetown.

(*The higher status élite*)

At the time of the study there was a clearly distinguishable élite in August Town, the members of which considered themselves to be superior to the rest of the village population, and who occupied positions which gave them some measure of control over the actions of other villagers. Its members were drawn together on the basis of the positions they held in the occupational system, or on the basis of their being light coloured. With the exception of the village chairman who was born in August Town, and was for many years head teacher of one of the schools, all were 'strangers' to the village with no kinship ties to any of the ordinary villagers. The group had no internal organization but was drawn together on the basis of its distinction from the rest of the village, and its focus of association was in party giving and bridge playing. The parties were occasions for status display and lavish consumption (relative to the incomes of the participants), and emphasis would be placed upon the 'right' way of doing things. The District Medical Officer, the District Commissioner, the Public Works overseer and the Police Inspector who all lived at Fort Nelson about one mile away, would be drawn into the round of social gatherings and party giving, because of their high status as government officials, and at the other end of the scale one family, the head of which was a truck driver but who owned a car (and also had living with him a very light coloured relative who was a school-teacher), would be drawn in on some occasions. One of the Portuguese store-keepers achieved membership of this élite, but only on account of his and his wife's

Georgetown connexions, and his membership of certain middle-class clubs in the city.

(*The school-teacher clique*)

The younger subordinate school-teachers formed a separate clique on their own. Many of them belonged to the village and had kinship ties within it, but they tended to mix with each other more than with anyone else, and they exercised leadership in practically all the church organizations and clubs. They were very conscious of their desire to 'improve' themselves and the village, and would be the most active members of any organization that started to initiate reform of any kind. Whilst their sincerity cannot be doubted, it must also be recognized that part of the motivation involved is to establish their own status as being both different from, and above, that which they desire to change. Countless movements aimed at improvement and 'moral uplift' have been initiated in August Town, but most of them have merely died a natural death without effecting any appreciable change in the structure of the village, or its moral system. They have, however, been important in providing a means of allowing persons who are changing their status to demonstrate their rôles, and their assimilation of different cultural standards, and they also serve to emphasize the differentiation of the minority from the mass, and thus preserve the status structure of the whole community.

The main status group differentiation within the village is schematically represented opposite, but it must be remembered that this is an abstract positional diagram and does not show the various empirical points of overlap due to individual participation in more than one group.

The reason why the village élite group does not harden into a hereditary village upper-class group, is that once persons have attained a position which would entitle them to be included in this group, they usually move out of the village. Even if they themselves do not leave, it is more than likely that their children will be sent to High School in Georgetown from where they may enter the civil service or the teaching or nursing professions without ever returning to the village. There is thus a regular turnover of the members of the village upper-class group, because most of them are 'strangers', and the few persons from the village who achieve higher status generally go off to other villages, or to Georgetown.

(*Differentiation within the main village group*)

The whole tenor of our argument so far has been to the effect that the main village group is a homogeneous (13) and relatively undifferentiated unit, but of course this is only true within the frame of reference we adopted, which directed our attention to the major status differences both within the village and within the colony as a whole. The main village group forms a localized sub-system of

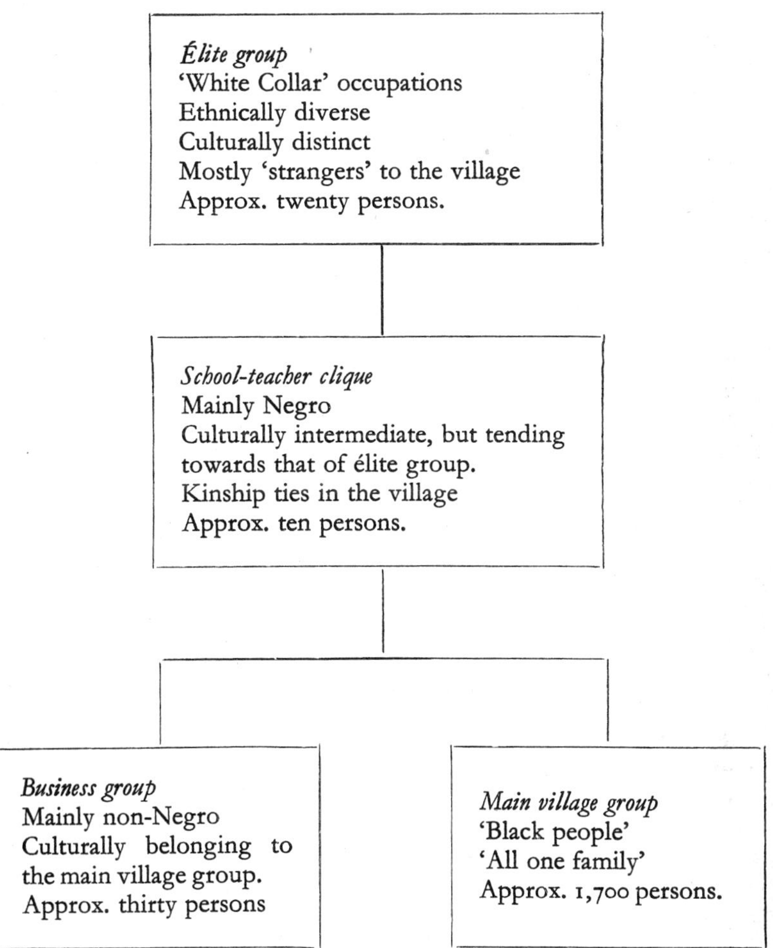

the total social system, but it is itself differentiated internally, without however producing any significant social stratification within itself. The 'band' of status differentiations within this group is narrow and non-institutionalized, and in fact the main pressures are operating to prevent its becoming wider, or in other words to prevent significant status differences from developing beyond a point which would destroy the solidarity of the group, and conflict with the major values of the total system. This does not mean that persons within the group do not aspire to be respected by their fellows or that there are no standards of value-judgement concerning behaviour; of course there are, and they are quite definitely enforced. Clearly the members of this group must share the values of the total social system, and they must recognize the superiority of those in superordinate positions for the social system to operate at all. It is significant that within the group a common opprobrious term is 'lawless' or 'unruly', and by implication it means that the person using the term considers that he conforms more closely to the pattern of 'respectable' behaviour embodied in the norms of the whole society. It is in fact in terms of these values that persons seek to validate their own sense of superiority **within** the main village group. Their failure conclusively to establish such superiority is always because they are 'black people', and of the village. Some persons are regular church-goers, good at making speeches, prosper financially or have steady jobs, and so on, and this entitles them to the respect of their fellow villagers provided they don't try to break the conventions of the group by 'playing great' or 'playing white people'. If they do, then they will be ridiculed and gossiped about and given a bad name. On the other hand some persons will fall below the standards of the group and the same sanctions will operate to prevent them continuing to do so. They may even have to leave the village if they are 'shamed' too much. It is of the utmost importance to note than even within the main Negro village group the term 'nigger man' is used as a term of abuse and there is the tendency to see beauty in a straight nose, a skin a shade lighter, or hair which is less 'kinky' or 'hard'. Mothers even pull their children's noses to make them longer. The negative evaluation of Negro characteristics operates even within the lowest status Negro group.

There are certain aspects of non-hierarchical differentiation which it is important to touch upon at this point. We described earlier the division of August Town into two primary territorial sections: Troy section on the one hand, and St. Paul's plus Belle Vue, on the other. The real division with a historical background, is between Troy and St. Paul's, and there is a definite myth (which may or may not correspond to historical fact) concerning the hostility which existed between the two sections (14). At the present time the distinction between the two sections is over-ridden by the primary membership of the village as a whole, but there are still numerous occasions on which persons refer to their membership of one or the other section, and whilst the primary criterion of membership is actual residence, it may be that a person who was born in Troy and now lives in St. Paul's may claim to be a Troy person. The distinction of belonging to one or the other section usually arises in situations of rivalry, hostility or antagonism, and each group characterizes the other in a derogatory way. Thus St. Paul's people are said to be secretive and un-co-operative, and it is said that if the members of one household heard a murder being committed in the next house they would close up their windows and keep quiet, rather than go and see what was happening. There is also a persistent rumour amongst Troy people that the members of St. Paul's section have a secret society at which they plan all kinds of nefarious activities. Troy people, on the other hand, are characterized as lawless and unruly, as great gossipers, and as people who are always ready to quarrel. In point of fact there is no distinguishable difference between the behaviour of the members of the two sections, and the sectional opposition is rarely expressed in any concerted form. There is always a certain amount of suspicion as to whether one or the other section is having an unfair proportion of village revenue spent on its drainage and irrigation works, and there is often difficulty in getting men from one section to carry out work on the dams and trenches of the other. Intersection rivalry in sports is reputed to occur, but this was never observed. Belle Vue is sometimes aligned with St. Paul's in this context, but there is a clear tendency for it to be regarded as a distinct and relatively neutral unit, a tendency reinforced by the fact that it has a number of households which are marginal to the village proper in that their members are East Indians, Coloured, or 'strangers' to the village. Most of these households are scattered throughout Belle Vue, generally away from the Public Road and they make Belle Vue into something of a 'fringe' area. (See map 3 at end of book.)

Both Troy and St. Paul's are further subdivided into two sections by the Public Road, but this division is more significant in Troy than in St. Paul's, probably because Troy has a larger population. The two sections of Troy are referred to as 'back-dam' and 'waterside', or 'back-dam' and 'sand-top', and whilst there is no tradition of mutual hostility between the two they tend to become separate neighbourhoods. Thus there will be more reciprocal visits between neighbours and kin within one section than between sections.

It is not surprising that these territorial distinctions should develop, and if one pushed the breakdown even further one could distinguish even smaller territorial nuclei of more intensive neighbourhood sentiments arising from the slightly greater frequency of interaction between households living close together. However, the extension of kinship, friendship, and various associational ties right through the village makes these smaller neighbourhood groups much less significant. The Public Road is the *locus* of all the principal shops, the communal water pipes, the market and various public meetings, and this becomes the focal point of the village where everyone meets everyone else.

Although the main division in church membership between the Congregational and Anglican churches does not have extensive ramifications in other spheres of activity, it is interesting to note that once again it is supposed to have had its origin in a situation of hostility. The story is that originally everyone in the village attended the Congregational or 'Mission' church, and when a dispute arose over the conduct of one of the ministers, the congregation split, and that faction which was most opposed to the action of the minister (he was supposed to have been carrying on an affair with his cook), left and joined the Anglican church at Fort Nelson. There does not appear to be any antagonism between the two churches at the present time, although there is rivalry between the schools, but the Anglican church is regarded as being 'outside' the village, and it is also referred to as the 'English' church. The Congregational church is the real village church, and has no members from outside the village, whilst the Anglican church draws its congregation from a number of villages along the coast, including East Indian communities. Not all villagers attend church, and certainly no more than half the village population has church membership, in the sense of being communicants at one or the other church. The number of persons attending church regularly, every time there is a service, is considerably less than this, and constitutes a core around which a more fluid group of sporadic attenders adheres. The more regular attenders are usually old men and women, and young married persons of both sexes, with a sprinkling of the more ambitious persons in the middle age-ranges. Thus all the school-teachers of both sexes will almost invariably be regular church-goers, and will usually take a leading part in the services, the clubs, Sunday schools, choir, etc. Many persons never go to church at all except on special occasions, but only one man in the village openly professed to be an atheist, and he would preach his views on the Public Road on Saturday evenings. Apart from the Congregational and Anglican church members and attenders, a few odd persons would go to a Seventh Day Adventist church farther down the coast, a few persons professed to be Jehovah's Witnesses, and a handful of persons would attend small Roman Catholic services held in the house of a Portuguese storekeeper. All the children in the village attended either the Congregational or the Anglican school where they received a liberal measure of religious instruction, and a large proportion of them attended church or Sunday School, depending on whether their parents could afford to buy them good clothes or not, including shoes, which are an important focus of attention for those who wish to establish their moral superiority and social dignity. Being a church member and a regular communicant is one method of establishing 'respectability'. Alone it is not sufficient to differentiate a person from membership of the main village group, but it tends to place him on a slightly higher status level within it. Membership of one church does not carry any hint of inferiority or superiority *vis-a-vis* membership of the other.

We said earlier that August Town expresses its common identity in the phrase—'all August Town is one family'—and it is certainly true that most persons can trace an extended series of kinship ties to other persons in the village. However, there are no real extended kinship groupings, which would function as groups engaging in corporate activities of any kind. Deriving from descent and kinship affiliation are a series of differentiations as to 'tribal' origin, and whilst these are worthy of note it would be misleading to stress their significance unduly. Most people in the village have some hazy idea as to whether they are Cromati, Kissi, Congo or Nyame. These are the terms employed in August Town, and for the first may be substituted the term 'Big Driver people'. 'Big Driver' is supposed to have been one of the original founders of the village who had been a 'driver' or overseer on the estate from which the ex-slaves came. He is reputed to have had a large number of children and is thought of as a semi-mythical ancestor for a large sector of the village population. No one can trace exact genealogical connexions through known stages back to this man, but persons may go back as far as they can (usually three generations) and then assert a connexion to 'Big Driver'. For most people the process is a less exact one and they will merely have heard from one or other of their parents that they are 'Big Driver' people. 'Big Driver' was supposed to be Cromati, or mixed Cromanti and Ibo, but since the concept of being 'Big Driver' people is itself rather ill-defined and not distinguished by any differentiation in custom of any kind, the exactitude of the African tribal origins is even less reliable. Nyame is a rather special designation, and the cultural and mythological correlates of this small group have been mentioned earlier (15).

All these differentiations within the main village group are cross-cutting, and only emerge in specific contexts where it becomes convenient for an individual to express his distinction from others. They carry no implications of superiority, but the interesting thing about them is that they are all ascriptive classifications. They classify persons as having the quality of 'belonging' to one or other of a series of categories, and the ones we have mentioned are only a few of the whole range of empirical differentiation. Sex, of course, is another, as is age, and the term 'we are grow match' (i.e. same age) is commonly used. They order the main village group into certain categories which in reality serve to include **all** the persons in this group in one or other category, and provide them with a network of relationships which counteracts any tendency to differentiation on the basis of specific performance of individuals. When two persons quarrel over something or other, the occasion serves to draw in the diffuse solidarities of many of these categories of persons. Territorial affiliation, 'tribal' belongingness, or kinship ties may all be invoked to abuse the antagonist, and this emphasizes the diffuse solidarity of the whole group rather than its subdivisions, for each occasion on which such an event takes place brings different alignments into play. The very fact that each individual has statuses in many different categories involves him in loyalties to each on different occasions, and the fact that there is no ranking as between the different categories means that he is unlikely to exploit his membership of one at the expense of his membership in others, in order to increase his status. In other words it is suggested that internal differentiation of this order may positively contribute to the integration of the more embracing system of the village by providing cross-cutting and overlapping zones of solidarity which build up to a more inclusive solidarity.

The differentiations which involve a variation in prestige are less easy to define and in fact the word 'prestige' has been used deliberately in the sense it is used by Nadel to indicate the very vagueness of the social situation (16). What is quite certain is that prestige is acquired by virtue of a more rigorous adherence to the norms of the primary value system, and there is more incentive to this kind of adherence where an individual has gone part of the way by securing a regular job, having been in the army, having been a teacher at one time, and so on.

Perseverance and Better Hope

The broad outlines of the pattern we have described for August Town apply to both Perseverance and Better Hope, but there are differences of degree in the empirical situations which are important, and throw considerable light on the processes we have described. Perseverance possesses less of the 'superstructure' of higher status groups than August Town, and Better Hope exhibits considerably more internal status differentiation. There is no 'higher status élite' in Perseverance, and the school-teacher clique is less sharply differentiated. The village is small and there is only one school, the head teacher and three male teachers of which are from outside the village. All share one house, and whilst they associate with each other more frequently than they do with any other persons, they nevertheless mix freely and on terms of relative familiarity with many other villagers. This is not to say that they are not accorded higher status, for they quite definitely are, and they exercise leadership rôles in many fields of village organization. The head teacher is the village chairman, and the younger male teachers take a leading part in the running of the church and church groups. The principal shops are once again run by non-Negroes, East Indians this time, and the rum-shop is owned by a mixed Negro-English family who actually live on a private estate outside the village. The economic depression of the whole area, and the lack of good farming land within the village has facilitated the spread of interests outside the village boundaries, but the territorial co-residential factors have, of course, operated to produce a local solidarity in the same way that they did in August Town. If anything this local solidarity is more marked in the case of Perseverance, and in place of the August Town quasi-historical mythologies of origin of the village, etc., Perseverance tends to be categorized as 'backward', 'primitive' and 'lawless'. It has a reputation for beating up policemen, which is only slightly less well known than its reputation for being perpetually flooded (17).

Better Hope, on the contrary, is a more 'respectable' village with a reputation for being more 'progressive', and as we have said it exhibits a higher degree of internal status differentiation than either of the other two villages. Its multiplicity of churches and clubs give scope for a relatively larger number of persons to occupy offices carrying a measure of prestige, and from the village upwardly mobile persons spread out into other parts of the colony to occupy positions as teachers, nurses, civil servants, skilled workmen and so on. Concomitantly there is a greater influx of 'strangers', and particularly of East Indians who settle in the village to become farmers.

SOCIAL CONTROL

In stressing the internal solidarity of the main village group and its lack of internal differentiation it is possible to give a grossly over-simplified picture of the kind of relations which obtain between co-villagers. If our analysis of the status system is correct, then one would expect a source of conflict or strain in the fact of the co-existence of values laying stress on achievement, and those laying stress on relatively uniform ascribed status in the group. We have said that too great a degree of internal differentiation is inhibited by various mechanisms such as the diffuse sanctions operating against anyone who 'plays great', or the great emphasis laid on liberal spending particularly at weddings, funerals, etc. Of course an important factor in preventing the consolidation of large land holdings or accumulation of property is the rule of equivalence of siblings in relation to inheritance.

Under such circumstances it becomes extremely important to any particular person that he should not get a 'bad name' in the village, which implies the loss of the esteem of his fellows, for esteem is the only source of this type of gratification open to him. We have seen how some individuals may try to raise their prestige in the village by a closer approximation to the norms of the next higher status group, or of the primary social system. At the other extreme there is a pre-occupation with trying to preserve a good reputation which results in an extreme sensitivity to insult, and leads to a great deal of litigation centring on this. Gossip or 'talking name' is the medium through which the actions of individuals are compared to the group norms, and in these, as in most small communities, it is pervasive and often vicious. Its effectiveness as a means of social control depends on the fact that it matters a great deal to the individual what is being said about him. Since he has no generalized universalistic reference point by which to fix his reputation, such as that which would be implied in being a doctor or a lawyer etc., he depends almost entirely on the reactions of other persons to his actions for his self-esteem. We are here getting into the realms of social control mechanisms within the local group, and since we have said that this constitutes a sub-system of the total social system, with its own partial sub-culture then it follows that there is a strong possibility of its having its own control systems distinct from those of the primary social systems. Empirically there is an overlap between the two of course, partly because conformity to the norms of the over-all system coincides at certain points with conformity to the norms of the sub-system, and partly because the institutions of control belonging to the primary system can be 'used' to ensure conformity to sub-system norms. Thus murder and serious assault are of serious moment at all levels of the society and are dealt with by the police and the courts, the instruments of the total political system. On the other hand inter-sex conflicts over the appropriate behaviour in pre-marital, marital or extra-marital affairs may be resolved by resort to gossip, or 'talking name', or to 'black magic' or obeah.

CONCLUSION

It should be clear from the foregoing analysis that we regard the study of the colony-wide system of social stratification as the starting point of a thorough understanding of the social structure of the villages we are discussing. The villages are local territorially based units whose members share deep interests, such as their ownership of the village land, their social relationships through kinship and marriage, their sharing of leisure time activities, griefs and joys. But they are not isolated units. Their members also share a common status in the ranking system of the colony and they perform similar kinds of tasks in the occupational system, being all replaceable one by another (allowing for sex and age differentiation of course). They share low status, and they do not occupy important positions of control. This low status is defined principally in terms of their ethnic identity as Negroes, and it is sharply contrasted with the position occupied by the members of the white group who occupy the most important control positions and enjoy the highest status.

The homogeneity of the village population is not absolute, and we have tried to show where the principal lines of differentiation lie. The school-teacher is the ideal type of the high status person in the village, and it is significant that the principal function of the school-teacher is to impart the values and culture of the total social system (as opposed to the rural Negro sub-group), to the rising generation. The school-teacher stands as the representative of those values which must take precedence over the values of the sub-group, if the colonial society is to function at all, and if the village is to be integrated into it.

Such a short analysis of the social structure of the total Guianese society cannot fail to be deficient in many respects, but the important point we wish to make is the lack of important status and occupational differentiation in the main village groups, and their unitary position in the over-all scheme of hierarchical social ranking, for this ties up very directly with certain aspects of family structure as we shall show in the next chapter.

CHAPTER IX

HYPOTHESES AND THE PROBLEM OF 'EXPLANATION'

In the preceding chapters we have examined most of the features of Guianese society which are necessary to the type of correlation we wish to make, and this chapter outlines our main hypothesis. We also deal briefly with the problem of 'explanation' as it has been conceived in relation to West Indian family life.

STATUS DIFFERENTIATION IN THE TOTAL SOCIAL SYSTEM AND THE INTERNAL STRUCTURE OF THE HOUSEHOLD GROUP

The crux of our argument lies in this:—

We maintain that the matri-focal system of domestic relations and household groupings, in the villages we have studied, can be reguarded as the obverse of the marginal nature of the husband-father rôle. We further argue that there is a correlation between the nature of the husband-father rôle and the rôle of men in the economic system and in the system of social stratification in the total Guianese society. Men, in their rôle of husband-father, are placed in a position where neither their social status nor their access to, and command of economic resources are of major importance in the functioning of the household group *at certain stages of its development*.

Such an argument requires a good deal of elaboration and we shall begin by attempting to summarize the main features of the status system and the family system as follows:—

Features of the status system

A. There is a scale of colour values at the extremes of which the 'white' or European complex is given positive value, and the 'black' or Negro complex is given negative value, and this serves as a basis for the hierarchical ranking of persons, and groups of persons, according to the 'colour' characteristics ascribed to them.

B. The other main basis of evaluation of a person's status is in terms of his performance in economic or occupational rôles, thereby making it possible for a limited number of persons to achieve higher status than that which is initially ascribed to them on the basis of their 'colour', though the ethnic component of a person's social character is never completely effaced as a factor in status placement. Achieved status is secondary to ascribed status, especially at the extreme ends of the colour scale, but the evaluation of performance in jobs, educational attainment, etc., can serve as a basis for upward mobility especially in the middle zone of the colour scale.

C. We may speak of a colour/class system in so far as the internal differentiation of the social system allocates differential facilities and rewards largely on the basis of position on the scale of socially evaluated colour differences, but the fact that performance criteria are taken into account keeps the system 'open' to a degree where we can speak of 'classes' which do not have an absolute one to one relation to ethnic factors.

D. Ethnic groups such as the Portuguese, Chinese and East Indians, which do not fit readily into the colour/class hierarchy, are able to infiltrate at all levels and to take over special functions where a relative lack of status-consciousness is an advantage, particularly in the retail and distributive trades. The development of a separate collectivity, primarily oriented towards a function implying the predominance of economic achievement, such as business enterprise, competition and efficiency, really conflicts with ascribed membership of groups, and it would seem to have been fortuitous that these ethnic groups came from societies where there was already a tradition of trading, shopkeeping, money-lending and so on. The market nexus of petty trading in British Guiana is interstitial to the ascriptively based social groupings but it has not developed very far towards becoming organized, or forming a primary focus of attention for the ordering of social relations, and in any case the larger scale marketing operations have been controlled by the higher status ethnic groups. The very multiplicity of operators in the lowest level of the marketing system (especially vendors of garden produce, fruits, etc.), is an indication of the tendency to spread the functions and prevent specialization from developing to a point where it would conflict with the ascribed low status of the operators. One special feature of a differentiated group in market operations is the necessity for 'affective neutrality', and this could most readily be found in the Chinese and Portuguese groups, where all other sections of the population did in fact regard them as being neutral in terms of the scale of colour values, and the symbolism connected with it (1).

E. In the villages studied, the model of the total social system tends to repeat itself, but since the village is only a section of the total society, it does not have the same degree of internal differentiation. The village 'upper-class' is either occupationally or ethnically differentiated in the sense that its members are either non-Negroes, or in high-status white-collar (usually government) jobs, and it shows its difference by means of 'diacritical' signs such as dress, speech pattern, marriage pattern, etc. (2).

F. The main village group tends to be solidary *vis-a-vis* the rest of the society, and status differentiation within it is discouraged since this would conflict with the main status differentiations within the total social system. However, there are both non-hierarchical differentiations (segmentations), and minor differential prestige positions within it, as well as the inevitable age and sex differentiations which are not directly relevant to the present discussion.

G. There is a variation in the degree of internal differentiation as between the three villages.

Main aspects of family structure

A. The household group tends to be matri-focal in the sense that a woman in the status of 'mother' is usually the *de facto* leader of the group, and conversely the husband-father, although *de jure* head of the household group (if present), is usually marginal to the complex of internal relationships of the group. By 'marginal' we mean that he associates relatively infrequently with the other members of the group, and is on the fringe of the effective ties which bind the group together.

B. Household groups normally come into being when a man and a woman enter a conjugal union (legal or common-law marriage), and set up house together in a separate dwelling. Either or both partners may have children which were born prior to the establishment of an effective conjugal union.

C. During the period when the woman is bearing children she will be most dependent on her spouse for economic support and most subject to his authority and control, but as her children grow older she becomes much more independent and acquires much greater security in her status as 'mother'.

D. Common-law marriage is a cultural characteristic of the lower class, and can be regarded as a permissive deviation from the norms of the total social system. The non-legal nature of the tie reflects the reluctance to establish a conclusive bond and is in accordance with the primary emphasis upon the mother-child relationship rather than the conjugal relationship.

E. There is a variation in the incidence of different types of conjugal union as between the three villages.

These two paradigms have been constructed in an attempt to compress into a more manageable form the relevant features of the two complexes we wish to correlate, and they are only intended as a brief summary of our previous descriptions.

It would seem that whilst biological relatedness is taken as a major focus of status ascription in the total social system, the unit of kinship which is emphasized in this respect is not the nuclear or extended family as such, but rather the widest possible kinship unit which is the ethnic group itself. Within this group two other points of reference become foci of differentiation in descending order of importance (from this point of view). They are territorial affiliation (membership of the local community), and matri-filiation. Matri-filiation as a basis of status ascription has a long history in the West Indies, and under the slave régime it was taken as defining legal status. The child of a slave woman and a free man always took its mother's legal status and became a slave (3). In the contemporary situation the relation to the mother almost invariably determines the place of residence of the child, for it is the services rendered to the child by the mother, such as 'care' in its broadest sense, which are amongst the main functions of the household group. In this respect it is significant that any woman will give any child a little food, and children quite often eat at their play-mates' homes or at the houses of kinsfolk if they happen to be there at meal times.

There is a sense in which we can take for granted the fact that the mother-child relationship will be a close one in any society, and the real problem then begins to centre on the way in which masculine rôles are integrated into the family system, and the way in which the mother-child relationship is structured to fit in with the general structure including the masculine rôle pattern (4).

In societies where kinship provides the basis for practically all the differentiation within the social system, the positions of prestige and control are almost invariably and totally vested in adult males and no matter whether the system is patrilineal, matrilineal or based on double unilineal descent, it is males in whom the principal rights over property and services are vested. The varying patterns of domestic organization may place these rights in different contexts, and even where the rights themselves are formally vested in women, as amongst the Hopi, it is still the males who control the exercise of these rights, and who hold positions of primary managerial authority (5).

It is clear from our discussions in previous chapters that the rôle of husband-father is by no means absent in lower-class Negro society in British Guiana, nor is it reduced to such insignificant proportions as we find in certain extreme matrilineal societies such as the traditional Nayar (6) or Menangkabau (7).

Amongst the Nayar a woman resides in the joint household (*taravad*) of her matri-lineage, and is visited by a series of lovers with whom she has sexual relations. Her children remain with her in the *taravad* where they come under the authority of the eldest male member of the group, who may be the woman's brother, mother's brother or even mother's mother's brother. The child's father, who is an outsider to the group (he may even belong to a different caste), has no economic, political or ritual functions in relation to the *taravad* of his children. His relationship to his child is confined to presenting certain customary gifts at the time of the birth. The rôle of husband-father is not completely absent from the Nayar system, but it is reduced to extremely limited proportions.

However, men do have vital economic, political, status, and ritual functions in relation to their own *taravad* and it is the existence of a tightly organized unilineal descent group, having strongly corporate functions, and laying stress upon the close interdependence of a set of brothers and sisters that makes the Nayar system completely different from that with which we are dealing in British Guiana. The Nayar are able to reduce the husband-father rôle to minimal proportions precisely because male rôles in relation to the *taravad* are so highly developed and the supportive activities of males in relation to women and children are embodied in the structure of the *taravad*. Virtually the only activities of men in relation to women which are left outside the sphere of the matri-lineage are those concerned with sexual activity and procreation.

In the bilaterally organized kinship system of the villages with which we are dealing, men are essential providers of economic support for women and children. Women can, and do, engage in money-making activities, but they cannot be economically self-sufficient. The question then arises as to how men's supportive functions shall be tied in to the family system. There are thus two distinct problems to be considered. The first concerns the male rôle in society, and here we have indicated that men are expected to earn money to contribute to the support of women and children. We have described in some detail the difficulties which face men in a society where there is little prospect of steady employment, and we have also stressed the fact that there is little occupational differentiation and correspondingly little hierarchical status differentiation amongst the village men. The second problem concerns the direction in which men are to offer their economic support, and this is the main problem we are to consider here. Economic support for women and children is located in a series of statuses, the principal ones being those of son, husband and lover. It is not located in a group, for in a bilaterally organized kinship system there is no enduring kinship-group structure available. For any particular woman with children the problem is to find a male in one of the above statuses to provide the necessary support. Chance factors inherent in the birth and death incidence render the likelihood of there being an individual *always* available to fill a given status somewhat uncertain, and therefore a situation such as the one in British Guiana has to be sufficiently fluid to permit of a choice of alternative persons. This is particularly the case in bilateral systems of narrow range.

One way of resolving this difficulty is to vest the functions of economic support in a husband-father who is selected from a wide range of possible individuals and this is precisely what happens in our case. However, the importance of the economic function of the husband-father becomes diminished as the woman passes her period of maximum dependence and becomes freed for economic activities of her own and as her sons begin to take over supportive functions. The reasons for this must be sought in the economic and stratification systems of the total social system.

In a society where the range of effective kinship ties is narrowed to a point where the nuclear family becomes a highly significant and relatively isolated unit, as in urban middle-class groups in the

United States, then the position of the husband-father in the primary status-determining occupational system, rather than in an extended kinship system, is a crucial one. In such a situation hierarchical mobility is normal and the husband-father determines the social status of the whole unit by virtue of his position in the occupational system. He becomes the peg on which the whole unit hangs.

In British Guiana the male member of the village groups neither has exclusive control over property and services, including the means of production for the livelihood of the household group, nor does he determine its status in the social system by virtue of his position in a graded occupational hierarchy, since this is already determined to a large extent by 'race' or 'colour', plus membership of the territorial unit which is the village. The important fact is that occupations are not hierarchically graded to any significant extent within the main Negro village groups, though the occupations of the Negro men are ranked low in the total occupational system in the same way that Negro men are ranked low in the colour scale. The male's participation in the occupational system does not affect the status of the other members of the household group, which is already defined by their racial characteristics and territorial affiliation. This is a very broad statement and only holds good for the relatively undifferentiated lowest status group. As soon as one approaches the upper fringe of this group, where prestige factors begin to operate, or get into the higher-status village group, then the occupation of the husband-father becomes significant, and there is a quite definite tendency for his position in the household group to be established, and for him to become a reference point for the other members of the group. In the urban middle-class certain other factors may intervene to tend to bring the focus of solidarity of the group back to the mother, particularly where the man marries a lighter coloured woman who then becomes a focus of attention for status placement on the colour scale (8). In the middle-class there is always this interplay between occupational factors, and 'colour' and/or 'cultural' factors. In the lowest status group the only basis for male authority in the household unit is the husband-father's contribution to the economic foundation of the group, and where there is both insecurity in jobs where males are concerned, and opportunities for women to engage in money-making activities, including farming, then there is likely to develop a situation where men's rôles are structurally marginal in the complex of domestic relations. Concomitantly, the status of women as mothers is enhanced and the natural importance of the mother rôle is left unimpeded.

Although we have had to present our argument rather forcefully in order to make it clear, there are certain reservations which must be entered. The analysis of family structure has shown quite clearly that the elementary family, consisting of a conjugal pair and their offspring is not atypical in the groups we have been considering, but is in fact the normal unit of co-residence, particularly at the stage when a father-figure is important in the socialization of the children. It is not within our competence to discuss the psychological implications of this fact but in any discussion of socialization it should be borne in mind that we are dealing with a social system where the *normal* unit of child-rearing is an elementary family unit. In particular cases of mental development it would be important to look for the deviations from this norm and in discussing the psychological component of values it may be necessary to bear in mind the nature of the father-child and mother-child relationships. In the three villages we have been discussing it would not be justifiable to treat these questions as if the normal pattern were for children to grow up without any kind of relationship to a father or father-surrogate, and high illegitimacy rates are not an indication of these relationships.

THE CULTURE-HISTORICAL APPROACH TO NEW WORLD NEGRO FAMILY ORGANIZATION

Writings on New World Negro family organization have tended to concentrate to some extent on the controversy as to whether the form of the New World Negro family is the result of the peculiar conditions obtaining on the plantations during the period of slavery or whether it can be seen as a modified survival of an 'African' family pattern. Equally plausible theories supported by historical evidence have been advanced on either side, and the polemical discussions have brought to light a considerable body of information and have been productive of many profound insights. It would seem, though, that there is a need for synchronic analysis, which attempts to understand the working of the system without any pre-conceptions as to its previous states. There is always a danger that the prior task of sociological analysis may be side-stepped when historical factors are prematurely introduced as 'explanatory' devices.

Professor and Mrs. Herskovits were, in a very real sense, the pioneers of anthropological study in the Caribbean area, and their work has had a profound influence on subsequent investigators, so that it is impossible to discuss the problems of the area without considering their work. It is beyond the scope of this book to offer a critical examination of the highly developed theoretical approach they brought to their studies, and we shall confine our discussion to the interpretations they present of some of the institutions of West Indian society. More particularly we shall consider those interpretations concerning the village of Toco in Trinidad which most nearly resembles August Town, Perseverance and Better Hope (9).

The Herskovitses are primarily concerned with the problem of law in history, or the processes of social change, and they suggest that two different drives work together to fashion civilization.

> There are first of all the forces that, without reference to cultural form as such, are constantly at work to maintain the balance between stability and change in every culture or, where different cultures are in close and continuous contact, to accelerate change. Then there are the unique historical sequences of events which, in any given instance, determine particular reactions in specific situations, and through this the particular forms that the institutions, beliefs, and values in a given culture will take at a given moment in its history (10).

In discussing Toco, they state explicitly that it will be necessary to comprehend both the general laws of cultural dynamics, and the particular historical forces bringing about change in Toco. These 'general laws of social dynamics' are relatively simple and are set out at length by Professor Herskovits in other publications. Principally they concern the idea of 'cultural focus', 'cultural retention', and 'reinterpretation' of 'borrowed' items of culture (11). Fundamental to the whole theory is the assertion that culture is learned, and culture is an all-embracing concept of which social organization is one 'aspect' (12). They demonstrate quite convincingly in the opening section of 'Trinidad Village' that one way of explaining the importance of women in the family structure of Toco, is to see this structure as a persistence of a part of the form of African family organization. In Africa each wife has her own hut which she inhabits with her children, and whilst those aspects of African social organization which were the field of male activity (the clan, and the extended family) were impossible to maintain under slavery conditions this basic structure of a woman and her children persisted through all the vissicitudes of slavery. The rôle of the father continued to be remote from the children and the wife as it was in Africa. Unfortunately there is an equally convincing 'explanation' of how this situation involving the importance of women in the family system might have arisen. Franklin Frazier has carefully documented the disruption in family life brought about by slavery and demonstrated how the natural unit of a woman and her children was the one most likely to survive, no matter what the antecedent form of family life might have been (13). It would seem difficult to make a choice between these two alternative 'explanations' and Henriques in a paper published in 1949, sought a compromise by giving each 'explanation' some credence (14). In his later work however he seems to have concentrated much more upon showing the relation between family structure and the differential factors of social status in terms of the colour/class system which originated in the slave society (15).

The main body of the book on Toco is concerned with descriptions of Toco life, and perhaps the most unsatisfying sections from our point of view are those on mating and the family. The distribution figures which are given must be considered of doubtful validity since they are not based on any sampling system. Figures on marital status are 'of a considerable proportion of the families in Toco and its immediate vicinity' whilst the number of children in 106 households was computed by asking persons to give the number of children in the households of their neighbours and friends (16). In a preliminary survey, this method of arriving at an idea of the composition of households from third parties was tried in August Town, and a subsequent first-hand census revealed a significant disparity in the two sets of figures.

At the beginning of Chapter V of 'Trinidad Village' the point is made that, 'The definition of the Toco family, in any functioning sense, must give a prominent place to the individual household' (17). With this we would agree whole-heartedly, and the disappointing fact is that the Herskovitses do not follow up this statement. Apart from citing one case, the typicality of which we are unable to assess, the chapter is mainly devoted to a discussion of child-birth, child-rearing and the life-cycle, which stresses those aspects which are most susceptible of analysis in terms of the authors' theory of persistence and reinterpretation of African culture. This becomes even more clear when we turn to the theoretical discussion in Chapter XI, when an attempt is made to indicate 'what of African custom has been retained, how this was integrated with the European conventions that were accepted, and how both these were reinterpreted in terms of one another' (18). It is precisely here that our main criticisms of this study must rest.

'The division of Toco society into socio-economic groups, although cast in Euro-American patterns, is in accord with African tradition, and has been reinforced by continued African sanctions' (19). This is the opening statement of a paragraph that seems to contain a number of statements which permit of much more rigorous formulation, for to contend that status differentiation is a survival of ancestral African patterns is forcing the facts a great deal. It is not even the form of status differentiation which is compared, but merely status differentiation *per se*. In the first place we are told very little of the real nature of rank differentiation in the village beyond the fact that some people are poor and others are comfortably off. Whilst in this paragraph it is stated that 'in both areas [Africa and Toco] there is conscious striving to better the status of the individual and his family' (20), we are left to assume that there is the possibility of considerable upward movility and are told absolutely nothing of the operative colour-class system.

In the discussion of marriage and mating we find the statement that 'here is a translation, in terms of the monogamic pattern of European mating, of basic West African forms that operate within a polygynous frame' (21). This refers of course to the dual system of legal marriage and 'keeping', and this is equated with the disappearance of bride-price payments, and the consequent loss of legal control of the father over the children, except where he gives them financial support. This idea is not developed to any great extent and we are left to guess just how the process of reinterpretation came about.

It is in the discussion of ritual and symbolism that the Herskovitses thesis is most convincing, and here their analyses are remarkably penetrating and well documented. This brings us up against the core of the problem, which concerns the validity of a theoretical system based upon an all-embracing concept of culture. Once the assertion is made that social structure is an aspect of culture, capable of transmission in exactly the same way as symbolism, the way is open for confusion. Our contention is that the Herskovitses fail to analyse the contemporary social system fully; treat structure and culture as being of the same order of generality; and fail to recognize that these two orders of social facts need to be treated within different frames of reference. Cultural symbols which are clearly derived from

Africa may serve as vehicles for the expression of new values in Toco, or in the West Indies generally, and the tracing of their origins and their new integration into a coherent system is an important task for anthropology, admirably tackled by the Herskovitses. Another impressive monographic study of this type is Miss Deren's study of Haitian Vodun cults (22). However, the study of social structure does not respond to the methods used by Prof. and Mrs. Herskovits, and the prior task of sociology in this field is the elucidation of the social structure of a functioning system within a general theoretical framework which permits of comparative study at a higher level of abstraction than the purely descriptive. The functional pre-requisites of social systems impose a limited number of possibilities of structuring, and this is particularly true if we begin to examine sub-systems of such a fundamental nature as domestic groups. That there should be similarities between domestic groups in Trinidad and West Africa is not surprising. There are similarities between domestic groups in Trinidad and Manchester and Cape Town and many other places, and a comparative study has to be based on a theoretical approach which is more refined than that of the culture concept. Perhaps one of the most persuasive arguments against the Herskovitses' interpretation of lower-class Negro family structure as a reinterpretation of basic African forms is the fact that in lower-class white society in the southern states of North America as described by Davis and Gardner one finds the same instability of marriage, and the same emphasis on the mother-child relationship (23). There are considerable differences of course, but the similarities are striking and certainly cannot be explained, either by a reference to 'African survivals' or 'European values' whatever that might mean in this context.

In *Life in a Haitian Valley* we find the same general approach to the problems as in *Trinidad Village*, but the method of analysis is laid out perhaps even more clearly. The book begins with three chapters entitled 'The African Heritage', 'What the Slaves Found in Haiti' and 'Working the Amalgam'. Here we are presented with a brief picture of two cultures; 'African' and 'French', and then given a hypothetical account of how these two entities mingled with each other to form 'Haitian' culture. Later on in the book we find such statements as:

> The Africans who peopled Haiti, coming from cultures where descent is counted solely on the side of the mother or the father, and coming into contact with the French, whose custom binds children with equal

strength to the families of both parents, molded both traditions into the social forms found today not only in Mirebalais, but in their essential outlines, throughout the Republic (24).

Although there is in Herskovits's work always the recognition of some kind of connectedness in social life, at the same time he does not hesitate to think in terms of the fusion of traits. He starts with two 'cultures' which are presumably some kind of integrated wholes, then permits them to come into contact, a process which results in the exchange of traits which then become reintegrated into a new whole, which can be explained in terms of the process of fusion of the two original 'cultures'. Lines of thought on the social system which is 'Haitian' are very poorly developed, but enough material of a descriptive nature is provided to enable us to guess that Haitian peasant society has many structural features in common with other similar societies throughout the West Indies. The equivalence of siblings in regard to inheritance is one such structural principle. There is also some indication of the fact that in Haitian peasant society, men are important as the heads of extended families held together by common interests in land, this being of supreme importance as an economic asset. However, we are not told whether women ever occupy this position, or of the distribution of rôles within the family. Most important of all, we are once again told practically nothing of the position of the Negro peasant in the social system of Haiti as a whole, and no mention is made of the contemporary colour/class system. That the identification of status with colour should have persisted in Haiti even after the virtual expulsion of the whites, says a great deal for the stability of the social system, and the values inherent in it, which developed under French Colonial rule. This is a phenomenon which cannot be derived from either Europe or Africa, but it is symptomatic of the selective bias of Herskovits's approach that this vitally important subject should have been omitted from serious consideration.

In the Negro communities of the southern states of the United States of America one finds many features of family life which are familiar to the student of West Indian Negro groups, and Franklin Frazier has produced a magnificently documented study of family organization in both the historical period when the Negroes were slaves, and in the present century (25). Taking the diametrically opposed view to that adopted by Herskovits, Frazier contends that the Negro in North America has been stripped of his cultural heritage, and that the various types of Negro family organization found today have arisen as the result of experience under the slave régime, and more lately by a process of successful assimilation of the culture of the whites.

> Within this world [the plantation] the slave mother held a strategic position and played a dominant rôle in the family groupings. The tie between the mother and her younger children had to be respected not only because of the dependence of the child upon her for survival but often because of her fierce attachment to her brood . . . On the whole, the slave family developed as a natural organization, based upon the spontaneous feelings of affection and natural sympathies which resulted from the association of the family members in the same household. Although the emotional interdependence between the mother and her children generally caused her to have a more permanent interest in the family than the father, there were fathers who developed an attachment for their wives and children (26).

It is this primary natural bond of mother and children which persisted through all the break-up of local communities that took place at the time of emancipation in North America, and despite all the laxity in sexual mores encouraged by a life of deprivation. Frazier recognizes that stable nuclear families consisting of a man, woman and their children developed when some of the ex-slaves 'managed to get some education and buy homes'. He says:

> This has usually given the father or husband an interest in his family and has established his authority. Usually such families sprang from the more stable, intelligent, and reliable elements in the slave population. The emergence of this class of families from the mass of the Negro population has created small nuclei of stable families with conventional standards of sexual morality all over the South. Although culturally these families may be distinguished from those of free ancestry, they have inter-married from time to time with the latter families. These families represented the highest development of Negro family life up to the opening of the present century (27).

The fact that the term 'Negro' is used in the United States to refer to any person possessing any proportion of Negro blood often tends to obscure certain colour differences which would be of paramount significance in the West Indies. However, Frazier does point out that the 'upper-class' Negroes were predominantly of mulatto origin and tended to preserve their traditions of descent from 'aristocratic' white families. The hierarchical grading within Negro society has been, and is, associated with differences in skin colour as in the West Indies, but, as Frazier points out, other factors have been operative as determinants of class status within the whole Negro group (28). What he calls 'cultural attainments', such as learning to speak 'the uncorrupted language of the cultured whites', have been important indices of higher rank, and these have usually been associated with economic success. But it is with the increased urbanization of the Negro that opportunities have arisen for a real division into socio-economic classes based primarily on occupational differentiation, and despite the inferior status of the Negro *vis-a-vis* the white group, considerable opportunity for social mobility based on economic achievement is in evidence. It is in the urban areas that Negroes begin to engage in business activities, primarily within the Negro group. However, even in the large cities of the United States of America the broad correlation of 'middle-class' status and lighter skin colour holds good, and there is the same tendency for upwardly mobile black men to marry lighter coloured women in order to consolidate their class status. Frazier brings this out very clearly in his chapter on the 'Brown Middle Class' (29). Ample confirmation of our main thesis is contained in Frazier's work, but in making judgments as to 'higher' and 'lower' development, he tends to shift attention from the structural correlations to a purely historical statement that a class differentiation has developed within the Negro group itself.

SOCIOLOGICAL STUDIES OF THE FAMILY IN THE BRITISH WEST INDIES

In 1946 Professor Simey published a book which has had considerable attention paid to it, both in Britain and in the West Indies (30). Simey's main interest was in describing the existing conditions in the British West Indian Colonies in such a way that adequate plans for social welfare and development could be formulated, and in this he was no doubt successful if one is to judge by the amount of administrative action which has subsequently been taken. However, our purpose is not to assess the adequacy of his proposals for improvement of social conditions, but to examine very briefly some of his statements about West Indian social organization, which have been accepted in many quarters as authoritative. Simey himself makes it perfectly clear that his conclusions are not based upon any intensive first-hand study, but are compounded of general impressions, insights from the work of other writers, and what he describes as wholly inadequate statistical data.

Simey is acutely aware of the class and colour distinctions which exist in West Indian society, and he devotes considerable space to exploring the psychological implications of these divisions, drawing heavily on the work of Dollard in the United States (31). However, it is not with this aspect of the work that we are concerned, but mainly with his discussion of the lower-class Negro family organization. It is important to realize that he sees the lower-class Negro population as existing in a state of chronic poverty, underfed, and depending on irregular employment for a meagre income. Citing Mr. Lewis Davidson he gives a classification of four types of family organization, this classification being based on data collected in seven different rural districts in Jamaica in 1943–4. The information refers to 270 families, but the samples were not random in a statistical sense. The four types are as follows:—

(*a*) *The Christian Family*, based on marriage and a patriarchal order approximating to that of Christian families in other parts of the world;

(*b*) *Faithful Concubinage*, again based on a patriarchal order, possessing no legal status, but well established and enduring for at least three years;

(*c*) *The Companionate Family*, in which the members live together for pleasure and convenience, and for less than three years; and

(*d*) *The Disintegrate Family*, consisting of women and children only, in which men merely visit the women from time to time, no pattern of conduct being established.

The percentages of the various 'types' are Christian families 20 per cent, Faithful Concubinage families 29 per cent and types (*c*) and (*d*) combined, 51 per cent (32).

To comment upon a piece of numerical information such as this with too much severity would be sheer pedantry, for it is doubtful whether Professor Simey would seriously claim the figures to be anything more than a rough guide. However, certain conclusions which are drawn from rather vague pieces of factual information such as this, do require comment. In the first place the categorization of families into the 'types' presented above suffers from the same drawbacks as that of Henriques's to which we referred earlier (33). It is extremely doubtful whether one could legitimately define any family group as really belonging to either category (*c*) or category (*d*). Category (*c*) may be only an early stage of category (*b*), and unless much more information is given about families included in category (*d*) we don't know whether they have previously been based on marriages or common-law marriages or whether they are incipient forms of category (*b*) or category (*c*). The distribution figures indicating the number of legal marriages (which is presumably what 'Christian families' are based on), are quite remarkably low and they disagree substantially with the kind of proportions we find in British Guiana (34) and with those reported by Henriques for Jamaica (35). The complete absence of any attempt to introduce a time perspective and see the various 'types' of family in their developmental aspect is a serious omission.

One of the conclusions reached by Simey, and here he is talking of the West Indies as a whole, is that:

> . . . the married state is something quite extraordinary, only open to those in higher walks of life, well endowed with worldly goods. Faithful concubinage is largely an economic institution. When the complementary wages earned by each partner form a more or less stable family income, then it may be assumed (there is no direct evidence for this) that this type of family is most secure.
>
> The working classes *all round the West Indies* are firmly convinced that a wife (as distinct from a 'keeper' or such like) should not be expected to work for wages outside the family, that the furnishings of the house should be something approaching a lower middle-class standard, and that the wife should have a servant (36).

It should be clear from the data presented in Section II of this book that the above statements are simply incorrect so far as the communities we have studied in British Guiana are concerned. Simey's statements would be explicable if they had been made by a member of the middle-class, or the lower middle-class, for this is exactly the kind of stereotype of lower-class life which one hears in the urban centres from persons of middle-class status.

In many ways the work of Dr. Henriques is a more refined development of that of Simey, for he is carrying out a detailed investigation of a limited set of problems in a specific area. The two books have much in common however, in so far as the treatment of the problems of family organization is concerned.

Henriques's approach to Jamaican society is quite different from that of Herskovits, the other principal anthropological student of the West Indies, since he is much more concerned with understanding Jamaican family life in relation to the contemporary colour-class system, and only has a recourse to history to demonstrate the importance of the social situation in which this system came to fruition (37). We may pass over Dr. Henriques's strictures that a European investigator would not be able to obtain information because of the attitudes towards Europeans, by reminding him that there are more ways of obtaining information than by asking questions. This is largely a matter of technique, and it must be admitted that there is a certain amount of difficulty involved for a European attempting to work with a coloured middle-class group, and obviously there would be fields of inquiry where one would expect a biased reaction, and any investigator who did not take this factor into account would be naïve in the extreme. Henriques's section on the colour/class system is descriptively sound, though there is very little attempt at any systematic analysis in relation to a general theory which would permit of comparison within a generalized framework. There is competent empirical correlation of the three factors of colour, economic position and family pattern, and we shall concentrate our attention on this latter aspect of the study, and particularly on the lower-class family organization.

There is a brief discussion of historical causative factors underlying the forms of Jamaican family life, and Henriques tends to reject Herskovits's thesis of the persistence of African elements, in favour of 'slavery' as a determining factor. By 'slavery' we presume Henriques means the whole social system of which slavery was an integral part in the West Indies. This is certainly a major advance on Herskovits's work, for it brings us one step nearer to a view of West Indian society which takes cognizance of the functioning system which developed, and exists today in the West Indies, and to a certain extent throughout the New World wherever Negro groups are to be found.

One of the main limitations of Henriques's work on Jamaican family structure is the lack of data which may be considered adequate for the type of analysis he attempts. Census figures are hardly satisfactory since they do not deal in the categories necessary for the analysis. Henriques stresses the importance of the domestic group as the central point of his analysis, but lacks the data to make more than very general statements concerning the distribution of various types. He distinguishes four types of household group:—

A. Christian family	*B.* Faithful concubinage
C. Maternal or Grandmother family	*D.* Keeper family.

However, he is fully aware that these categories are not rigid, and mentions, without much further demonstration of the point, that any given household could experience all four categorical states during its existence through time. This is a crucial point, for the classificatory scheme presented is essentially the result of trying to deal with the material by means of a rigidly synchronic view of empirical data. Henriques speaks of the 'typical monogamous family' as if it were in a category quite apart from the other three, and if in fact this is so, it is extremely important. He asserts that in this type of family, meals tend to be taken in common, and it is implied that such a family normally has a servant of some kind. Unfortunately we don't know just how 'normal' this is, though obviously some precise measure of normality in this context is required. Eating together or not eating together is an important index to internal family relations, and if in fact there is such a basic difference between families of Henriques Type *A*, and Types *B* and *D*, in this respect, then we are faced with a situation which differs radically from that reported for other parts of the West Indies. Since it is estimated that a good many people get married after having lived together for some time, do they then change their eating habits? The situation as reported for Jamaica is so different from that in British Guiana that it raises important issues concerning the rôle of marriage in lower-class family life in the two areas.

The census figures quoted for the distribution of household heads by sex and conjugal status are tantalizingly vague. The largest category of female heads is listed as 'single' but we have no means of telling how many of these persons are separated, common-law widows, or women who have never cohabited with a man at all. This is equally true for the male heads in this category.

So far we have been dealing with the empirical aspects of this section of the monograph only, but it is clear that the vagueness in reporting of specific facts is connected with the absence of a generalized frame of reference by which such facts could be ordered. In the concluding chapter of the book Henriques comes much nearer to formulating a general hypothesis concerning Jamaican society when he shows that domestic groupings in the lower-class are in part a function of the economic and colour/class system, within a general framework of what he has termed a *disnomic* society. However, the implications of this approach are not at all clearly worked out. He refers to 'poverty' as if it were in itself a causal factor, instead of being merely a relative measurement of wealth, whereas, it would be more satisfactory to take poverty as a correlate of low social status which is the important social fact.

CROSS-CULTURAL COMPARISONS

We have already had occasion to contrast certain features of Guianese Negro family structure with those found in societies as widely different as the Nayar of Malabar (38), the Hopi of Arizona (39), and so on, but if the hypothesis we developed earlier in this chapter is correct then it may be possible to test it against situations where a similar structural complex appears to exist. This is not to claim that we are establishing the hypothesis by rigorous cross-cultural comparison of a statistically valid nature, but by a limited comparison we should be able to suggest lines for further inquiry.

Latin America

The area which is broadly designated 'Latin America' contains within it several sub-areas where the autochthonous groups of American Indians form a substantial proportion of the population. Generally speaking these Indian groups are over-laid with Spanish and mixed Spanish-Indian groups, the three groups being arranged in some kind of hierarchy in approximately the same fashion that we find Negro, Coloured and White groups in the British West Indies. A great deal of anthropological work has been carried out in these communities, primarily by North American scholars, and it is proposed to examine firstly, one community study undertaken by Dr. John Gillin in Peru during a six-months field trip in 1944 (40). The series of studies of which this is a part were concerned primarily with problems of acculturation in mixed Indian-European rural communities. In a foreword Julian H. Steward says: 'They [the studies] are essentially acculturational, the various communities selected for investigations ranging in degree of assimilation from self-sufficient and self-contained preliterate Indian groups to strongly mestizoized, literate, Spanish-speaking villages, which are more or less integrated into national life' (41).

The conception of the studies is basically similar to that propounded by Robert P. Redfield in his classic monograph on the differential 'Westernization' of Yucatan communities, and in many ways it resembles the culture-historical approach used by Herskovits in his study of West Indian Negro communities (42). At the moment we are less concerned with the general theoretical approach, than with the reported facts, but we must bear in mind that Gillin was working within the tradition of 'culture contact' studies.

Moche lies on the coast of Peru, seven miles from the city of Trujillo on the road to Lima. Its aboriginal population is descended from the people who possessed the archaeological culture known as *Mochica*, but although there is a consciousness that the present day Mocheros are a distinctive group, being more 'Indian' and more conservative than other coastal villagers, there is no historical tradition in the community of descent from an ancient Peruvian civilization. Moche itself is one of a series of villages, which are generally known as 'Mochica villages' but there is no organization uniting them as such, no common tradition of origin, and although social intercourse between their inhabitants tends to be more frequent than with other communities, it is by no means exclusively so. Spanish is the only language spoken, all the original Indian languages having disappeared. The inhabitants of Moche are not all Indian, and the classification of the Peruvian National Census for 1940 gave the following figures for Moche district (43).

	MALE	FEMALE	TOTAL
White and Mestizo	914	978	1,892
Indians	921	928	1,849
Yellow (Chinese and Japanese) ..	12	2	14
Undeclared	10	8	18
Negro	None	None	None
Total Population			3,773

Gillin says that the above figures must be taken cautiously especially as regards the division into Indian, Mestizo and White. As far as he is concerned the principal internal division in Moche is between 'true Mocheros' and *forasteros*. The latter are 'strangers' and seem to include the 'whites' as well as a large number of 'Peruvians' who would probably fall into the category of Mestizo rather than pure Indian. In any case Gillin is of the opinion that the 'pure Indian' element is not, strictly speaking, racially pure, but the term 'Indian' includes both racial and cultural characteristics. There are some 500 *forasteros* as opposed to 3,178 'true Mocheros', and they rarely engage in agriculture as do the Mocheros. He characterizes the 'true Mocheros' as being 'more Indian' than outsiders, thus giving an ethnic designation to this group despite the apparent discrepancy with the census figures. This would seem to indicate that many of the 'true Mocheros' group returned themselves as

Mestizo, despite their general classification in a sociological sense as 'Indian'.

The economy of the village is based upon irrigation agriculture, the surplus produce being sold in the towns, but an increasing number of Mocheros work for cash wages outside the village. It is in no sense a subsistence economy, and cash crops are important. The Mocheros women engage in trade, selling the farm produce, but nevertheless,

> trading, as an occupation in itself, seems to hold little interest for the people. All retail establishments in Moche pueblo itself are in the hands either of *forasteros* or of *extanjeros*, and I am not aware that any Mochero has left the community to set up or take part in a strictly trading or commercial enterprise elsewhere (44).

The Chinese and Japanese are shopkeepers, tinsmiths and traders, as are a few of the other *forasteros*. There is a sense of marked difference between the Mocheros and *forasteros* and Gillin suggests that 'the resistance and reserve toward *forasteros* shown by Mocheros in their personal relations is rooted in fear for their land' (45).

So far we have a general background picture of a situation not very different from that with which we have been dealing in British Guiana. The 'true Mocheros' would correspond roughly to what we have designated the 'Negro' community in August Town, for example. There we have referred to a village 'upper-class' and to various Chinese, Portuguese and Coloured elements which are set off in greater or lesser degree from the bulk of the village population. It is also true that the Negro villagers of August Town are not racially pure in a biological sense, but they are regarded as 'black people'. Both within Moche and within August Town there is a lack of business initiative on the part of most people, and nearly all shops etc., are in the hands of *forasteros*, and Chinese and Portuguese, respectively. Both communities are based on mixed wage earning and subsistence economies. Both 'true Mocheros' and the 'black people' of August Town are low status groups in a total society stratified in terms of an ethnic class system. Structurally they are comparable.

Mocheros live in houses that are quite different in construction from those in our Guianese villages, but they are about the same size and the furnishings are similar with Guiana being a little better off as regards the number of display items. Gillin asserts that there are no social classes which are 'formally defined and recognized in

Moche, but there are differences in wealth or expenditure . . .' (46). The areas of land owned and worked by Mocheros are small, and the average holding is about 3.9 acres, composed of scattered plots of less than 1,000 square metres. Land is inherited in both lines and,

> Transfer from the older to the younger generation is made by gift before death, by written testament, and by customary division if the deceased has died intestate. In the latter case, my informants tell me that it has been customary for the spouse to receive half of the property in life trust, as it were, with the remainder *divided equally among the children* and their mother's share reverting, share and share alike, to them on her death (47). [My italics.]

Since land still forms a most important basis for money-making in Moche, where the trend towards working outside the community for wages is still developing, there are a great number of legal disputes over land. This contrasts with the situation in the Guianese communities, but the type of inheritance is identical, with all children getting an equal share (48).

Gillin's data on family organization and household composition are rather meagre, for as he says, he never actually lived in the community, and the field tour was not long enough to collect adequate statistical data. However, he noted immediately the dominant position of women. They control finances and whilst the men are responsible for agricultural production, the women do all the marketing and handle all domestic funds. Families keep a small amount of savings for sickness or funerals in much the same way Guianese villagers keep a 'canister', but these are never large. Shops only extend limited credit, so that there is no chronic indebtedness.

The normal Moche household contains only a nuclear family of spouses and their unmarried children. Although the man is nominal head of the household, it is the woman who is the dominant partner controlling the finances and the running of the household. 'Both parents discipline the children, although infants are handled almost exclusively by women' (49). Where quarrels occur between spouses, beating of men by the women is as common as the opposite (50). We are told very little else about the internal relationships of household members.

There is the familiar pattern of early heterosexual activity, and illegitimacy is common. The offspring of youthful affairs suffer no social disabilities.

As a result of these affairs not a few girls have children, called *niños de la calle*, 'children of the street'. They are not thrown out of the house or disowned by outraged fathers, nor, in fact, is any serious obstacle put in the way of their continued normal social development. If the father of the child is economically suitable to the girl, her parents will try to force the pair into setting up a household together; if not, the girl and her child continue to live with her parents. Practically all such girls eventually settle down with some man and form a family without any great social stigma attached either to them or to the child. Men do not disdain to marry or to set up a household with an unmarried mother. The main bar to illicit unions is Church disapproval. The guilt felt on this score, however, is somewhat assauged by having illegitimate children properly baptized in the church (51).

Marital customs also follow very closely those found in Guiana, and Gillin distinguishes three types of marriage—*de facto, de jure* and *de religio*—corresponding to customary, legal and church marriage, though he says that legal or civil marriage is rarely found without church marriage (52).

'An informal type of marriage, more common that the formal, is accomplished by the couple simply starting to live together . . .' (53). Couples live together in customary unions for long periods of time, often converting the union into a legal and religious marriage after the birth of children. Divorce is practically unknown, but marriages break up, and the couples may settle in customary unions with other persons. There are no organized and lasting kin groups wider than the immediate family, but Gillin mentions the fact that

> There are a few exceptions in which a group of siblings and other kinsmen maintains a certain solidarity and unity. In all cases the unity seems to be imposed by the personal influence of a 'matriarch', an old woman, usually the mother of the siblings (54).

This is admittedly vague, but the very fact that it is noted is significant from our point of view.

Without carrying our comparison further into the realms of religion, magical beliefs, drinking habits, etc., enough has been cited to show that there are striking similarities between this Peruvian community and the Negro villages of Guiana on the other side of the continent. The similarities are particularly interesting since the Mocheros are not Negroes, nor do any Negroes live in Moche district, which means that the structural forms we find there cannot be explained away in terms of an African heritage. What is even more interesting is that Moche social structure is clothed in a completely different set of customs, manners, beliefs etc. In other words it is culturally distinct from the Negro communities of the West Indies.

From Gillin's discussion of the cultural position of Moche, at the end of his report, it seems clear that the Mocheros are sufficiently integrated into Peruvian life for them to share a large number of the common values of Peruvian society. In this sense Moche is much more 'mestizoized' than a community such as the Mexican village of Tepoztlan studied by Redfield and Lewis, or the pueblo of San Luis Jilotepeque, Guatemala, described by Tumin (55). In San Luis the Indians appear to retain a considerable degree of cultural autonomy and maintain an internal prestige hierarchy which is related to the holding of 'offices' requiring a good deal of skill in matters of Indian ritual. Here also the family system appears to accord a much greater degree of importance to the husband-father rôle which is consonant with the greater importance of the farm as the sole basis of subsistence and the participation of men in the positively valued Indian prestige hierarchy (56).

Tepoztlan presents a much more fluid situation than that found in San Luis Jilotepeque. Redfield maintained that there were clear-cut differences between the low status group of *tontos,* and the higher status group of *correctos,* the latter being more versed in the culture of the city. Lewis contends that this division does not correspond to any real division of the population into social groups, but merely represents an ideal dichotomy in value judgments about the behaviour of individuals. However he does imply that there is some form of social stratification within the village, and it is clear that wealth differences, cultural differences and racial differences all enter into the determination of status, at least to some extent, though from Lewis's descriptions we are unable to assess just how far. Since the status system of the village is not adequately related to the wider social system of Mexico, we must regard the discussion as inadequate from our point of view, but it does seem fairly clear that cultural and economic differentiations override racial distinctions to a more marked degree than they do in the West Indies. Lewis does not dwell upon the variability of family structure with socio-economic status, but speaking of the internal relations of the household group he says:—

> In contrast to the wife's central rôle within the home, the husband's actual participation in family and household affairs is minimal. His work,

with the exception of hauling water and making occasional repairs in and around the house, is outside the home. The division of labor is clear-cut, and the husband, except in emergencies, never does anything in connection with the house or children. For the majority of men, the home is a place where they have their physical needs attended to. Men are away from home a good part of the day, and sometimes for several days at a time, depending upon their work and the season of the year.

The history of Tepoztlan has been such that men frequently were forced to leave the village for long periods, and it is interesting to speculate on the effect of this on family life. We know that many Tepoztecans had to work in the mines of distant Taxco and on far away haciendas during the early sixteenth century. This pattern continued in modified form throughout the colonial period and until the Revolution. Before the Revolution, large numbers of men worked on the neighbouring haciendas and returned to the village only once every two weeks. Even today, about 150 men work on the haciendas during four to six months of the dry season, returning home once a week. With the husband away, the wife was not only head of the family but also often had to find means of supporting herself and the children until his return (57).

Elsewhere Lewis describes the family system as being strongly patriarchal, and clearly we must not be misled into thinking that wherever we find matri-focal household groups we must also find men without any form of authority or control. Even in the villages with which we are concerned in British Guiana it would be untrue to say that men have absolutely no authority, but even so the use of the word 'patriarchal' in relation to the situation as reported for Tepoztlan is, to say the least, uninformative. In a society such as Nupe which is technically patrilineal, Nadel points out quite clearly that a 'real' situation can exist where authority in the household is largely surrendered to women on account of their command of economic resources (58). In Tepoztlan the situation is not dissimilar, though the rôle of men as providers is as well marked as it is in British Guiana.

If Lewis had provided more data on the variation of family type with socio-economic status we should have been in a better position to utilize his work for comparison. The ethnic distinctions in Tepoztlan are obviously of less direct importance than they are in the West Indies, and from this point of view there may be much to be learned of the possible lines of development in the West Indies if ascriptively based status differentiations give way even more to status based on criteria of achievement. From Lewis's remarks on the lack of eagerness to 'get on' in the world, it seems likely that there is at least a section of the village community where the 'ethos' is not much different to that found in our villages.

Scotland

The Scottish mining community studied by a team of British anthropologists in 1948–50 provides us with a unit of comparison which has the advantage of having practically no similarity of historical background to the Guianese case. One member of the research team, Miss Shirley Wilson, concentrated upon a study of the neighbourhood and family complex and it is to her work we shall refer (59). It must be admitted at the outset that there is considerable danger in a comparison of this kind, of abstracting certain facts from their context, but the limited material available on this Scottish community seems suggestive enough to warrant its inclusion here.

Although she calls her dissertation 'The Family and Neighbourhood in a British Community', it is really a study of the family in relation to the variability in the status system. Social status is largely correlated with territorial clustering in the sense that each street in the town seems to be ranked in some way, although there are some streets inhabited by a series of families belonging to different parts of the status scale. Miss Wilson decided that it is impossible to draw rigid lines dividing the population into various 'classes', and she tries to see the situation as a 'gradient' of statuses with persons tending towards one of two sets of polar values and polar types. On the one hand there is the 'lower-status' pole, and on the other the 'white-collar higher-status' pole. Persons tending towards the 'lower-status' end of the scale can be separated off into a group characterized by a whole series of factors of which occupation is the most significant. The occupational scale is divided into 'dirty' and 'clean' jobs and this corresponds to the major status division. Miss Wilson develops her thesis with skill, showing how there is a basic dichotomy in social values between the two main status groups. The higher status group is the socially mobile group imbued with values laying stress on the importance of 'getting on', and the moral necessity for improving one's status; in short that complex of values sometimes referred to as the Protestant ethic (60). What interests us particularly is the fact that it is possible to separate out so clearly a lower status group which is occupationally differentiated, recruited mainly by birth, and tending to cluster in territorial units.

It is characterized by its own internal value system which gives it a solidarity lacking in the higher status groups, and it is the nature of these values that we find so strikingly similar to those in our Guianese villages. In contrast to the higher status group there is no emphasis on 'getting on' in terms of rising up an occupational ladder, and jobs within the lower status range are ranked in terms of the immediate remuneration. Lower status group values always stress the present, and there is no emphasis placed on planning, saving, or working towards long term goals involving a change in status.

> . . . in the ideology of the lower status people, success has radically different implications; it does not bring primarily an increase in social status. Success is often interpreted more simply in terms of getting money (61).

Emphasis on the short term goal is evident in other spheres, such as the use of leisure. Whereas the higher status conception of leisure is that it should be used 'constructively' and devoted to activities which either emphasize, or improve, social status, the lower status group demands immediate relaxation in its leisure time and contrasts play very strongly with work.

> Generally for people in manual and unskilled jobs, enjoyment and pleasure from leisure activities is held to exist when these are divorced from the aspects of learning and of the long term moral benefit. The completeness of the contrast between work and play is emphasized by people in the lower status jobs (62).

Patterns of consumption and expenditure are also radically different as between the two groups.

> Generally, higher status expenditure tends to be concentrated on the collection of material goods, or on such activities as higher education which brings some measurable and observable result in terms of increased status, whereas lower status expenditure is devoted mainly to more consumable objects. (63).

'Homes of very low status are sometimes devoid of all furniture and equipment apart from a few necessary items' (64). For the 'white collar' group, 'the "Moral" use of expenditure is considered to be that which is status giving or status-revealing' whilst for the lower status group 'saving and thrift are sometimes thought to signify "meanness" ' (65).

It is clear even from the very brief summary given above that there is a basic similarity in the values of the lower status group described by Miss Wilson, and in the Negro groups studied in Guiana. Both groups occupy low status in a stratified society, though of course in Guiana, skin colour presents a more permanent and distinguishing badge of status and inhibits mobility to a greater extent. Nevertheless, the Scottish community displays the same general characteristics, and even though upward mobility is theoretically possible for the lower status group, it does not prevent an acceptance of low status, and a development of solidarity which lays stress on this acceptance and discourages upward mobility. Miss Wilson sees quite clearly that ideas about the nature of the total society will vary from group to group, and she says,

> The emphasis on democracy is less evident among lower-status people than among higher-status people and the society is sometimes spoken of as divided by 'class barriers'. This is an interesting reflection of the weaker social mobility of lower status people; since they neither value it, or achieve it to the same extent, they tend to assume that it cannot and does not exist' (66).

The pre-occupation with status which is characteristic of the higher status group means that the family system must be compatible with the social mobility of its members. There is a shrinkage of kin ties and a relative isolation of the conjugal family as in America (67). Greater stress is laid upon clique and association membership which can be manipulated to improve status, and even within the elementary family the internal relationships are adjusted to allow or even encourage the mobility of children at the expense of the solidarity of the family itself. The occupation of the husband-father becomes of prime importance in determining the status of the family as a unit, but on the other hand the necessity for children to try to improve on their acquired hereditary status means that elementary families tend to liquidate themselves in the shortest possible time. In the lower status group the situation is quite different, and whereas the upper status woman feels that she must not interfere with her married children, the lower status woman often takes over the upbringing of her daughter's children almost completely. Even when higher status people live quite close to kinsfolk there is the feeling that one must not 'interfere', and the self-sufficiency of the conjugal unit is always stressed.

> Among lower status people, not only do relatives often live near to each other, since they are not scattered by the demands of social mobility, but the affectional relationships may be close and the sentimental tie is often expressed in day-to-day life, through the sharing of leisure time contacts, the borrowing of household articles and money, the informal visiting of homes, the care of the children and so on (68).

Of particular interest to us is the strong emphasis laid upon the bond between mother and daughter, and the social importance of 'Mum'. Young married couples often live with the wife's parents, and even if they don't, married daughters may visit their mothers every day and they go to the cinema together, do their shopping together, etc. The sharing of a household with the wife's mother is not regarded as merely a temporary expedient, and Wilson records one case where a couple lived with the wife's mother for eighteen years before they got a home of their own. In 1946, 40 per cent of the children born in the town, to town mothers, were born at the home of the maternal grandparents and only a few of these were in the streets of the three highest grades.

The maternal grandmother takes a significant part in the upbringing of the child, and where both mother and grandmother live in the same house the grandmother may take over completely to all intents and purposes.

> At least three-quarters of the children in low-grade streets are bottle-fed so that even the intimate physical act of nourishment is taken from the mother and transferred to the grandmother (69).

So far as marriage is concerned the lower status girl places great emphasis on 'fate', good looks, and luck in finding a partner and is but little concerned about status compatibility as are higher status individuals. Sex and physical attractiveness become important elements, and one labourer's daughter said 'All the people I know say that marriage is 90 per cent bed. And that's what I think' (70). In the lower status group, the proportion of civil marriages as opposed to church marriages is much higher than in the higher status groups, and a civil marriage is regarded as a sign of social inferiority, implying an element of impermanence. Divorce occurs almost solely in the lower status group, and in the period January 1940 to May 1950 there were eighty-eight divorces, and only four of the individuals involved came from streets in the upper three grades, all the rest coming from the three lowest grades of streets. Forty-six of the men and fifty-four of the women came from mining families.

Illegitimacy is both more frequent and less severely condemned in lower status families, and of 117 illegitimate births recorded between 1940 and 1949, only six of the mothers came from streets in the three upper grades. Nearly one third of all first born children in the community are either illegitimate or premaritally conceived, but the pressure to conformity results in many girls getting married before the first child is born so that the illegitimacy rate is much lower than it would otherwise be. Wilson relates the limitation of family size in the higher status groups to the desire for upward mobility, and remarks on the much more fatalistic attitude towards repeated pregnancies in the lower status homes where a greater number of children doesn't matter so much, since there is less concern for giving them all a good start on the road to higher status.

In the lower status group, adolescence is less marked by inter-generational conflict than in those groups where status differences between parents and children are becoming more marked, for since there is a tendency towards uniformity of type of occupation in the lower status group there is less emphasis on increasing social differentiation. Eating habits vary considerably between the two groups and the lower status homes place little emphasis on regular meal times at which everyone sits down together. There is more buying from fish-and-chip shops, cake-shops etc., and children are given food at odd intervals rather than at set meal times.

Miss Wilson deals only cursorily with the conjugal relationship, and tells us very little of the position of men in relation to their families of procreation, but it seems clear that the stress on matri-filiation in the lower status groups, exemplified by the frequency of matri-local residence and the close bond between mother and married daughter, tends to shift the focus of the household to the woman. It would be wrong to assume complete identity between this Scottish family structure and that found in British Guiana. In the Scottish case the total social situation is much more culturally homogeneous, and legal marriage is much more widely accepted as the normal framework for conjugal unions and child-bearing. Miss Wilson's analysis does bring out the correlation between a lengthened matri-line and the maternal-grandmother rôle on the one hand, and low status involving a negative emphasis on status mobility on the other. It suggests that the general principles which enter into the structuring of Guianese Negro households may be operative here, but a great deal more research would have to be done on this type of urban community before an adequate case could be maintained.

CONCLUSION

Without extending the range of our discussion any further it is evident that we have raised many fundamental problems merely by juxta-posing the material from several different 'culture areas' as we have done. What we have done, essentially, is to take two main features of the social systems we have dealt with; social stratification and family structure; and describe some aspects of their inter-relations in the different societies. We started out by trying to understand the structure of the family in three village communities in British Guiana, and an attempt was made to analyse this structure as fully as possible in the main section of this work. Inevitably we came up against the old problem of whether the nature of family relations in New World Negro society is to be explained in terms of historical factors such as the survival of African patterns of behaviour, the peculiar conditions existing on the slave plantations, or whether we could advance more plausible hypotheses in terms of the functional requirements of an on-going social system. It has been remarked that there is a fundamental similarity between the types of family structure found in Negro communities all over the New World, and of course if one regards this unit as a clearly defined 'culture area', there is a tendency to try to explain its unity and peculiar characteristics in terms of a set of factors peculiar to it alone. The very concept of culture held by the majority of scholars who have worked in the area has tended towards this type of analysis, for culture in this sense is essentially an historical concept, and culture contact becomes a process of exchange of culture traits over a period of time. The same type of analysis has been employed by scholars working in the Latin-American field, and it seems truly remarkable that the two areas—Latin American and New World Negro—should have been treated in such a completely separatist manner. If the same kind of approach had been adopted towards the problems of African anthropology it is difficult to see how the advances in comparative social structure in Africa could have developed. Had societies been classified according to their complexes of culture traits alone, without reference to their structure, then presumably a book such as *African Political Systems* or *African Systems of Kinship and Marriage* could never have been written (71).

Throughout Latin America and the Caribbean area we are dealing with societies that all exhibit similar structural features, and this gives the whole region a unity which is not to be found in a comparison of the particular cultural symbols through which that structure is given meaning. Admittedly both areas have been subject to not dissimilar sequences of historical events, since both have been areas of colonization of European powers. But since quite different 'cultures' have been involved, Amerindian and African, we should expect the resulting situation to be quite different in the two areas. In terms of our definition of culture, we do in fact find that the contemporary 'cultures' in the two areas are very different indeed. Radcliffe-Brown speaks of a 'cultural tradition' as the process of handing down knowledge, skills, ideas, belief, tastes and sentiments, which are thus acquired by other persons through the learning process (72). A more precise and systematic statement, and one with which we would substantially agree is made by Talcott Parsons, when he says 'It is [such] a shared symbolic system which functions in interaction which will here be called a *cultural tradition*' (73). If culture is a system of shared symbolic meanings which make communication possible in an ordered social life, then it is the way in which actions are carried out that interests us when discussing 'culture'. Thus, when a Mochero dies, the church bells are rung in almost the same way that they are in August Town, but when the *velorio* is held on the night following the death, although it seems to have exactly the same functions as a Guianese 'wake' in expressing a sense of communal loss etc., the details of the way in which the body is laid out, the women weep, and so on are quite different.

If we look at all the societies we have mentioned in this section we find a correlation between low social status in a stratified society, and a type of family system in which men seem to lack importance as authoritarian figures in domestic relations. These are facts of social structure, and the arrangement of these structural elements is basically similar despite marked variations in their corresponding cultural complexes in different societies. We are really dealing with sub-systems of the several societies, although certain aspects of the total societies are basically comparable. In all cases the sub-groups with which we are most immediately concerned constitute relatively solidary groups, differentiated with respect to other groups in the society, but internally relatively undifferentiated so far as status is concerned.

If our analysis is correct then it raises certain issues of general importance. It would suggest that there is a rewarding field for comparative study between Latin American and West Indian societies using a structural frame of reference. The relations of racial or ethnic groups become special cases of a general theory of social stratification, and 'acculturation' has to be seen in the light of continuing social differentiations of a certain kind.

Cultural traditions of certain ethnic sub-groups may be found to persist as indices of status differentiation rather than as a result of geographical isolation. Leach has graphically shown how even linguistic differences can persist between households in one local community provided there is a structural base for such cultural differentiation, and his conclusion that culture and structure appear to vary independently is borne out by our researches, though there is always the possibility that the independent variability is merely apparent at the particular level of abstraction at which we are working (74).

CHAPTER X

CONCLUSION

In this study we have attempted to present a series of ethnographic observations in such a way that they would serve to clarify certain specific problems concerning the nature of family structure in the communities with which we were concerned. The most important conclusions which emerge from the study concern the relations between the configuration of domestic relations and the position which the family and its members occupy in the total social system. This is exactly the kind of problem with which social anthropologists have been concerned in societies in other parts of the world; societies where 'the total social system' has often been represented by a 'tribe', internally differentiated on a kinship-defined basis. Such societies have generally been characterized by the absence of a developed technology and economy, and by a very rudimentary division of labour. Domestic rôles have often been closely associated with political and economic rôles, in the sense that the former have often been the starting point of the definition of the latter.

In British Guiana we have been faced with an entirely different situation, but we have tried to elucidate the structural framework of social relations by the same general method of approach as that used by social anthropologists working in what are usually termed 'primitive' societies. We have adhered to the theoretical principle that the unit of study is a whole society; in this case the whole of British Guiana is taken as constituting the total social system from an analytical point of view, but we have been concerned with particular aspects of the total social structure, isolated for special study according to a theoretical scheme. We have taken the colour/class divisions to represent the major lines of differentiation within the total social system, and it is in the nature of the functional unity of the society that the units so differentiated are hierarchically arranged, being allocated different statuses, different degrees of political power and different social functions. Every social system has internal differentiations of this order, but we have been primarily concerned with the basis on which the differentiation takes place rather than with the social function of the differentiation itself. It has been our contention that a primary base line for the differentiation of function, and of status, is the fact of ethnic identity, and this fact has important implications for the study of domestic relations. It would be a complete and complicated study in itself to analyse even the formal aspects of the total social system in full, and it must be made quite clear that we have not attempted to do this. Enough has been clarified to make it possible to state that in the villages with which we are most concerned we find that the bulk of the population constitutes a cohesive group bound by ties of kinship and territorial affiliation, and occupying a low position in the status system, both on account of the position of its members in the scale of values relating to ethnic characteristics, and because of the nature of the occupational, political, and other functions which they fulfil. In this case, ethnic characteristics are merely a convenient factor by which status and functions can be ascribed to individuals and groups. In other societies, as our comparison with a Scottish mining community shows, such cohesive low status groups can exist without the presence of an ethnic distinguishing 'badge', and other bases of ascription of status may exist such as birth into a particular family, possession of certain cultural characteristics and so on. Even in British Guiana, status and occupation can be changed to some extent by various means we have termed 'achievement', after Linton, but the institutionalized social values of the total social system lay less stress upon achievement than upon ascribed characteristics, and there is not a high rate of mobility in the status scale.

In Chapter I we laid out as concisely as possible the facts which are necessary to an understanding of the position of the Negro communities in the historical development of the colony, and in the present-day economic system. We described the systems of drainage and irrigation which are necessary to make the Guiana coastlands habitable and agriculturally productive, and we also dwelt upon the necessity for some kind of political organization in order to operate them effectively. Whilst ecological factors have been of great importance in determining the lay out of the clusters of dwellings and farm lands which we call villages, it is a striking fact that there are no really highly developed political institutions at the village level, with a series of important offices held by members of the main village group who would control the activities of their fellow villagers. There are such institutions, of course, in the form of the Local Authorities, but the tendency is for the really important control functions to be delegated to persons occupying offices in the wider social system of which the village is only a part. Thus there has not developed *within* the villages any really important rank differentiation of a political kind, and such political functions as are carried out at the village level are usually thrust upon school teachers, i.e., persons who derive higher status from other specialized functions. The villages are not self-contained economic entities with their own internal division of labour supplying all their needs, neither are they specialized units of production in the over-all system. They are largely reservoirs of labour on the one hand, and their inhabitants are small scale farmers and stock-rearers on a part-time basis on the other. This has always been the case from the date of their establishment as villages.

In our discussion of the household group and the kinship system in Part II, we have had to break a good deal of new ground so far as discussions of West Indian family life are concerned. It has long been known that the lower-class Negro family all over the New World tended to be matri-focal, and controversies have arisen as to why this should be so. This book has attempted to throw light on this question, as well as examining in some detail exactly what 'matri-focal' implies in the three villages we have studied. It seems likely that the detailed anthropological study of family structure, concentrating upon variations within this one 'culture area', are only just beginning, and by carrying out a series of studies concentrating upon the 'depth' analysis of specific problems such as that attempted here, it will be possible to build up a body of comparative material which can be integrated with the more extensive problem analyses undertaken by sociologists.

We have shown quite conclusively that the normal type of domestic unit in British Guiana comes into being as the result of a man and a woman entering a conjugal union of some kind, and that the elementary, or nuclear, family is the normal type of co-residential unit, particularly at that stage of development where the children are young. The variations from this norm arise as the result of the strength of the mother-child relationship and the relative weakness of the conjugal bond, and they generally result in the emergence of the typically solidary unit of a woman, with her daughters and their children.

There is a sense in which the conjugal tie is always a potentially weak one in every society, for in a matrix of close kinship relations, it is the only non-kinship relationship, and it has to be buttressed by moral and legal rules which are compatible with other features of the social structure. These may be stronger or weaker in each case depending on the way in which the elementary family is integrated into wider structures, and there are some matrilineal societies where the conjugal tie, and the father-child relationship, may be regarded as being extremely tenuous.

In our particular case there are no such extreme conditions, and in so far as the conjugal tie can be considered 'weak', its weakness is not correlated with the existence of matrilineal descent groups, but rather with the relative unimportance of the jural position of the father in relation to the children, without there being any comparable relation of the child to its mother's brother or mother's lineage. The functions which the husband-father performs are minimal and are almost solely confined to providing food, shelter and clothing for his spouse and her children, though of course he has important functions in the socialization of the children, even if these imply no more than just existing as a father-figure.

The consideration of a strongly patrilineal society such as the Tallensi throws interesting light on the Guianese situation, and can be held to constitute a source of valuable 'negative evidence' (1). In societies such as this the position of the husband-father in the domestic unit is firmly fixed. As head of the compound he is head of a corporate property-owning group, and all rights of possession over land, stock, buildings, food etc., may be vested in him so long as he occupies this position. He has very definite rights over the procreative powers of his wife or wives, these rights being transferred to him in customarily defined ways, usually through payment of a bride-price. The children belong to the segment of the patrilineage of which he is head, and their important social statuses are fixed by virtue of their membership of that lineage, and hence by reference to the father. The husband-father is not only head of the domestic group or compound, so far as its internal relationships are concerned, but he also occupies a position in the political system by virtue of his headship of that unit, and it is in this way that the family system is so closely integrated into wider social structures. The dual rôle of the husband-father in two systems is crucial.

In the case of rural Guiana Negro groups, the child's relationship to his father is not a crucial one in fixing his social position. This position is fixed by his birth as a member of the whole Negro group, and of the village community. In Section III we tried to show why the position of the husband-father in the social status hierarchy is not immediately important for the rest of the family. We pointed out that as soon as we leave the lower-class group, and begin to consider the middle and upper classes, then there is a tendency for the position of the husband-father in the occupational system to be important to the rest of the family, in so far as it is status-determining. Other problems arise of course, with which we have not dealt, such as the situation which exists when the wife-mother is of lighter complexion, and can therefore claim higher status on account of her position in the 'colour' hierarchy.

Much confusion about the nature of lower-class family life in the West Indies has arisen as the result of taking verbal statements from members of the middle-class, or even of the lower-class, too much at their face value, and regarding them as statements of fact rather than as symbolic statements of a state of inter-group relationship. It is a part of the mythology of the West Indies that the lower-class Negro is immoral and promiscuous, and that his family life is 'loose' and 'disorganized', and unless it is clearly recognized that such myths are an integral part of the system of relationships between various groups, reflecting value judgements inherent in their status rankings, then serious bias may be introduced into objective study. Differential standards of sexual morality reflect group differentiations of another order, and in fact, far from being completely promiscuous, sexual relations in the villages are quite definitely regulated within the limits imposed by the family structure. Village gossip often turns around specific couples and this gossip is never indifferent to what is taking place, and in itself it constitutes a means of regulating sexual relationships. There are very few 'don't care' girls, and the concern they show for what is being said about them shows that they do really 'care' about public opinion. Admittedly the limits of permissiveness are considerably broader than those found in middle-class English society, but this does not mean that there is no moral constraint whatsoever.

The specific comparisons with other societies made in Chapter IX have shown that similar structural principles may be found in other societies with a different cultural tradition and historical background. Merely to formulate the questions leading to such a comparison is a step forward in analysis, and the answers would seem to justify our contention that it is imperative to explore fully the interrelations between the co-existing parts of the social system before trying to 'explain' certain social facts in terms of their antecedent states over a long time span. Such 'explanations' are not invalid or without value, but they are not sociological explanations, and they may side-step the crucial issues of sociological analysis.

This book has been concerned with one set of problems only, and in seeking to clarify them it has often been necessary to treat whole sectors of the social organization of British Guiana in a very cursory manner. This is inevitable when one is dealing with an area where so little research has been carried out and where one must give at least a brief indication of the nature of the background in which the main problems are set. If the deficiencies of this work are recognized, it is hoped that it will stimulate other scholars to make good those deficiencies and to help in the building of a more adequate understanding of the social processes operating in this most fascinating corner of the West Indies.

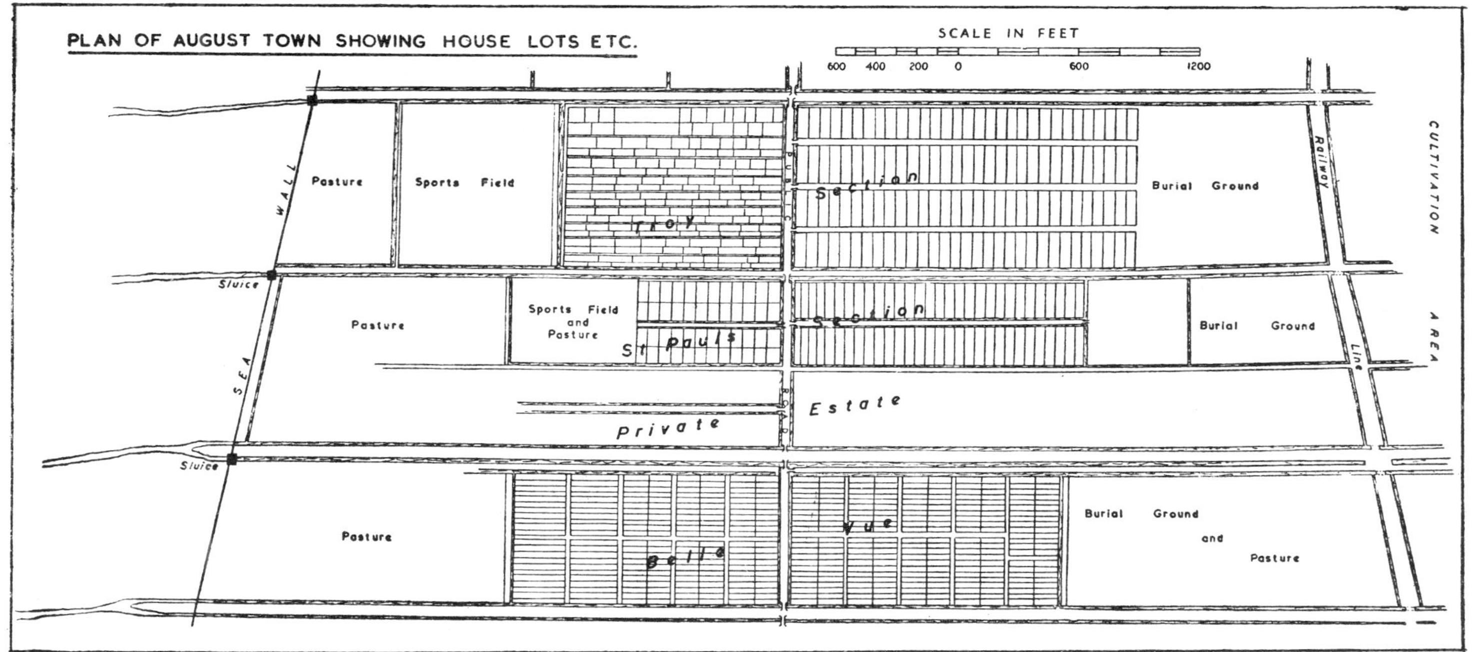

MAP 3

PLAN OF AUGUST TOWN SHOWING HOUSE LOTS, ETC.

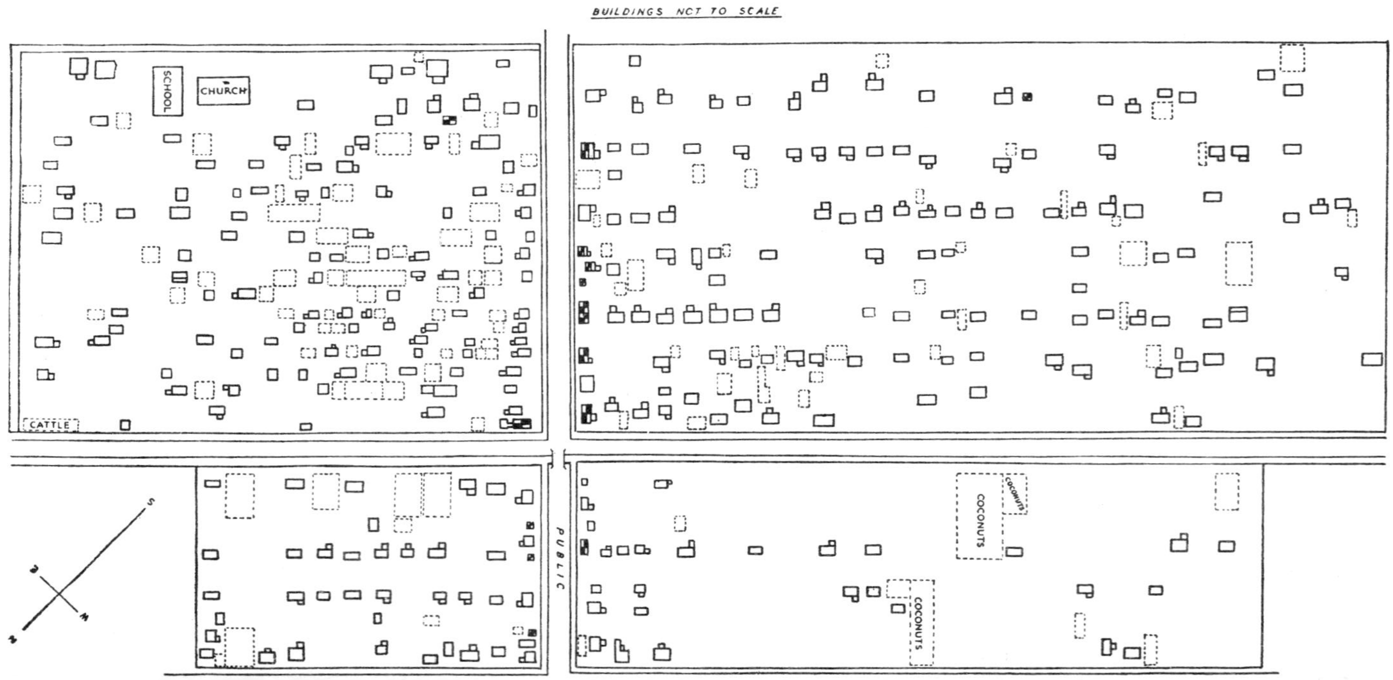

BUILDINGS NOT TO SCALE
SCHOOL
CHURCH
CATTLE
PUBLIC
COCONUTS
COCONUTS
COCONUTS
S
W
E
N

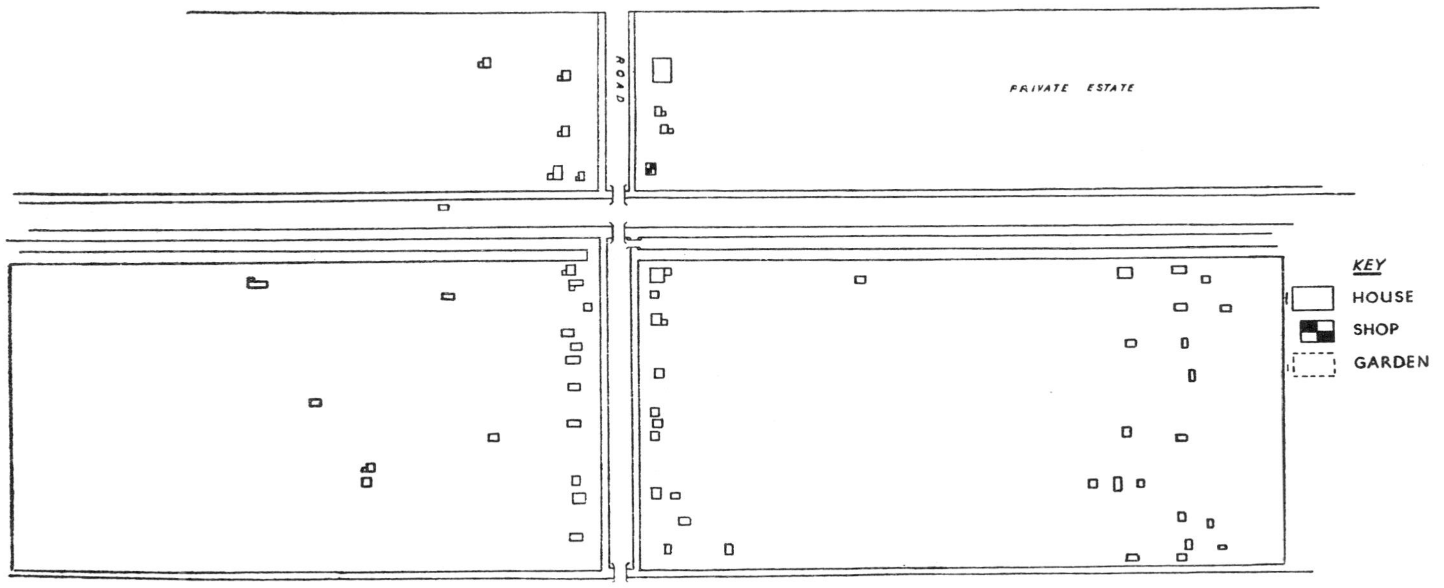

MAP 4

SKETCH PLAN OF AUGUST TOWN SHOWING LAYOUT OF VILLAGE, HOUSES, AND SHOPS

NOTES

CHAPTER I—INTRODUCTION *pages 3–47*

(1) Warner (1952) p. 33.
(2) Braithwaite (1953) p. 39.
(3) See Nadel (1951) for a discussion of field-work techniques. Also Evans-Pritchard (1951) pp. 64–85.
(4) See Fortes (1949 b), p. 54 and (1953) pp. 32–3, 35 for a discussion of this point.
(5) Masefield (1950) p. 22.
(6) Pinckard (1806).
(7) See Williams, E. (1942), (1944) and Henriques (1953).
(8) See Leyburn (1941).
(9) Rodway cited by Cameron (1934) Bk. I, pp. 108–9.
(10) The present-day burial societies are amongst the most vigorous and long-lived village organizations. They provide members with the financial means for a proper funeral and 'wake', and many of them provide sickness benefits as well.
(11) The pickled cheeks of cow or pig.
(12) Pinckard (1806) Vol. II, pp. 246–7.
(13) See Herskovits, M. J. and S. F. (1934).
(14) See Henriques (1953) p. 15 and Edwards (1796).
(15) Pinckard (1806) Vol. III p. 403. In a footnote Pinckard states that sugar began to replace cotton on many estates shortly after the time of writing.
(16) Farley (1954).
(17) See Cruikshank (1919).
(18) See Rodway (1891–4) Vol. III p. 106.
(19) See Barton Premium (1805) pp. 60, 69, 70–1, 133.
(20) Cameron (1934) Bk. II, p. 8.
(21) ibid. p. 12.
(22) Rodway (1891–4) Vol. III p. 103.
(23) See Williams, E. (1942).
(24) Pinckard (1806) Vol. II p. 351 and pp. 358–67.
(25) Sch. B. 1916/No. 768—Deeds Registry—New Amsterdam, British Guiana.
(26) 1841 C.O. III/82—Governor Light to Russell, 26 Jan. 1841—Encl.
(27) See p. 213.
It was impossible to check whether previous inter-marriages had taken place between the two sections since the church registers had been destroyed by fire a short time before I arrived in the village.
(28) See pp. 23–5.
(29) Cameron (1934). I am much indebted to this writer for his account of the history of the Guianese villages.

(30) Hinden (1950) pp. 53–70.

(31) Obeah is a generalized term for witchcraft, black magic and sometimes white magic. See Beckwith (1929), Williams, J. J. (1933) pp. 108–41 and Trevor (1950) pp. 87–115 and p. 467.

(32) See Barton Premium (1850).

(33) The names of the original proprietors of Belle Vue section appear on a plan drawn up in 1863 by A. F. Baird, sworn Land Surveyor, and have been compared with the names appearing on the agreement reproduced on pp. 16–18. The original copy of this plan is held in the Lands and Mines Department, Georgetown, British Guiana.

(34) Balata is collected from the wild Bullet tree (*Mimusops balata* of the order *Sapotoceae*). It is used in the manufacture of *gutta percha*.

(35) Kirke (1898) pp. 143–4.

(36) Simey (1946).

(37) Hinden (1950).

(38) Laing (1949).

(39) See Smith (1955) and *Report of the British Guiana Constitutional Commission 1954* (Cmd. 9274) (H.M.S.O., London).

(40) Smith (1955) p. 76.

(41) One dollar (B.W.I.) = four shillings and two pence or fifty-five cents (U.S.).

(42) *Colonial Reports—British Guiana 1951*, London: H.M.S.O. (1953) p. 50.

(43) This rather casual method of cultivating rice is in sharp contrast to the painstaking care which most East Indians lavish upon their rice crops. Certainly the Negro farmers could get higher yields if they devoted more time and attention to the crop, but they argue that they can be earning money elsewhere, and it does not pay them to stay in the village. They also assert that Negro women and children will not spend long periods of time in a flooded padi-field transplanting seedlings. The whole pattern of activities in the Negro villages is much more oriented towards the acquisition of cash wages, and the idea of a whole family turning out to work a rice farm under the direction of a male head is quite alien. This fact, rather than climatic factors or 'racial character', must be regarded as being of the greatest importance in moulding the attitudes towards methods of cultivation.

(44) See Cameron (1934) Bk. II, p. 61.

(45) I was told by one informant that a certain clergyman resident on the West Coast of Berbice acted as a recruiting agent for the bauxite companies at one time, and that it was he who persuaded the first men from August Town to go and take jobs at Kwakwani.

(46) Out of his earnings at Kwakwani or McKenzie a man may send as much as five or six dollars per week back to relatives in the village, particularly to his mother and to the mother of his children. In addition to this he will probably accumulate savings in order to buy land or build a house in the village, or to help his mother with the building of a house, payment of rates, etc.

(47) See pp. 207–8.

(48) Cumper (1953) p. 33.

(49) Wilson (1953) p. 336.

(50) See pp. 218–20.

CHAPTER II—THE HOUSEHOLD *pages* 51–69

(1) *Avicennia nitida* (Jacq.) or Black mangrove.

(2) *Euterpe oleracea.*

(3) These are basically stories of the Anansi cycle. See Henriques (1953) p. 25 and Trevor (1950) p. 423. In British Guiana the term 'Nancy' story is generalized to include all folk tales.

(4) See Smith (1955).

(5) See p. 143.

(6) See Table I, p. 43.

CHAPTER III—ECONOMIC FEATURES OF THE HOUSEHOLD GROUP *pages* 70–93

(1) There is a widespread belief that when the Dutch were in possession of the colony, many of the planters used to bury hoards of gold coins, and that with supernatural help, particularly in the form of spirit possession or through dream messages, it is possible to discover these hoards of 'Dutch money'.

(2) See pp. 61–5.

(3) During the course of the field tour in August Town, a series of daily household budgets were collected and for some households they extended over a period of two months. Unfortunately these have been lost, and the case presented here is one of a small series collected in Perserverance. It would correspond fairly closely to the food consumption of a household in either of the other two villages.

(4) See p. 57.

(5) See p. 145.

(6) Bales (1953) pp. 144–5.

(7) The census carried out by the Economics Division of the Department of Agriculture. See Blaich (1952).

(8) 'Rôti' is the local name for the East Indian bread or *chapati.*

(9) See p. 56.

(10) See pp. 52–53.

(11) The institution of 'throwing a box' is a method of obtaining credit. A number of people undertake to make regular periodic contributions to a 'box holder' and each time the contributions are made, one of the participants draws the whole amount. Similar institutions have been described for Africa and other parts of the West Indies. See Bascom (1952) and the correspondence colums of *Man* (Vol. LIII).

(12) Straw (1953).

(13) See p. 43.

CHAPTER IV—COMPOSITION OF THE HOUSEHOLD GROUP *pages* 94–107

(1) Herskovits, M. J. and S. F. (1947) p. 164.

(2) Simey (1946) p. 84.

(3) Kerr (1952) p. 56.

(4) Henriques (1953).

(5) Simey (1946).

(6) Henriques (1953), p. 105–6.

(7) Fortes (1949 b).

(8) A similar system of classification of household groups by members' relationships to each other has been adopted by the South West Cape Survey cited in *Small Towns of Natal—Natal Regional Survey, Additional Report No. 3*, University of Natal Press (1953).

(9) Fortes (1949 b) p. 84.

CHAPTER V—THE TIME FACTOR IN RELATION TO THE STRUCTURE OF THE HOUSEHOLD GROUP *pages* 108–141

(1) See Henriques (1953) and Simey (1946).
(2) See Braithwaite (1953) p. 122.
(3) See p. 61.
(4) Henriques (1953) p. 105.
(5) *Census of the Colony of British Guiana, 9th April 1946*. Government Printer, Kingston, Jamaica (1949).
(6) Compare this with the situation amongst the Tiv as reported by Bohannen and cited by Fortes (1953) p. 34.
'A Tiv may claim to be living with a particular group of relatives for purely personal reasons of convenience or affection. Investigation shows that he has in fact made a choice of where to live within a strictly limited range of non-lineage kin.'
(7) This is consonant with the change in the pattern of domestic relations described earlier in this chapter.
(8) See Rattray (1927) pp. 59–62.
(9) Christaller (1933) p. 599.
(10) It is noticeable that the god-parent relationship seems to be much weaker than that reported for some other parts of the West Indies, and particularly for areas with a strong Catholic background. In Mexico and other parts of Latin America the god-parent relationship is of great importance, providing ties between many more persons than the god-parents and god-child. See Lewis (1951), Gillin (1945) and Tax (1952). The custom seems to work as a method of transforming local ties into quasi-kinship ties within a territorial and religious community.
(11) See Kerr (1952) p. 35.
(12) In the register of births for the August Town area fifteen children were registered as being born to unmarried mothers from August Town, and in no case was the father's name entered in the register.
(13) van Gennep (1909) pp. 57–93.
(14) Great stress is laid on speaking 'grammatical' English in school, and the whole educational system is based on the pattern of denominational school education which was prevalent in Britain at the beginning of the twentieth century. For a good description of Jamaican rural schools, which would apply with slight modifications to British Guiana, see Kerr (1952). See also Lamming (1953) for a novelist's semi-autobiographical account of school life in Barbados.
(15) Kerr (1952) p. 168.
(16) See p. 171.
(17) See Nadel (1954) p. 179.
(18) Kerr (1952) p. 80.
(19) See Parsons (1949).
(20) See pp. 168–9.
(21) See pp. 62–3.

CHAPTER VI—THE NORMS OF DOMESTIC GROUPING *pages* 142–150

(1) Richards (1950) p. 246.
(2) See pp. 99–101.
(3) See Fortes (1949b) p. 58.
(4) See Homans (1950) Ch. 11 and Parsons (1952) pp. 300–1.
(5) Homans (1950) p. 276.

(6) See Parsons (1949) and Centers (1949).

CHAPTER VII—THE KINSHIP SYSTEM *pages* 151–187

(1) For example, see Rees (1951).
(2) Radcliffe-Brown (1950), p. 81.
(3) See Fortes (1949b) and (1950).
(4) See p. 58n(3).
(5) Smith (1955) p. 73.
(6) See Henriques (1953) p. 137, n.l.
(7) The term 'kinna' is almost identical with the Dutch Guiana Bush Negro term 'tchina', and has approximately the same, if a somewhat more restricted meaning. In Surinam the taboo is also acquired from the father. See Herskovits, M. J. and F. S. (1934), p. 137. According to the Herskovitses the word is of Bantu origin.

It should be noted that in the Gold Coast the word for 'taboo' is very similar, and the Guiana term 'kinna' is probably derived from it. In Ashanti the word 'Kyiri' or 'Kyi' means taboo. Christaller (1933) p. 297 and p. 300 gives the following meanings (amongst others) for the term 'Kyi' or 'Kyiri':

1. To dislike, or to loathe.
2. To abstain from, to avoid, to consider forbidden and unclean.

See also Rattray (1929) p. 415.

The Tallensi (North Gold Coast) use the word 'Kiher' for 'taboo'. See Fortes (1945) p. 67.

The concept of 'kinna' is not so highly developed in British Guiana as it is in Surinam, and sharing the same 'kinna' has no special significance.

(8) See p. 143.
(9) Schneider (1953) p. 228.
(10) See p. 143.
(11) See Braithwaite (1953).
(12) See Henriques (1953).
(13) A small bundle made up of ribs from the leaves of the manicole palm (*Euterpe oleracea*).
(14) See Trevor (1950) pp. 115–21.
(15) See Rattray (1916) p. 48.
(16) By deviance, in this context, we mean failure to conform to the expectations of what constitutes normal behaviour for someone in his position as a member of *the village*, and not of Guianese society as a whole.
(17) Nadel (1954) pp. 163–206.
(18) Pronounced Kweh-Kweh.
(19) In this case 'marriage' almost certainly did not imply legal marriage in church as it does today.
(20) This would be a fond-name. See p. 161.
(21) Dennett (1902).
(22) See Simey (1946) pp. 183–4.
(23) This terminological usage may be contrasted with that reported by Rees for rural Wales, where marriage involves a change in the way the man is addressed. Prior to marriage when he is living on his father's farm, he is known by his own christian name followed by the name of the farm (e.g., John Ty Uchaf—John of the farm Uchaf). See Rees (1951).
(24) See Rattray (1916) p. 18 and (1923) p. 139.
(25) Durkheim (1952).

CHAPTER VIII—THE FAMILY SYSTEM IN THE CONTEXT OF GUIANESE SOCIETY

pages 191–220

(1) Braithwaite (1953).

(2) This 'mixed' group would not correspond exactly with our 'coloured' category, since we would rarely include persons of mixed Negro and East Indian descent. These persons are likely to identify with either the Negro or the East Indian groups for most social purposes.

(3) The term 'ascription' is used as defined by Linton (1936) p. 115.

(4) Parsons (1952) pp. 132–6.

(5) Henriques (1953) p. 168.

(6) Leach (1954) p. 285.

(7) Braithwaite (1953) pp. 46–63.

(8) This is not to say that leaders of the various churches have not spoken out against social injustice when they have seen it, but the churches as organizations have concentrated on 'moral uplift' within the existing social framework for the most part. The various Negro revivalist churches belong to a rather different category and cannot be dealt with here. Their main activities have been located in the city rather than in the urban areas.

(9) Braithwate (1953) pp. 40–1.

(10) Redfield (1941).

(11) Speaking of the increasing division of labour in societies, and the substitution of organic for mechanical solidarity, he says:—

'This social type [organic] rests on principles so different from the preceding that it can develop only in proportion to the effacement of that preceding type. In effect, individuals are here grouped, no longer according to their relations of lineage, but according to the peculiar nature of the social activity to which they consecrate themselves. Their natural milieu is no longer the natal milieu, but the occupational milieu. It is no longer real or fictitious consanguinity which marks the place of each one, but the function which he fills. No doubt, when this new organization begins to appear, it tries to utilize the existing organization and assimilate it. The way in which functions are divided thus follows, as faithfully as possible, the way in which society is already divided. The segments, or at least the groups of segments united by special affinities become organs. It is thus that the clans which together formed the tribe of the Levites appropriated sacerdotal functions for themselves among the Hebrew people. In a general way, classes and castes probably have no other origin nor any other nature; they arise from the multitude of occupational organizations being born amidst the pre-existing familial organization. But this mixed arrangement cannot long endure, for between the two states that it attempts to reconcile, there is an antagonism which necessarily ends in a break. It is only a very rudimentary division of labor which can adapt itself to those rigid, defined moulds which were not made for it. It can grow only by freeing itself from the framework which encloses it. As soon as it has passed a certain stage of development, there is no longer any relation either between the immutable number of segments and the steady growth of functions which are becoming specialized, or between the hereditarily fixed properties of the first and the new aptitudes that the second calls forth. The social material must enter into entirely new combinations in order to organize itself upon completely different foundations. But the old structure, so far as it persists, is opposed to this. That is why it must disappear.' Durkheim (1947), pp. 182–3.

(12) See Kirke (1898) pp. 42–4.

(13) The term 'homogeneous' is used here in the sense outlined by Fortes (1953) p. 36. 'A working definition I make use of is that a homogeneous society is ideally one in which any person, in the sense given to this term by Radcliffe-Brown in his recent (1950) essay, can be substituted for any other person of the same category without bringing about changes in the social structure.'
(14) See p. 14.
(15) See p. 181.
(16) Nadel (1951) p. 171.
(17) Its reputation for beating up policemen is greatly exaggerated, and is merely one aspect of the generally bad relations which exist between the public and a police force which is isolated in semi-military barracks, rather than being resident amongst the rural population.

CHAPTER IX—HYPOTHESES AND THE PROBLEM OF 'EXPLANATION' *pages* 221–254

(1) See Parsons (1952), pp. 59–61.
(2) This term is used in the sense defined by Nadel (1951) pp. 45–7.
(3) See Cousins (1935).
(4) See Radcliffe-Brown (1950) p. 77.
(5) See Eggan (1949).
(6) Gough (1952).
(7) Josselin de Jong (1951).
(8) See Braithwaite (1953).
(9) M. J. and S. F. Herskovits (1947).
(10) ibid, pp. 5–6.
(11) M. J. Herskovits (1945).
(12) M. J. Herskovits (1952).
(13) Frazier (1939).
(14) Henriques (1949).
(15) Henriques (1953).
(16) M. J. and S. J. Herskovits (1947) pp. 105–6.
(17) ibid, p. 104.
(18) ibid, p. 228.
(19) ibid, p. 228.
(20) ibid, p. 228.
(21) ibid, p. 293.
(22) Deren (1953).
(23) Davis (1941) pp. 133–6.
(24) M. J. Herskovits (1937) pp. 122–3. Although it is stated that the slaves came from 'cultures where descent is counted solely on the side of the mother or father', the inaccuracy of this statement may be judged by reference to Radcliffe-Brown (1952) p. 15. This paper was originally written in 1924 and published shortly afterwards.
(25) Frazier (1939).
(26) ibid pp. 481–2.
(27) ibid pp. 483–4.
(28) Using the term 'Negro' in the sense it is used in the United States.
(29) Frazier (1939) p. 420.
(30) Simey (1946).
(31) Dollard (1937).
(32) Simey (1946) pp. 82–3.

(33) See p. 95.
(34) See pp. 99, 116–19.
(35) Henriques (1953).
(36) Simey (1946) p. 85.
(37) Henriques (1953) pp. 11–41.
(38) See pp. 225–6.
(39) See p. 225.
(40) Gillin (1945).
(41) ibid, p. vii.
(42) See Redfield (1941).
(43) Gillin (1945) p. 8.
(44) ibid, p. 13.
(45) ibid, p. 71.
(46) ibid, p. 42.
(47) ibid, p. 71.
(48) See Smith (1955).
(49) Gillin (1945) p. 98.
(50) ibid, p. 99.
(51) ibid, p. 95.
(52) ibid, p. 99.
(53) ibid, p. 97.
(54) ibid, p. 101.
(55) Redfield (1930); Lewis (1951); Tumin (1952).
(56) This situation would seem to approximate more closely to that found in the case of East Indian groups in British Guiana. No thorough studies have been carried out yet, but on the basis of superficial observation I would say that the position of the husband-father in the East Indian groups is much more stable and secure than in the Negro groups, and the East Indians have by no means given up the high value placed upon the solidarity of the family as a work unit.
(57) Lewis (1951) p. 321.
(58) See Nadel (1942).
(59) Wilson (1953).
(60) See Weber (1930).
(61) Wilson (1953) p. 76.
(62) ibid, p. 56.
(63) ibid, p. 57.
(64) ibid, p. 58.
(65) ibid, p. 60.
(66) ibid, p. 78.
(67) See Parsons (1949).
(68) Wilson (1953) pp. 234–5.
(69) ibid, p. 237.
(70) ibid, p. 255.
(71) Fortes and Evans-Pritchard (1940); Radcliffe-Brown and Daryll Forde (1950).
(72) Radcliffe-Brown (1952) p. 4.
(73) Parsons (1952) p. 11.
(74) Leach (1954) pp. 288–90.

CHAPTER X—CONCLUSION *pages* 255–260

(1) Fortes (1945) and (1949a).

BIBLIOGRAPHY

Section A contains only works referred to in the text and footnotes of this book whilst section B is a short list of some of the lesser known works on the Negro villages of British Guiana which were consulted by the author.

Section A

BALES, R. F. 1953. 'The Equilibrium Problem in Small Groups' in *Working Papers in the Theory of Action* (by Talcott Parsons, Robert F. Bales and Edward A. Shils), (Glencoe, Illinois).

BARTON PREMIUM (Pseud.) 1850. *Eight Years in British Guiana* (London).

BASCOM, W. R. 1952. 'The *Esusu*: A Credit Institution of the Yoruba', *Journal of the Royal Anthropological Institute*. Vol. LXXXII.

BECKWITH, M. W. 1929. *Black Roadways: A Study of Folk Life in Jamaica* (Chapel Hill).

BLAICH, O. P. 1952. *Agriculture in British Guiana. Census 1952* (Georgetown, British Guiana).

BRAITHWAITE, L. 1953. 'Social Stratification in Trinidad: A Preliminary Analysis', *Social and Economic Studies*, Vol. 2 (Kingston, Jamaica).

CAMERON, N. E. 1934. *The Evolution of the Negro*. 2 Vols. (Georgetown, British Guiana).

Census of the Colony of British Guiana, 9th April 1946. Published 1949 (Kingston, Jamaica).

CENTERS, R. 1949. *The Psychology of Social Classes* (Princeton University Press).

CHRISTALLER, J. G. 1933. *Dictionary of the Asante and Fante Language Called Tshi (Twi)* (Basel).

COUSINS, W. M. 1935. 'Slave Family Life in the British Colonies 1800–34', *Sociological Review*. Vol. 27 (London).

CRUIKSHANK, J. G. 1919. 'African Immigration after Emancipation', *Timehri, Journal of the Royal Agricultural and Commercial Society of British Guiana*. Third Series, Vol. VI (Georgetown, British Guiana).

CUMPER, G. E. 1953. 'Two Studies in Jamaican Productivity', *Social and Economic Studies*, Vol. I (Kingston, Jamaica).

DAVIS, A. et al. 1941. *Deep South* (Chicago).

DENNETT, R. E. 1902. 'Laws and Customs of the Fjort or Bavili Family, Kingdom of Loango', *Journal of the African Society*. Vol. I (London).

DEREN, M. 1953. *Divine Horsemen: The Living Gods of Haiti* (London).

DOLLARD, J. 1937. *Caste and Class in a Southern Town* (Yale University Press).

DURKHEIM, E. 1947. *The Division of Labor in Society* (trans. G. Simpson). (Glencoe, Illinois).

EDWARDS, BRYAN. 1796. 'Introductory Account containing observations on the Disposition, Character, Manners and Habits of Life, of the Maroons' in *The Proceedings of the Governor and Assembly of Jamaica in regard to the Maroon Negroes* (John Stockdale, Piccadilly, London)

EVANS-PRITCHARD, E. E. 1951. *Social Anthropology* (London).

FARLEY, R. 1954. 'The Rise of the Peasantry in British Guiana", *Social and Economic Studies*. Vol. 2 (Kingston, Jamaica).

FORTES, M. 1945. *The Dynamics of Clanship Among the Tallensi* (Oxford).

—— 1949a. *The Web of Kinship Among the Tallensi* (Oxford).

—— 1949b. 'Time and Social Structure: An Ashanti Case Study' in *Social Structure: Studies Presented to A. R. Radcliffe-Brown* (Ed. M. Fortes) (Oxford).

—— 1950. 'Kinship and Marriage among the Ashanti' in *African Systems of Kinship and Marriage* (Ed. A. R. Radcliffe-Brown and D. Forde) (Oxford).

—— 1953. 'The Structure of Unilineal Descent Groups', *American Anthropologist*. Vol. 55.

FORTES, M., AND EVANS-PRITCHARD, E. E. (Eds.). 1940. *African Political Systems* (London).

FRAZIER, F. 1939. *The Negro Family in the United States* (Chicago).

GILLIN, J. 1945. *Moche: A Peruvian Coastal Community* (Smithsonian Institution, Institute of Social Anthropology, Publication No. 3) (Washington, D.C.).

GOUGH, K. 1952. 'Changing Kinship Usages in the Setting of Political and Economic Change among the Nayars of Malabar', *Journal of the Royal Anthropological Institute*. Vol. LXXXII.

HENRIQUES, F. 1949. 'West Indian Family Organization', *American Journal of Sociology*. Vol. LV.

—— 1953. *Family and Colour in Jamaica* (London).

HERSKOVITS, M. J. 1937. *Life in a Haitian Valley* (New York).

—— 1945. 'Problem, Method and Theory in Afroamerican Studies', *Afroamerica*. Vol. 1 (Mexico).

—— 1949. *Man and His Works* (New York).

HERSKOVITS, M. J. AND F. S. 1934. *Rebel Destiny: Among the Bush Negroes of Dutch Guiana* (New York).

—— 1947. *Trinidad Village* (New York).

HINDEN, R. (Ed.). 1950. *Local Government and the Colonies*. (Ed. R. Hinden). *A Report to the Fabian Colonial Bureau* (London).

HOMANS, G. F. 1950. *The Human Group* (London and New York).

JOSSELIN DE JONG, P. E. 1951. *Menangkabau and Negri Sembilan: Socio-Political Structure in Indonesia* (Leiden).

KERR, M. 1952. *Personality and Conflict in Jamaica* (Liverpool).

KIRKE, H. 1898. *Twenty-Five Years in British Guiana* (London).

LAING, M. B. 1949. 'Local Government in British Guiana', *Caribbean Quarterly*. Vol. I (Port of Spain, Trinidad).

LAMMING, G. 1953. *In the Castle of my Skin* (London).

LEACH, E. R. 1954. *Political Systems of Highland Burma: A Study of Kachin Social Structure* (London).

LEWIS, O. 1951. *Life in a Mexican Village: Tepoztlan Restudied* (Urbana, Illinois).

LEYBURN, J. G. 1941. *The Haitian People* (New Haven).

LINTON, R. 1936. *The Study of Man* (New York).

MASEFIELD, G. B. 1950. *Agriculture in the British Colonies* (Oxford).

NADEL, S. F. 1942. *A Black Byzantium* (Oxford).

—— 1951. *The Foundations of Social Anthropology* (London).

—— 1954. *Nupe Religion* (London).

PARSONS, TALCOTT. 1949. 'The Kinship System of the Contemporary United States' in *Essays in Sociological Theory, Pure and Applied* (Glencoe, Illinois).

—— 1952. *The Social System* (London).

PINCKARD, G. 1806. *Notes on the West Indies: Written during the Expedition under the Command of the Late General Sir Ralph Abercromby* (3 Vols.) (Longman, Hurst, Rees and Orme, London).

RADCLIFFE-BROWN, A. R. 1950. 'Introduction' to *African Systems of Kinship and Marriage* (Ed. by A. R. Radcliffe-Brown and D. Forde) (London).

—— 1952. *Structure and Function in Primitive Society* (London).

RATTRAY, R. S. 1916. *Ashanti Proverbs* (Oxford).

—— 1923. *Ashanti* (Oxford).

—— 1927. *Religion and Art in Ashanti* (Oxford).

—— 1929. *Ashanti Law and Constitution* (Oxford).

REDFIELD, R. 1930. *Tepoztlan: A Mexican Village* (Chicago).

—— 1941. *The Folk Culture of Yucatan* (Chicago).

REES, A. D. 1951. *Life in a Welsh Countryside* (Cardiff).

RICHARDS, A. 1950. 'Some Types of Family Structure Amongst the Central Bantu' in *African Systems of Kinship and Marriage* (Eds. A. R. Radcliffe-Brown and D. Forde) (London).

RODWAY, J. 1891–4. *History of British Guiana from 1668* (3 Vols.) (Georgetown, British Guiana).

—— 1912. *Guiana: British, Dutch and French* (London).

SCHNEIDER, D. M. 1953. 'Yap Kinship Terminology and Kin Groups', *American Anthropologist*, Vol. 55.

SIMEY, T. S. 1946. *Welfare and Planning in the West Indies* (Oxford).

Small Towns of Natal (Natal Regional Survey, Additional Report No. 3) (University of Natal Press) 1953.

SMITH, R. T. 1955. 'Land Tenure in Three Negro Villages in British Guiana', *Social and Economic Studies*. Vol. 4 (Kingston, Jamaica).

STRAW, K. H. 1953. 'Some Preliminary Results of a Survey of Income and Consumption Patterns in a Sample of Households in Barbados', *Social and Economic Studies*. Vol. I (Kingston, Jamaica).

TAX, SOL, et al. 1952. *Heritage of Conquest* (Glencoe, Illinois).

TREVOR, J. C. 1950. 'Aspects of Folk Culture in the Virgin Islands'. Unpublished Ph.D. dissertation. (Cambridge University Library).

TUMIN, M. M. 1952. *Caste in A Peasant Society* (Princeton, New York).

VAN GENNEP, A. 1909. *Les Rites de Passage* (Paris).

WARNER, L. W. 1952. *Structure of American Life* (Edinburgh).

WEBER, MAX. 1930. *The Protestant Ethic and the Spirit of Capitalism* (Trans. Talcott Parsons) (London).

WILLIAMS, E. 1942. *Capitalism and Slavery* (Chapel Hill, North Carolina).

—— 1944. *The Negro in the Caribbean* (Panaf Service Ltd., Manchester).

WILLIAMS, J. J. 1933. *Voodoos and Obeahs: Phases of West Indian Witchcraft* (New York).

WILSON, C. S. 1953. 'The Family and Neighbourhood in a British Community', Unpublished M.Sc. dissertation (Cambridge University Library).

Section B

BRONKHURST, H. V. P. 1883. *The Colony of British Guiana and its Labouring Population* (London).

—— 1888. *Among the Hindus and Creoles of British Guiana* (London).

CROOKALL, L. 1898. *British Guiana, or Work and Wanderings Among the Creoles and Coolies, the Africans and Indians of the Wild Country* (London).

CRUIKSHANK, I. G. 1918. 'King William's People'. *Timehri* (Third Series, Vol. VI) (Georgetown, British Guiana).

IN THURN. 1884. 'The Three Counties of Berbice, Demerara and Essequibo under the Dutch', *Timehri* (Vol. III) (Georgetown).

JENMAN, G. S. 1885. 'Balata and the Balata Industry' *Timehri* (Vol. IV) (Georgetown).

MACARTHUR, S. J. 1912. 'Our People', *Timehri* (Third Series, Vol. III) (Georgetown).

RUSSELL, W. 1886a. 'Land Titles', *Timehri* (Vol. V) (Georgetown).

—— 1886b. 'Rice', *Timehri* (Vol. V) (Georgetown).

WALLBRIDGE. 1911. 'Fifty Years Recollections of British Guiana', *Timehri* (Third Series, Vol. I) (Georgetown).

INDEX

INDEX

The International Library of
Sociology
and Social Reconstruction

Edited by W. J. H. SPROTT
Founded by KARL MANNHEIM

ROUTLEDGE & KEGAN PAUL
BROADWAY HOUSE, CARTER LANE, LONDON, E.C.4

CONTENTS

PRINTED IN GREAT BRITAIN BY HEADLEY BROTHERS LTD
109 KINGSWAY LONDON WC2 AND ASHFORD KENT

GENERAL SOCIOLOGY

Brown, Robert. Explanation in Social Science. *208 pp. 1963. (2nd Impression 1964.) 25s.*

Gibson, Quentin. The Logic of Social Enquiry. *240 pp. 1960. (3rd Impression 1968.) 24s.*

Homans, George C. Sentiments and Activities: Essays in Social Science. *336 pp. 1962. 32s.*

Isajiw, Wsevelod W. Causation and Functionalism in Sociology. *165 pp. 1968. 25s.*

Johnson, Harry M. Sociology: a Systematic Introduction. *Foreword by Robert K. Merton. 710 pp. 1961. (5th Impression 1968.) 42s.*

Mannheim, Karl. Essays on Sociology and Social Psychology. *Edited by Paul Keckskemeti. With Editorial Note by Adolph Lowe. 344 pp. 1953. (2nd Impression 1966.) 32s.*

Systematic Sociology: An Introduction to the Study of Society. *Edited by J. S. Erös and Professor W. A. C. Stewart. 220 pp. 1957. (3rd Impression 1967.) 24s.*

Martindale, Don. The Nature and Types of Sociological Theory. *292 pp. 1961. (3rd Impression 1967.) 35s.*

Maus, Heinz. A Short History of Sociology. *234 pp. 1962. (2nd Impression 1965.) 28s.*

Myrdal, Gunnar. Value in Social Theory: A Collection of Essays on Methodology. *Edited by Paul Streeten. 332 pp. 1958. (3rd Impression 1968.) 35s.*

Ogburn, William F., and Nimkoff, Meyer F. A Handbook of Sociology. *Preface by Karl Mannheim. 656 pp. 46 figures. 35 tables. 5th edition (revised) 1964. 45s.*

Parsons, Talcott, and Smelser, Neil J. Economy and Society: A Study in the Integration of Economic and Social Theory. *362 pp. 1956. (4th Impression 1967.) 35s.*

Rex, John. Key Problems of Sociological Theory. *220 pp. 1961. (4th Impression 1968.) 25s.*

Stark, Werner. The Fundamental Forms of Social Thought. *280 pp. 1962. 32s.*

FOREIGN CLASSICS OF SOCIOLOGY

Durkheim, Emile. Suicide. A Study in Sociology. *Edited and with an Introduction by George Simpson. 404 pp. 1952. (4th Impression 1968.) 35s.*

Professional Ethics and Civic Morals. *Translated by Cornelia Brookfield. 288 pp. 1957. 30s.*

Gerth, H. H., and Mills, C. Wright. From Max Weber: Essays in Sociology. *502 pp. 1948. (6th Impression 1967.) 35s.*

Tönnies, Ferdinand. Community and Association. *(Gemeinschaft und Gesellschaft.) Translated and Supplemented by Charles P. Loomis. Foreword by Pitirim A. Sorokin. 334 pp. 1955. 28s.*

SOCIAL STRUCTURE

Andreski, Stanislav. Military Organization and Society. *Foreword by Professor A. R. Radcliffe-Brown. 226 pp. 1 folder. 1954. Revised Edition 1968. 35s.*

Cole, G. D. H. Studies in Class Structure. *220 pp. 1955. (3rd Impression 1964.) 21s. Paper 10s. 6d.*

Coontz, Sydney H. Population Theories and the Economic Interpretation. *202 pp. 1957. (3rd Impression 1968.) 28s.*

Coser, Lewis. The Functions of Social Conflict. *204 pp. 1956. (3rd Impression 1968.) 25s.*

Dickie-Clark, H. F. Marginal Situation: A Sociological Study of a Coloured Group. *240 pp. 11 tables. 1966. 40s.*

Glass, D. V. (Ed.). Social Mobility in Britain. *Contributions by J. Berent, T. Bottomore, R. C. Chambers, J. Floud, D. V. Glass, J. R. Hall, H. T. Himmelweit, R. K. Kelsall, F. M. Martin, C. A. Moser, R. Mukherjee, and W. Ziegel. 420 pp. 1954. (4th Impression 1967.) 45s.*

Jones, Garth N. Planned Organizational Change: An Exploratory Study Using an Empirical Approach. *About 268 pp. 1969. 40s.*

Kelsall, R. K. Higher Civil Servants in Britain: From 1870 to the Present Day. *268 pp. 31 tables. 1955. (2nd Impression 1966.) 25s.*

König, René. The Community. *232 pp. Illustrated. 1968. 35s.*

Lawton, Denis. Social Class, Language and Education. *192 pp. 1968. (2nd Impression 1968.) 25s.*

McLeish, John. The Theory of Social Change: Four Views Considered. *About 128 pp. 1969. 21s.*

Marsh, David C. The Changing Social Structure in England and Wales, 1871-1961. *1958. 272 pp. 2nd edition (revised) 1966. (2nd Impression 1967.) 35s.*

Mouzelis, Nicos. Organization and Bureaucracy. An Analysis of Modern Theories. *240 pp. 1967. (2nd Impression 1968.) 28s.*

Ossowski, Stanislaw. Class Structure in the Social Consciousness. *210 pp. 1963. (2nd Impression 1967.) 25s.*

SOCIOLOGY AND POLITICS

Barbu, Zevedei. Democracy and Dictatorship: Their Psychology and Patterns of Life. *300 pp. 1956. 28s.*

Crick, Bernard. The American Science of Politics: Its Origins and Conditions. *284 pp. 1959. 32s.*

Hertz, Frederick. Nationality in History and Politics: A Psychology and Sociology of National Sentiment and Nationalism. *432 pp. 1944. (5th Impression 1966.) 42s.*

Kornhauser, William. The Politics of Mass Society. *272 pp. 20 tables. 1960. (3rd Impression 1968.) 28s.*

Laidler, Harry W. History of Socialism. Social-Economic Movements: An Historical and Comparative Survey of Socialism, Communism, Co-operation, Utopianism; and other Systems of Reform and Reconstruction. *New edition. 992 pp. 1968. 90s.*

Lasswell, Harold D. Analysis of Political Behaviour. An Empirical Approach. *324 pp. 1947. (4th Impression 1966.) 35s.*

Mannheim, Karl. Freedom, Power and Democratic Planning. *Edited by Hans Gerth and Ernest K. Bramstedt. 424 pp. 1951. (3rd Impression 1968.) 42s.*

Mansur, Fatma. Process of Independence. *Foreword by A. H. Hanson. 208 pp. 1962. 25s.*

Martin, David A. Pacificism: an Historical and Sociological Study. *262 pp. 1965. 30s.*

Myrdal, Gunnar. The Political Element in the Development of Economic Theory. *Translated from the German by Paul Streeten. 282 pp. 1953. (4th Impression 1965.) 25s.*

Polanyi, Michael. F.R.S. The Logic of Liberty: Reflections and Rejoinders. *228 pp. 1951. 18s.*

Verney, Douglas V. The Analysis of Political Systems. *264 pp. 1959. (3rd Impression 1966.) 28s.*

Wootton, Graham. The Politics of Influence: British Ex-Servicemen, Cabinet Decisions and Cultural Changes, 1917 to 1957. *316 pp. 1963. 30s.*

Workers, Unions and the State. *188 pp. 1966. (2nd Impression 1967.) 25s.*

FOREIGN AFFAIRS: THEIR SOCIAL, POLITICAL AND ECONOMIC FOUNDATIONS

Baer, Gabriel. Population and Society in the Arab East. *Translated by Hanna Szöke. 288 pp. 10 maps. 1964. 40s.*

Bonné, Alfred. State and Economics in the Middle East: A Society in Transition. *482 pp. 2nd (revised) edition 1955. (2nd Impression 1960.) 40s.*

Studies in Economic Development: with special reference to Conditions in the Under-developed Areas of Western Asia and India. *322 pp. 84 tables. 2nd edition 1960. 32s.*

Mayer, J. P. Political Thought in France from the Revolution to the Fifth Republic. *164 pp. 3rd edition (revised) 1961. 16s.*

CRIMINOLOGY

Ancel, Marc. Social Defence: A Modern Approach to Criminal Problems. *Foreword by Leon Radzinowicz. 240 pp. 1965. 32s.*

Cloward, Richard A., and **Ohlin, Lloyd E.** Delinquency and Opportunity: A Theory of Delinquent Gangs. *248 pp. 1961. 25s.*

Downes, David M. The Delinquent Solution. A Study in Subcultural Theory. *296 pp. 1966. 42s.*

Dunlop, A. B., and McCabe, S. Young Men in Detention Centres. *192 pp. 1965. 28s.*

Friedländer, Kate. The Psycho-Analytical Approach to Juvenile Delinquency: Theory, Case Studies, Treatment. *320 pp. 1947. (6th Impression 1967). 40s.*

Glueck, Sheldon and **Eleanor.** Family Environment and Delinquency. *With the statistical assistance of Rose W. Kneznek. 340 pp. 1962. (2nd Impression 1966.) 40s.*

Mannheim, Hermann. Comparative Criminology: a Text Book. *Two volumes. 442 pp. and 380 pp. 1965. (2nd Impression with corrections 1966.) 42s. a volume.*

Morris, Terence. The Criminal Area: A Study in Social Ecology. *Foreword by Hermann Mannheim. 232 pp. 25 tables. 4 maps. 1957. (2nd Impression 1966.) 28s.*

Morris, Terence and **Pauline,** assisted by **Barbara Barer.** Pentonville: A Sociological Study of an English Prison. *416 pp. 16 plates. 1963. 50s.*

Spencer, John C. Crime and the Services. *Foreword by Hermann Mannheim. 336 pp. 1954. 28s.*

Trasler, Gordon. The Explanation of Criminality. *144 pp. 1962. (2nd Impression 1967.) 20s.*

SOCIAL PSYCHOLOGY

Barbu, Zevedei. Problems of Historical Psychology. *248 pp. 1960. 25s.*

Blackburn, Julian. Psychology and the Social Pattern. *184 pp. 1945. (7th Impression 1964.) 16s.*

Fleming, C. M. Adolescence: Its Social Psychology: With an Introduction to recent findings from the fields of Anthropology, Physiology, Medicine, Psychometrics and Sociometry. *288 pp. 2nd edition (revised) 1963. (3rd Impression 1967.) 25s. Paper 12s. 6d.*

The Social Psychology of Education: An Introduction and Guide to Its Study. *136 pp. 2nd edition (revised) 1959. (4th Impression 1967.) 14s. Paper 7s. 6d.*

Homans, George C. The Human Group. *Foreword by Bernard DeVoto. Introduction by Robert K. Merton. 526 pp. 1951. (7th Impression 1968.) 35s.*

Social Behaviour: its Elementary Forms. *416 pp. 1961. (3rd Impression 1968.) 35s.*

Klein, Josephine. The Study of Groups. *226 pp. 31 figures. 5 tables. 1956. (5th Impression 1967.) 21s. Paper 9s. 6d.*

Linton, Ralph. The Cultural Background of Personality. *132 pp. 1947. (7th Impression 1968.) 18s.*

Mayo, Elton. The Social Problems of an Industrial Civilization. With an appendix on the Political Problem. *180 pp. 1949. (5th Impression 1966.) 25s.*

Ottaway, A. K. C. Learning Through Group Experience. *176 pp. 1966. (2nd Impression 1968.) 25s.*

Ridder, J. C. de. The Personality of the Urban African in South Africa. A Thematic Apperception Test Study. *196 pp. 12 plates. 1961. 25s.*

Rose, Arnold M. (Ed.). Human Behaviour and Social Processes: an Interactionist Approach. *Contributions by Arnold M. Rose, Ralph H. Turner, Anselm Strauss, Everett C. Hughes, E. Franklin Frazier, Howard S. Becker, et al. 696 pp. 1962. (2nd Impression 1968.) 70s.*

Smelser, Neil J. Theory of Collective Behaviour. *448 pp. 1962. (2nd Impression 1967.) 45s.*

Stephenson, Geoffrey M. The Development of Conscience. *128 pp. 1966. 25s.*

Young, Kimball. Handbook of Social Psychology. *658 pp. 16 figures. 10 tables. 2nd edition (revised) 1957. (3rd Impression 1963.) 40s.*

SOCIOLOGY OF THE FAMILY

Banks, J. A. Prosperity and Parenthood: A study of Family Planning among The Victorian Middle Classes. *262 pp. 1954. (3rd Impression 1968.) 28s.*

Bell, Colin R. Middle Class Families: Social and Geographical Mobility. *224 pp. 1969. 35s.*

Burton, Lindy. Vulnerable Children. *272 pp. 1968. 35s.*

Gavron, Hannah. The Captive Wife: Conflicts of Housebound Mothers. *190 pp. 1966. (2nd Impression 1966.) 25s.*

Klein, Josephine. Samples from English Cultures. *1965. (2nd Impression 1967.)*

1. Three Preliminary Studies and Aspects of Adult Life in England. *447 pp. 50s.*
2. Child-Rearing Practices and Index. *247 pp. 35s.*

Klein, Viola. Britain's Married Women Workers. *180 pp. 1965. (2nd Impression 1968.) 28s.*

McWhinnie, Alexina M. Adopted Children. How They Grow Up. *304 pp. 1967. (2nd Impression 1968.) 42s.*

Myrdal, Alva and **Klein, Viola.** Women's Two Roles: Home and Work. *238 pp. 27 tables. 1956. Revised Edition 1967. 30s. Paper 15s.*

Parsons, Talcott and **Bales, Robert F.** Family: Socialization and Interaction Process. *In collaboration with James Olds, Morris Zelditch and Philip E. Slater. 456 pp. 50 figures and tables. 1956. (3rd Impression 1968.) 45s.*

Schücking, L. L. The Puritan Family. *Translated from the German by Brian Battershaw. 212 pp. 1969. About 42s.*

THE SOCIAL SERVICES

Forder, R. A. (Ed.). Penelope Hall's Social Services of Modern England. *288 pp. 1969. 35s.*

George, Victor. Social Security: Beveridge and After. *258 pp. 1968. 35s.*

Goetschius, George W. Working with Community Groups. *256 pp. 1969. 35s.*

Goetschius, George W. and **Tash, Joan.** Working with Unattached Youth. *416 pp. 1967. (2nd Impression 1968.) 40s.*

Hall, M. P., and **Howes, I. V.** The Church in Social Work. A Study of Moral Welfare Work undertaken by the Church of England. *320 pp. 1965. 35s.*

Heywood, Jean S. Children in Care: the Development of the Service for the Deprived Child. *264 pp. 2nd edition (revised) 1965. (2nd Impression 1966.) 32s.*

An Introduction to Teaching Casework Skills. *190 pp. 1964. 28s.*

Jones, Kathleen. Lunacy, Law and Conscience, 1744-1845: the Social History of the Care of the Insane. *268 pp. 1955. 25s.*

Mental Health and Social Policy, 1845-1959. *264 pp. 1960. (2nd Impression 1967.) 32s.*

Jones, Kathleen and **Sidebotham, Roy.** Mental Hospitals at Work. *220 pp. 1962. 30s.*

Kastell, Jean. Casework in Child Care. *Foreword by M. Brooke Willis. 320 pp. 1962. 35s.*

Morris, Pauline. Put Away: A Sociological Study of Institutions for the Mentally Retarded. *Approx. 288 pp. 1969. About 50s.*

Nokes, P. L. The Professional Task in Welfare Practice. *152 pp. 1967. 28s.*

Rooff, Madeline. Voluntary Societies and Social Policy. *350 pp. 15 tables. 1957. 35s.*

Timms, Noel. Psychiatric Social Work in Great Britain (1939-1962). *280 pp. 1964. 32s.*

Social Casework: Principles and Practice. *256 pp. 1964. (2nd Impression 1966.) 25s. Paper 15s.*

Trasler, Gordon. In Place of Parents: A Study in Foster Care. *272 pp. 1960. (2nd Impression 1966.) 30s.*

Young, A. F., and **Ashton, E. T.** British Social Work in the Nineteenth Century. *288 pp. 1956. (2nd Impression 1963.) 28s.*

Young, A. F. Social Services in British Industry. *272 pp. 1968. 40s.*

SOCIOLOGY OF EDUCATION

Banks, Olive. Parity and Prestige in English Secondary Education: a Study in Educational Sociology. *272 pp. 1955. (2nd Impression 1963.) 32s.*

Bentwich, Joseph. Education in Israel. *224 pp. 8 pp. plates. 1965. 24s.*

Blyth, W. A. L. English Primary Education. A Sociological Description. *1965. Revised edition 1967.*

1. Schools. *232 pp. 30s. Paper 12s. 6d.*
2. Background. *168 pp. 25s. Paper 10s. 6d.*

Collier, K. G. The Social Purposes of Education: Personal and Social Values in Education. *268 pp. 1959. (3rd Impression 1965.) 21s.*

Dale, R. R., and Griffith, S. Down Stream: Failure in the Grammar School. *108 pp. 1965. 20s.*

Dore, R. P. Education in Tokugawa Japan. *356 pp. 9 pp. plates. 1965. 35s.*

Edmonds, E. L. The School Inspector. *Foreword by Sir William Alexander. 214 pp. 1962. 28s.*

Evans, K. M. Sociometry and Education. *158 pp. 1962. (2nd Impression 1966.) 18s.*

Foster, P. J. Education and Social Change in Ghana. *336 pp. 3 maps. 1965. (2nd Impression 1967.) 36s.*

Fraser, W. R. Education and Society in Modern France. *150 pp. 1963. (2nd Impression 1968.) 25s.*

Hans, Nicholas. New Trends in Education in the Eighteenth Century. *278 pp. 19 tables. 1951. (2nd Impression 1966.) 30s.*

Comparative Education: A Study of Educational Factors and Traditions. *360 pp. 3rd (revised) edition 1958. (4th Impression 1967.) 25s. Paper 12s. 6d.*

Hargreaves, David. Social Relations in a Secondary School. *240 pp. 1967. (2nd Impression 1968.) 32s.*

Holmes, Brian. Problems in Education. A Comparative Approach. *336 pp. 1965. (2nd Impression 1967.) 32s.*

Mannheim, Karl and Stewart, W. A. C. An Introduction to the Sociology of Education. *206 pp. 1962. (2nd Impression 1965.) 21s.*

Morris, Raymond N. The Sixth Form and College Entrance. *231 pp. 1969. 40s.*

Musgrove, F. Youth and the Social Order. *176 pp. 1964. (2nd Impression 1968.) 25s. Paper 12s.*

Ortega y Gasset, José. Mission of the University. *Translated with an Introduction by Howard Lee Nostrand. 86 pp. 1946. (3rd Impression 1963.) 15s.*

Ottaway, A. K. C. Education and Society: An Introduction to the Sociology of Education. *With an Introduction by W. O. Lester Smith. 212 pp. Second edition (revised). 1962. (5th Impression 1968.) 18s. Paper 10s. 6d.*

Peers, Robert. Adult Education: A Comparative Study. *398 pp. 2nd edition 1959. (2nd Impression 1966.) 42s.*

Pritchard, D. G. Education and the Handicapped: 1760 to 1960. *258 pp. 1963. (2nd Impression 1966.) 35s.*

Richardson, Helen. Adolescent Girls in Approved Schools. *Approx. 360 pp. 1969. About 42s.*

Simon, Brian and Joan (Eds.). Educational Psychology in the U.S.S.R. *Introduction by Brian and Joan Simon. Translation by Joan Simon. Papers by D. N. Bogoiavlenski and N. A. Menchinskaia, D. B. Elkonin, E. A. Fleshner, Z. I. Kalmykova, G. S. Kostiuk, V. A. Krutetski, A. N. Leontiev, A. R. Luria, E. A. Milerian, R. G. Natadze, B. M. Teplov, L. S. Vygotski, L. V. Zankov. 296 pp. 1963. 40s.*

SOCIOLOGY OF CULTURE

Eppel, E. M., and M. Adolescents and Morality: A Study of some Moral Values and Dilemmas of Working Adolescents in the Context of a changing Climate of Opinion. *Foreword by W. J. H. Sprott. 268 pp. 39 tables. 1966. 30s.*

Fromm, Erich. The Fear of Freedom. *286 pp. 1942. (8th Impression 1960.) 25s. Paper 10s.*

The Sane Society. *400 pp. 1956. (4th Impression 1968.) 28s. Paper 14s.*

Mannheim, Karl. Diagnosis of Our Time: Wartime Essays of a Sociologist. *208 pp. 1943. (8th Impression 1966.) 21s.*

Essays on the Sociology of Culture. *Edited by Ernst Mannheim in co-operation with Paul Kecskemeti. Editorial Note by Adolph Lowe. 280 pp. 1956. (3rd Impression 1967.) 28s.*

Weber, Alfred. Farewell to European History: or The Conquest of Nihilism. *Translated from the German by R. F. C. Hull. 224 pp. 1947. 18s.*

SOCIOLOGY OF RELIGION

Argyle, Michael. Religious Behaviour. *224 pp. 8 figures. 41 tables. 1958. (4th Impression 1968.) 25s.*

Nelson, G. K. Spiritualism and Society. *313 pp. 1969. 42s.*

Stark, Werner. The Sociology of Religion. A Study of Christendom.
Volume I. Established Religion. *248 pp. 1966. 35s.*
Volume II. Sectarian Religion. *368 pp. 1967. 40s.*
Volume III. The Universal Church. *464 pp. 1967. 45s.*

Watt, W. Montgomery. Islam and the Integration of Society. *320 pp. 1961. (3rd Impression 1966.) 35s.*

SOCIOLOGY OF ART AND LITERATURE

Beljame, Alexandre. Men of Letters and the English Public in the Eighteenth Century: 1660-1744, Dryden, Addison, Pope. *Edited with an Introduction and Notes by Bonamy Dobrée. Translated by E. O. Lorimer. 532 pp. 1948. 32s.*

Misch, Georg. A History of Autobiography in Antiquity. *Translated by E. W. Dickes. 2 Volumes. Vol. 1, 364 pp., Vol. 2, 372 pp. 1950. 45s. the set.*

Schücking, L. L. The Sociology of Literary Taste. *112 pp. 2nd (revised) edition 1966. 18s.*

Silbermann, Alphons. The Sociology of Music. *Translated from the German by Corbet Stewart. 222 pp. 1963. 32s.*

SOCIOLOGY OF KNOWLEDGE

Mannheim, Karl. Essays on the Sociology of Knowledge. *Edited by Paul Kecskemeti. Editorial note by Adolph Lowe. 352 pp. 1952. (4th Impression 1967.) 35s.*

Stark, W. America: Ideal and Reality. The United States of 1776 in Contemporary Philosophy. *136 pp. 1947. 12s.*
The Sociology of Knowledge: An Essay in Aid of a Deeper Understanding of the History of Ideas. *384 pp. 1958. (3rd Impression 1967.) 36s.*
Montesquieu: Pioneer of the Sociology of Knowledge. *244 pp. 1960. 25s.*

URBAN SOCIOLOGY

Anderson, Nels. The Urban Community: A World Perspective. *532 pp. 1960. 35s.*

Ashworth, William. The Genesis of Modern British Town Planning: A Study in Economic and Social History of the Nineteenth and Twentieth Centuries. *288 pp. 1954. (3rd Impression 1968.) 32s.*

Bracey, Howard. Neighbours: On New Estates and Subdivisions in England and U.S.A. *220 pp. 1964. 28s.*

Cullingworth, J. B. Housing Needs and Planning Policy: A Restatement of the Problems of Housing Need and "Overspill" in England and Wales. *232 pp. 44 tables. 8 maps. 1960. (2nd Impression 1966.) 28s.*

Dickinson, Robert E. City and Region: A Geographical Interpretation. *608 pp. 125 figures. 1964. (5th Impression 1967.) 60s.*
The West European City: A Geographical Interpretation. *600 pp. 129 maps. 29 plates. 2nd edition 1962. (3rd Impression 1968.) 55s.*
The City Region in Western Europe. *320 pp. Maps. 1967. 30s. Paper 14s.*

Jackson, Brian. Working Class Community: Some General Notions raised by a Series of Studies in Northern England. *192 pp. 1968. (2nd Impression 1968.) 25s.*

Jennings, Hilda. Societies in the Making: a Study of Development and Redevelopment within a County Borough. *Foreword by D. A. Clark. 286 pp. 1962. (2nd Impression 1967.) 32s.*

Kerr, Madeline. The People of Ship Street. *240 pp. 1958. 28s.*

Mann, P. H. An Approach to Urban Sociology. *240 pp. 1965. (2nd Impression 1968.) 30s.*

Morris, R. N., and **Mogey, J.** The Sociology of Housing. Studies at Berinsfield. *232 pp. 4 pp. plates. 1965. 42s.*

Rosser, C., and **Harris, C.** The Family and Social Change. A Study of Family and Kinship in a South Wales Town. *352 pp. 8 maps. 1965. (2nd Impression 1968.) 45s.*

RURAL SOCIOLOGY

Chambers, R. J. H. Settlement Schemes in Africa: A Selective Study. *Approx. 268 pp. 1969. About 50s.*

Haswell, M. R. The Economics of Development in Village India. *120 pp. 1967. 21s.*

Littlejohn, James. Westrigg: the Sociology of a Cheviot Parish. *172 pp. 5 figures. 1963. 25s.*

Williams, W. M. The Country Craftsman: A Study of Some Rural Crafts and the Rural Industries Organization in England. *248 pp. 9 figures. 1958. 25s.* (*Dartington Hall Studies in Rural Sociology.*)

The Sociology of an English Village: Gosforth. *272 pp. 12 figures. 13 tables. 1956.* (*3rd Impression 1964.*) *25s.*

SOCIOLOGY OF MIGRATION

Humphreys, Alexander J. New Dubliners: Urbanization and the Irish Family. *Foreword by George C. Homans. 304 pp. 1966. 40s.*

SOCIOLOGY OF INDUSTRY AND DISTRIBUTION

Anderson, Nels. Work and Leisure. *280 pp. 1961. 28s.*

Blau, Peter M., and **Scott, W. Richard.** Formal Organizations: a Comparative approach. *Introduction and Additional Bibliography by J. H. Smith. 326 pp. 1963.* (*4th Impression 1969.*) *35s. Paper 15s.*

Eldridge, J. E. T. Industrial Disputes. Essays in the Sociology of Industrial Relations. *288 pp. 1968. 40s.*

Hollowell, Peter G. The Lorry Driver. *272 pp. 1968. 42s.*

Jefferys, Margot, with the assistance of Winifred Moss. Mobility in the Labour Market: Employment Changes in Battersea and Dagenham. *Preface by Barbara Wootton. 186 pp. 51 tables. 1954. 15s.*

Levy, A. B. Private Corporations and Their Control. *Two Volumes. Vol. 1, 464 pp., Vol. 2, 432 pp. 1950. 80s. the set.*

Liepmann, Kate. Apprenticeship: An Enquiry into its Adequacy under Modern Conditions. *Foreword by H. D. Dickinson. 232 pp. 6 tables. 1960.* (*2nd Impression 1960.*) *23s.*

Millerson, Geoffrey. The Qualifying Associations: a Study in Professionalization. *320 pp. 1964. 42s.*

Smelser, Neil J. Social Change in the Industrial Revolution: An Application of Theory to the Lancashire Cotton Industry, 1770-1840. *468 pp. 12 figures. 14 tables. 1959.* (*2nd Impression 1960.*) *50s.*

Williams, Gertrude. Recruitment to Skilled Trades. *240 pp. 1957. 23s.*

Young, A. F. Industrial Injuries Insurance: an Examination of British Policy. *192 pp. 1964. 30s.*

ANTHROPOLOGY

Ammar, Hamed. Growing up in an Egyptian Village: Silwa, Province of Aswan. *336 pp. 1954.* (*2nd Impression 1966.*) *35s.*

Crook, David and **Isabel.** Revolution in a Chinese Village: Ten Mile Inn. *230 pp. 8 plates. 1 map. 1959.* (*2nd Impression 1968.*) *21s.*

The First Years of Yangyi Commune. *302 pp. 12 plates. 1966. 42s.*

Dickie-Clark, H. F. The Marginal Situation. A Sociological Study of a Coloured Group. *236 pp. 1966. 40s.*

Dube, S. C. Indian Village. *Foreword by Morris Edward Opler. 276 pp. 4 plates. 1955. (5th Impression 1965.) 25s.*

India's Changing Villages: Human Factors in Community Development. *260 pp. 8 plates. 1 map. 1958. (3rd Impression 1963.) 25s.*

Firth, Raymond. Malay Fishermen. Their Peasant Economy. *420 pp. 17 pp. plates. 2nd edition revised and enlarged 1966. (2nd Impression 1968.) 55s.*

Gulliver, P. H. The Family Herds. A Study of two Pastoral Tribes in East Africa, The Jie and Turkana. *304 pp. 4 plates. 19 figures. 1955. (2nd Impression with new preface and bibliography 1966.) 35s.*

Social Control in an African Society: a Study of the Arusha, Agricultural Masai of Northern Tanganyika. *320 pp. 8 plates. 10 figures. 1963. (2nd Impression 1968.) 42s.*

Ishwaran, K. Shivapur. A South Indian Village. *216 pp. 1968. 35s.*

Tradition and Economy in Village India: An Interactionist Approach. *Foreword by Conrad Arensburg. 176 pp. 1966. (2nd Impression 1968.) 25s.*

Jarvie, Ian C. The Revolution in Anthropology. *268 pp. 1964. (2nd Impression 1967.) 40s.*

Jarvie, Ian C. and **Agassi, Joseph.** Hong Kong. A Society in Transition. *396 pp. Illustrated with plates and maps. 1968. 56s.*

Little, Kenneth L. Mende of Sierra Leone. *308 pp. and folder. 1951. Revised edition 1967. 63s.*

Lowie, Professor Robert H. Social Organization. *494 pp. 1950. (4th Impression 1966.) 50s.*

Mayer, Adrian C. Caste and Kinship in Central India: A Village and its Region. *328 pp. 16 plates. 15 figures. 16 tables. 1960. (2nd Impression 1965.) 35s.*

Peasants in the Pacific: A Study of Fiji Indian Rural Society. *232 pp. 16 plates. 10 figures. 14 tables. 1961. 35s.*

Smith, Raymond T. The Negro Family in British Guiana: Family Structure and Social Status in the Villages. *With a Foreword by Meyer Fortes. 314 pp. 8 plates. 1 figure. 4 maps. 1956. (2nd Impression 1965.) 35s.*

DOCUMENTARY

Meek, Dorothea L. (Ed.). Soviet Youth: Some Achievements and Problems. *Excerpts from the Soviet Press, translated by the editor. 280 pp. 1957. 28s.*

Schlesinger, Rudolf (Ed.). Changing Attitudes in Soviet Russia.

2. The Nationalities Problem and Soviet Administration. Selected Readings on the Development of Soviet Nationalities Policies. *Introduced by the editor. Translated by W. W. Gottlieb. 324 pp. 1956. 30s.*

Reports of the Institute of Community Studies

(*Demy 8vo.*)

Cartwright, Ann. Human Relations and Hospital Care. *272 pp. 1964. 30s.*

Patients and their Doctors. A Study of General Practice. *304 pp. 1967. 40s.*

Jackson, Brian. Streaming: an Education System in Miniature. *168 pp. 1964. (2nd Impression 1966.) 21s. Paper 10s.*

Jackson, Brian and **Marsden, Dennis.** Education and the Working Class: Some General Themes raised by a Study of 88 Working-class Children in a Northern Industrial City. *268 pp. 2 folders. 1962. (4th Impression 1968.) 32s.*

Marris, Peter. Widows and their Families. *Foreword by Dr. John Bowlby. 184 pp. 18 tables. Statistical Summary. 1958. 18s.*

Family and Social Change in an African City. A Study of Rehousing in Lagos. *196 pp. 1 map. 4 plates. 53 tables. 1961. (2nd Impression 1966.) 30s.*

The Experience of Higher Education. *232 pp. 27 tables. 1964. 25s.*

Marris, Peter and **Rein, Martin.** Dilemmas of Social Reform. Poverty and Community Action in the United States. *256 pp. 1967. 35s.*

Mills, Enid. Living with Mental Illness: a Study in East London. *Foreword by Morris Carstairs. 196 pp. 1962. 28s.*

Runciman, W. G. Relative Deprivation and Social Justice. A Study of Attitudes to Social Inequality in Twentieth Century England. *352 pp. 1966. (2nd Impression 1967.) 40s.*

Townsend, Peter. The Family Life of Old People: An Inquiry in East London. *Foreword by J. H. Sheldon. 300 pp. 3 figures. 63 tables. 1957. (3rd Impression 1967.) 30s.*

Willmott, Peter. Adolescent Boys in East London. *230 pp. 1966. 30s.*

The Evolution of a Community: a study of Dagenham after forty years. *168 pp. 2 maps. 1963. 21s.*

Willmott, Peter and **Young, Michael.** Family and Class in a London Suburb. *202 pp. 47 tables. 1960. (4th Impression 1968.) 25s.*

Young, Michael. Innovation and Research in Education. *192 pp. 1965. 25s. Paper 12s. 6d.*

Young, Michael and **McGeeney, Patrick.** Learning Begins at Home. A Study of a Junior School and its Parents. *About 128 pp. 1968. 21s. Paper 14s.*

Young, Michael and **Willmott, Peter.** Family and Kinship in East London. *Foreword by Richard M. Titmuss. 252 pp. 39 tables. 1957. (3rd Impression 1965.) 28s.*

The British Journal of Sociology. *Edited by Terence P. Morris. Vol. 1, No. 1, March 1950 and Quarterly. Roy. 8vo., £3 annually, 15s. a number, post free. (Vols. 1-18, £8 each. Individual parts £2 10s.*

All prices are net and subject to alteration without notice

1268 H.B.